Computers Inc.
Japan's Challenge to IBM

Harvard East Asian Monographs
144

Subseries on the History of
Japanese Business and Industry

Japan's rise from the destruction and bitter defeat of World War II to its present eminence in world business and industry is perhaps the most striking development in recent world history. This did not occur in a vacuum. It was linked organically to at least a century of prior growth and transformation. To illuminate this growth a new kind of scholarship on Japan is needed: historical study *in the context of a company or industry* of the interrelations among entrepreneurs, managers, engineers, workers, stockholders, bankers, and bureaucrats, and of the institutions and policies they created. Only in such a context can the contribution of particular factors be weighed and understood. It is to promote and encourage such scholarship that this subseries is established, supported by the Reischauer Institute of Japanese Studies and published by the Council on East Asian Studies at Harvard.

Albert M. Craig
Cambridge, Massachusetts

COMPUTERS INC.
Japan's Challenge to IBM

MARIE ANCHORDOGUY

Published by COUNCIL ON EAST ASIAN STUDIES, HARVARD
UNIVERSITY, and distributed by HARVARD UNIVERSITY PRESS,
Cambridge (Massachusetts) and London   1989

Index by John Gates

The Council on East Asian Studies at Harvard University publishes a monograph series and, through the Fairbank Center for East Asian Research and the Reischauer Institute of Japanese Studies, administers research projects designed to further scholarly understanding of China, Japan, Korea, Vietnam, Inner Asia, and adjacent areas. Publication of this volume has been assisted by a grant from the Shell Companies Foundation.

Library of Congress Cataloging-in-Publication Data

Anchordoguy, Marie.
Computers Inc. : Japan's challenge to IBM / Marie Anchordoguy.
p.   cm.—(Harvard East Asian monographs ; 144)
Revision of the author's thesis.
Bibliography: p.
Includes index.
ISBN 0-674-15630-7
1. Computer industry—Japan.   I. Title.   II. Series.
HD9696.C63J29   1989
338.4'7004'0952—dc20   89-7913
CIP

To my mother and father
Dorothy and Arnold Anchordoguy

Contents

Tables

Appendix Tables

Figures

Abbreviations

AI   artificial intelligence
AIST   Agency for Industrial Science and Technology (MITI)
AT&T   American Telephone and Telegraph
BOJ   Bank of Japan
CDL   Joint Computer Development Laboratories (Fujitsu, Hitachi, and Mitsubishi)
CPU   central processing unit
DIPS   Dendenkōsha Information Processing System (NTT)
ECL   Electrical Communications Laboratory (NTT)
ETL   Electrotechnical Laboratory (MITI)
FBI   Federal Bureau of Investigation (U.S.)
FILP   Fiscal Investment and Loan Program
GATT   General Agreement on Tariffs and Trade
GE   General Electric Company
HEMT   high electronic mobility transistor
IBJ   Industrial Bank of Japan
IBM   International Business Machines (U.S.)
IC   integrated circuit
ICOT   Institute for New Generation Computer Technology
IMF   International Monetary Fund
IPA   Information-Processing Promotion Association
JDB   Japan Development Bank
JECC   Japan Electronic Computer Company
JEIDA   Japan Electronics Industry Development Association
JIEB   Japan Import-Export Bank
JIPDEC Japan Information-Processing Development Center
JREB   Japan Real Estate Bank
JSDC   Joint System Development Corporation

LDP	Liberal Democratic Party
LTCB	Long-Term Credit Bank of Japan
LSI	large-scale integrated circuit
MB	megabyte
MITI	Ministry of International Trade and Industry
MOF	Ministry of Finance
MOS	metal-oxide semiconductor
MPT	Ministry of Post and Telecommunications
ms	millisecond
NEC	Nippon Electric Company
NTIS	NEC-Toshiba Information Systems, Inc.
NTT	Japan Telegraph and Telephone Co.
OECD	Organization for Economic Cooperation and Development
OS	operating system
PC	personal computer
PIPS	Pattern Information Processing Project (MITI)
RAM	random access memory
RCA	Radio Corporation of America
ROM	read only memory
R&D	research and development
Sigma	Software Industrialized Generator and Maintenance Aids
TI	Texas Instruments (U.S.)
TRON	Real-Time Operating System Nucleus
VAN	value-added network
VLSI	very large-scale integrated circuit
WTC	World Trade Corporation (IBM)

Acknowledgments

In writing this book, I have received generous guidance and support from many people and institutions.

My research was funded by a Fulbright-Hays Dissertation Fellowship, a Japan Foundation Dissertation Fellowship, a postdoctoral fellowship at the Reischauer Institute of Japanese Studies at Harvard University, and the Division of Research of the Harvard Business School. I am very grateful to these institutions for enabling me to complete this book.

I am indebted to many people in the United States who have given me guidance on this study. My greatest debt is to Chalmers Johnson of the University of California, San Diego, and David Vogel of the University of California, Berkeley. They assisted me throughout the dissertation stage and in revising the work into a book. They have been a source of constant encouragement, always assuring me that what I was doing was not only good but also important. I would like to express my deepest gratitude to them for their comments and support.

I would also like to thank John C. Campbell, David Friedman, Robert Harris, Richard Holton, George Lodge, Thomas McCraw, James McKenney, Richard Samuels, Bruce Scott, Richard Vietor, and Ezra Vogel. Comments from members of the Business History Seminar at the Harvard Business School, where I presented a paper on this topic, helped me in revising the manuscript.

In Japan, my greatest debt is to Nakano Mutsuji and Tanaka

Akiyoshi, who helped me gain a greater understanding of how Japan's political economy works. Their constant erncouragement, kindness, and willingness to answer my numerous questions were invaluable. I would also like to thank Aiso Hideo, Chūma Kiyofuku, Inose Hiroshi, Iwaba Hiroshi, Kajiwara Yasushi, Konishi Akira, Kuwahara Yutaka, Maeda Norihiko, Miyano Motoyuki, Sakai Yoshio, Tajiri Yasushi, Toda Iwao, Uekusa Masu, Yamamoto Kinko, Yonekura Seiichirō, and Yoshioka Tadashi. The general managers of the Research Department of the Japan Electronic Computer Company, first Ishii Yoshiaki and later Isahai Kenji, generously allowed me to spend months using their private collection of documents on the industry; the staff of their department was also very helpful, always willing to photocopy material for me and rejuvenate me with tea and sweets. The faculty of Tokyo University's Economics Department, where I was a research fellow, and the staff of its library also helped me.

I am grateful to the Council on East Asian Studies for the publication of this book. I thank my editor, Florence Trefethen, for making the manuscript easier to read. Two anonymous reviewers also helped strengthen the manuscript.

I thank the publishers of *International Organization* and the *Political Science Quarterly* for granting me permission to use in this book material that first appeared in articles in their journals.

Finally, I thank my husband, Leslie Helm. Without his encouragement and faith in me, the work simply would not have been completed. This book is dedicated to my mother and father, who instilled in me the desire to learn and provided me with the opportunity to make my first visit to Japan a decade and a half ago.

Despite all of the generous assistance I have received, I alone am responsible for the interpretations and conclusions in this study of Japan's efforts to nurture a domestic computer industry.

Computers Inc.

Japan's Challenge to IBM

ONE

Market-Conforming Policies

In the chilly pre-dawn of a New England fall, Naruse Jun, a senior engineer of Hitachi, and Alan Garretson, his paid Silicon Valley consultant, met in a dark isolated parking lot with their "contact." They exchanged two ID badges for an envelope full of cash. The three drove to Pratt and Whitney, a maker of aircraft engines, and passed doors secured with armed guards and combination locks on their way to the computer room. There Naruse got what he wanted: a look at IBM's 3380 computer disk drive. After he snapped some photos, the three slipped back out into the morning. This was just one of many such cloak-and-dagger missions Hitachi employees undertook from 1981 to 1982 to fill a long shopping list of IBM technologies they wanted to acquire. On 22 June 1982, Hitachi wired $525,000 to Garretson's bank account to pay for the "consulting." The game was over. The elaborate FBI sting had caught employees of Hitachi red-handed.[1]

That Garretson was an undercover FBI agent was not surprising. What was unusual was how close IBM worked with the FBI to develop this elaborate sting. IBM has always defended its proprietary technology. But this time the scale of the operation and the publicity it drew were more reminiscent of a high-security Soviet counterespionage program than a mere effort to protect trade secrets. IBM had targeted the Japanese. Why was IBM, which dominates some 55 percent[2] of the world computer market, worrying about Japanese computer firms? No doubt concern over protection of its trade secrets was involved; but surely it had been for years. Why hit now? IBM was, for the first time, taking the Japanese challenge seriously. While U.S. giants like General Electric and RCA quit the computer business and other U.S. mainframe companies such as National Cash Register (NCR), Burroughs, Honeywell, and Sperry Rand (UNIVAC) were growing weaker year by year, a vibrant computer industry composed of three major computer companies and several small ones had emerged in Japan. Two of Japan's largest makers—Fujitsu and Hitachi—were successfully making computers that could be run on IBM software. By the late 1970s, they were selling mainframes that even Westerners agreed were superior in performance to IBM's. While there was no danger that they would take over the world mainframe computer market in the foreseeable future, Japanese firms had steadily increased their share. Fujitsu, Hitachi, and NEC were supplying mainframes to U.S. and European firms such as Honeywell, Amdahl, National Advanced Systems, Sperry, Siemens, BASF, and ICL. Only in Japan had local firms been able to roll back IBM's market share to below 30 percent; Fujitsu has a larger share of the Japanese market than IBM, and NEC is close on IBM's heels. Given the opportunity, IBM was happy to respond.

To the Japanese, the *IBM Supai Jiken* (IBM Spy Incident) symbolized the ever-present threat of an IBM so powerful it could squash its Japanese competitors. For two decades, the Japanese computer firms had grown in the shadow of this threat. A key ingredient in their survival and healthy growth was their partnership with the government.

In a free market, where the firms with the lowest-priced, highest-quality computers win, there is no question but that today the market for computers in Japan would be dominated by IBM. In the late 1950s and early 1960s, no Japanese company could have acquired the huge sum of money to make the investment necessary to develop computers; no bank would have put out the funds for such an outlandish adventure; and Japanese customers would not have purchased drastically inferior domestic machines even if they were cheaper than IBMs. The Japanese government and electronics companies decided, however, that to leave the potentially huge Japanese computer industry to the vagaries of the free market would be unwise in the long run. It would make the nation hostage to IBM's technological whims and would hinder Japanese companies' abilities to compete in related areas such as telecommunications and computer-controlled power stations. Moreover, the computer would be the core of a whole range of high-technology products in the future. The government decided to help domestic companies develop the financial and technological clout necessary to stand up to IBM—to help local firms develop a *Hi no Maru* Computer, a truly Japanese machine.[3]

The government needed to create a market environment in which Japanese companies would be willing to invest heavily to develop and manufacture sophisticated computers and users would be willing to purchase them. Japan did this in several ways. One was to restrict the number and type of machines that IBM and other foreign companies could sell in Japan. Foreign investment was controlled to prevent foreign firms from buying local companies and setting up wholly owned subsidiaries to produce in Japan. Subsidies, low-interest loans, and loan guarantees gave the companies access to capital for investment in R&D and computer production. Finally, carefully monitored production, sales, R&D, and price cartels allowed them to avoid some of the potentially wasteful aspects of competition—cutthroat price wars, redundant R&D, and uneconomic scales of production—while still requiring that they compete in the final marketplace. These policies influenced the market structure of the industry and the behavior of the computer firms in two primary ways: They reduced the costs and risks of entering and operating in the computer business to encourage the firms to make the heavy investment necessary to become competitive; and they reduced the number of companies operating in each market segment to help the firms gain economies of scale in R&D and production. Hammered out by the public and private sector, these policies were generally structured in ways that did not completely shelter the firms from competition and that required them to make better products to survive in the long term.

Did these policies help or hinder the industry's development? Were they necessary or sufficient conditions for the emergence of a competitive computer industry? The government certainly did not single-handedly create a viable computer industry. It was the firms that invested, developed the technology, and ultimately produced high-quality, low-cost machines. Citizens, through their huge savings in government-controlled post-office savings accounts, provided the funds at low interest rates to the corporate sector. And heavy demand for computers was stimulated by the rapidly expanding economy as a whole. These market factors were crucial components of the success story. Managers based investment, pricing, and production decisions on their expectations of their competitors' actions—this competition undoubtedly drove the industry's development. But this was not unfettered market competition; the government shaped competition by altering profit expectations; in a free market, IBM would have monopolized the industry, making profit expectations for potential Japanese entrants negative. Because the government controlled IBM, the domestic makers were able to view the industry as potentially profitable, and entered the market based on this expectation of profit. Though at best a partial explanation of Japan's success in computers, the role of the Japanese government in the success story needs to be systematically explored.

The focal point of this book is the government's role—how it used protection and promotion policies to alter competition in the computer industry, and how and to what extent this intervention accelerated the industry's development. According to classical economic theory, protecting companies from foreign competition makes them lazy—it grants them a monopoly or, at least, a cozy, collusive oligopoly in which they can set high prices and produce low-quality, technologically unsophisticated products. Unable to purchase better imported goods, the consumer has no choice but to accept high prices for a low-quality product or forego the product altogether. Subsidies have a similar effect: With enough government aid to stay in business profitably, companies have little motivation to take the extra steps necessary to become more productive and profitable. The implicit threat that subsidies will be discontinued if profits become excessive also discourages the firms from cutting costs and improving product design, quality, and technology. Yet, despite rather extensive protection and subsidization, the Japanese computer firms are producing high-quality, competitive mainframes. Indeed, while government intervention can lead to a technologically sluggish and inefficient industry, it need not. Governments can structure their policies in ways that spur an industry's development by leaving intact market incentives to cut costs and improve quality and technology.

The Japanese view of the state's role in industrial development can be better understood if contrasted with that of the United States. With different histories, these nations have very different government-business relationships and views about the appropriate role of the government in an economy. Nations like the United States, with democratic pasts and an early industrial revolution, have experienced "atomistic forms of capitalism," while late developers like Japan, with feudal pasts and an eagerness to catch up with the industrialized nations, have seen a more positive role for government in economic development.[4] Indeed, the Japanese state played the leading role in Japan's industrialization in the late 1800s. Fearing colonization by Europe or the United States—another invasion by the black ships and the blue eyes—the state became actively involved in building up the army and strengthening the economy. In contrast, entrepreneurs sparked the U.S. industrial revolution; the government's primary involvement in the late 1800s was to *regulate* business.

The degree of government intervention is not what delineates the differences between the U.S. and Japanese views of the appropriate role of the state in the economy; rather it is the type of intervention, by whom, and for what purpose. The U.S. government intervenes to create and maintain "fair" competition—to make sure that all players play the competitive game by the same rules. Japan is much less concerned with the rules of the playground; her primary objective is to win the game.

Chalmers Johnson calls states concerned with "fair play" regulatory states and those concerned with results developmental states.

A regulatory, or market rational, state concerns itself with the forms and procedures—the rules, if you will—of economic competition, but it does not concern itself with substantive matters. . . . The developmental, or plan-rational, state, by contrast, has as its dominant feature precisely the setting of such substantive social and economic goals.[5]

The U.S. regulatory state believes that, the closer a market gets to perfect competition, the more efficient it is, and the better the society's resources are allocated. According to this view, rooted in the ideas of Adam Smith, competition among many small firms, none large enough to influence price, leads to the best product at the lowest price; government intervention by definition creates market inefficiencies and is only justified to correct so-called "market failures," which occur when consumers have inadequate information about products, when the cost of externalities such as pollution are borne by people other than the offending firm, or in cases of natural monopolies like utilities where economies of scale make it most efficient for one firm to run an industry. Thus, while the U.S. government has intervened to promote the housing, agriculture, and defense industries—cases in which it felt the market failed—it is not involved in deciding what portfolio of industries U.S. firms should be in nor in systematically encouraging some industries and discouraging others. Instead, it generally leaves such decisions to the market. Indeed, the U.S. regulatory state believes, as classical economic theory suggests, that industrial policies that promote one industry over another distort market forces and lead to a suboptimal allocation of resources. Protectionism and subsidization, two key components of industrial policy, reduce competition and thereby encourage inefficient production and slow technological progress. The theory does makes an exception for "infant industries," recognizing that government intervention in the market may be important to stimulate an industry in its initial stage of development; yet Japanese industries that are providing the most competition to American firms—steel, automobiles, machine tools, and semiconductors—have received continuous assistance far past what most economists would define as the infant stage.

The view that the government is at best a necessary evil has resulted in an antagonistic relationship between government and businesses in the United States.[6] In Japan, there is a very different view of the role of the government that has resulted in a more cooperative relationship between the public and private sectors. The Japanese believe that government intervention, in some cases, can actually help industries develop faster and more efficiently than they would under perfect competition. Untouched by the ideology of laissez faire, the Japanese do not see competition as having intrinsic value in itself; in fact, when Fukuzawa Yukichi introduced the word "competition" (*kyōsō,* with *kyō* meaning race and *sō* fight) to the Japanese public in his translation of an economics text in the late nineteenth century, he was criticized for introducing an unJapanese value.[7] The Japanese do not think that the invisible hand of the market, left to itself, will bring about the changes necessary to make an economy internationally competitive. Competition is considered

> inefficient, resulting in firms too small, firms unable to cope with cyclical changes, unable to compete effectively in international trade. Competition is not regarded as conducive to technological progress.[8]

The Japanese perspective, the result of a historically successful experience with bureaucratic leadership and close government-business relations going back to the eighteenth century, does not completely reject the U.S. view. Japanese agree that, in principle, the optimum allocation of resources in an economy should be left to the market, but they believe that there are cases where the market mechanism will not bring about the optimal solution. Indeed, the market can be crude and inefficient; competition in the short term can knock out firms that, over the long run, might be economic successes. External shocks, like a sharp rise in oil prices or the introduction of new technology, can threaten firms that, if temporarily cushioned by the government, could build up their resources for long-term competitiveness. Government mediation is also deemed necessary to prevent *katō kyōsō* or "excessive competition,"[9] where cutthroat price competition can lead to bankruptcy and leave all the firms in the industry without money to invest. Though it buffers some firms in the short term, the Japanese government has generally been ruthless in demanding competitiveness in the long term; if a firm gets off track, performing poorly even in good times, the government allows competition to determine whether it will survive or perish. Far from rejecting the market mechanism, the Japanese mercilessly, though selectively, exploit it. The Japanese call this mix of market elements and state intervention a "planned market economy system" (*keikakuteki shijō keizai hōshiki*), [10] a term similar to the French *dirigiste* state-led economy.

The Japanese are not the only ones who believe that, in some cases, short-term market distortions, often deliberately created by government policies, can accelerate long-term industrial development. Joseph Schumpeter saw capitalism as an evolutionary process in which competition consists of a series of "revolutions" caused by innovations of dominant firms. Price competition was not what mattered; rather what counted was

> competition which commands a decisive cost or quality advantage and which strikes not at the margins of profits and the outputs of the existing firms but at their foundations and their very lives. [11]

To Schumpeter, market distortions, such as those caused by oligopoly, price cooperation, and subsidization, could, in some cases, bring about faster long-term technological advancement; short-term market imperfections could help create long-term competitive advantages. The prominent U.S. economist, F.M. Scherer, agrees that, while it is important to use resources efficiently at any point in time, "dynamic performance" is what really counts in the long run. [12]

Cooperation among firms can actually be more efficient by wasting fewer resources than a system of perfect competition. G.B. Richardson, focusing on the role of the market in regulating investment, points out that, when demand suddenly increases, the market mechanism has no signal to tell some firms to invest to meet the new demand and others to restrain from investing; if all producers invest, the result will be excess capacity. He suggests that coordination of investment to meet demand may be necessary to provide firms with enough information on which to base their investment decisions. [13]

Price cooperation can prevent many of the wasteful effects of cut-throat price competition. Price wars can reduce the profits of all firms in an industry, leaving none with resources to invest; even worse, they can let the most inefficient firm "win," only because that firm is the biggest and can hold out longer. Indeed, as Almarin Phillips explains:

> Each firm is free to compete with quality and advertising. Each may vary its output or add new products. Each may alter its system of distribution . . . most important, each is legally free to violate the agreement at will, a point which causes the ambitious cartel manager no little worry.[14]

Purely competitive conditions can be particularly inappropriate for bringing about certain types of technological advances. Schumpeter, Galbraith, Villard, and others argue that it is large firms that have the resources and economies of scale to invest huge sums in R&D for long-term, high-cost, risky projects; that only large firms can undertake numerous projects such that successes and failures will to some degree average out; and that only firms that have enough control over the market to reap the rewards of innovation will innovate.[15] True, in many cases smaller firms are the real inventers, but it is the large firms that have the resources to apply basic inventions to products for the marketplace quickly and cheaply.[16] If a country is technologically backward and is able to purchase technology, the role of small inventive firms may be less important. Nonetheless, there has to be a balance in the size of companies in an industry. According to Scherer,

> A bit of monopoly power in the form of structural concentration is conducive to invention and innovation . . . but very high concentration has a favorable effect only in rare cases, and more often it is apt to retard progress by restricting the number of independent sources of initiative and by dampening firms' incentive to gain market position through accelerated R&D . . . What is needed for rapid technical progress is a subtle blend of competition and monopoly.[17]

If one accepts the notion that firm size and market share can influence technological progress, the possibility arises that government policies that shape market structure can trigger technological development.

Classical economists themselves are beginning to revise their theories as a result of the Japanese experience. The new international economists [18] suggest that industrial policies can play a positive role in industrial development by correcting "market failures," such as the market's inability to deal with economies of scale, learning curves, and spillover effects, issues that economists have assumed away for generations. Reluctantly, they admit that, in some cases, government intervention can lead to a more efficient allocation of resources than the free market over the long term. Other scholars, such as Scott and Lodge and Tyson and Zysman, also suggest that targeting policies can change factor endowments and thereby create comparative advantages. [19]

The distinction between those who argue that government intervention can, under some circumstances, accelerate market forces and those who believe that, the more competitive the market, the more advanced and lower-priced the products will be is mirrored in the two principal schools of thought explaining Japan's rapid economic growth in the postwar period. Proponents of the "Market Explanation" argue that Japan's economic development has followed the same pattern as that of the United States and Europe: Market competition sparked industrial development. In this view, developmental states do not exist; states may provide a conducive environment for growth but do not significantly influence it. In contrast, proponents of the government-business relations or "Japan Inc." explanation view Japan as a development state in which a close government-business relationship facilitates government intervention in an economy to promote strategic industries. They acknowledge that market competition has been a necessary and critical ingredient, but also argue that Japan's industrial policy has contributed significantly to economic success. [20]

James Abegglen has used the term "Japan Inc." to compare Japan's government-business relationship with the relationship between a U.S. conglomerate's corporate headquarters and its various divisions:

> A conglomerate can channel cash flows from low-growth to high-growth areas and apply the debt capacity of safe, mature businesses to capitalize rapidly growing but unstable ventures. It can move into a dynamic new

industry and bring to it financial power that no existing competitor can match.[21]

In this conceptualization of Japan's political economy, the bureaucracy, guiding the economy in close cooperation with big business, rules; and the Liberal Democratic Party (LDP), the weakest of the three actors participating in the policymaking process, reigns.[22] This separation is possible because the Japanese legislative and judicial branches of government "fend off the numerous interest groups in the society, which if catered to would distort the priorities of the developmental state."[23] Industrial policy is thus strategic planning at the national level, and MITI men the strategic planners.

There is significant disagreement among the proponents of the "Japan Inc." explanation over just how tight and smooth-running the government-business machine is. All agree that there is far more conflict than the metaphor implies, but some, like Johnson, see the bureaucracy as guiding the economy; others, like Richard Samuels, see the private sector as having the upper hand in the government-business coalition driving Japan's industrial development.[24] This present study suggests that the interaction is not sufficiently clear-cut to be considered either "state-led" or "private-sector-led."

The view of an elite government-business partnership guiding the development of strategic industries is disputed by other academics who emphasize the role of economic factors such as market competition and high rates of savings and investment in Japan's spectacular economic development. "The main impetus to growth has been private—business investment demand, private saving, and industrious and skilled labor operating in a market-oriented environment."[25] According to this view, most persuasively argued by Hugh Patrick and Henry Rosovsky in *Asia's New Giant,* a well-educated labor force, high rates of investment, and the rapid introduction of technology have fueled Japan's high growth rates. By the mid-1950s, the authors note, Japan already had a labor force that matched Europe's in terms of educational level; these workers were able to move easily into the new jobs that opened up as Japan grew. Moreover, Japanese firms were quick to introduce new technology into industry by purchasing advanced machinery, licensing technology, and reading the vast store of information available in the

West on new technological developments.[26] The combination of heavy investments (made possible by high savings rates) and the introduction of new technology led to rocketing rates of labor productivity and economic growth. While they acknowledge that the government played a role in economic growth, Patrick and Rosovsky primarily emphasize the importance of the government's decision to keep taxes low by spending little on social overhead and defense.[27]

Patrick and Rosovsky are not alone in emphasizing the importance of market factors in Japan's economic take-off. James Abegglen and George Stalk Jr., in *Kaisha,* for example, focus on the role of corporate strategies in the Japanese success story: "Companies, not societies, compete for markets; companies, not governments, trade; and in the end it is companies that prosper or stagnate—in Japan, as well as in the United States or Europe."[28]

Few would question the critical role of the points enumerated by Patrick, Rosovsky, and others about the importance of market competition and corporate strategies in Japan's economic development. Nor would many quibble with the "Japan Inc." characterization of Japan as a country where government and business tend to work hand in hand. Both approaches contribute substantially to our understanding the stimulants to Japan's rapid economic expansion. But studies need not be limited to focusing on either the state or the market. In fact, viewing Japan's success as either the result of private market forces or state policy obfuscates a more comprehensive analysis of the factors triggering Japan's economic explosion. The critical question is how the government and market interacted to produce the highest rates of growth the world has ever experienced.

This book is by no means the first to look at Japan's industrial policy in depth, although its attempt to integrate the "market" and "state-policy" approaches to analyze the impact of policies on market competition in an industry has not earlier been sufficiently explored. Because of the many types of industrial policy, their various objectives, and the different academic approaches that can be used to analyze them, the steadily mounting number of studies have not yet made a dent in the topics that need to be covered. As Hugh

Patrick, skeptical of any positive effects of industrial policy, concedes:

> Industrial policy may have had some success in accelerating the growth rate. The problem is that we do not yet have detailed, definitive studies which settle once and for all the issue of the degree and nature of the effectiveness of Japanese industrial policy.[29]

Among the most probing works on Japan's industrial policy is Chalmers Johnson's *MITI and the Japanese Miracle*. Johnson analyzes the ministry in charge of Japan's industrial policy, the ways policies are developed and implemented, and how they have influenced the economy from 1925 through 1975. He concludes that the Ministry of International Trade and Industry (MITI), through industrial policies, guided the economy into industries that triggered Japan's high growth rates. Johnson provides a wealth of detail about the key institutions and people that helped shape Japan's industrial policies. While the breadth of Johnson's analysis does not allow for detailed examinations of specific industries, this author and many others use his study as a base of knowledge from which to explore specific cases.[30]

Several studies suggest that Japanese government policies have changed competition in industries in ways that have increased efficiency and accelerated technological advances. Leonard Lynn, in a study of foreign technology acquisition in Japan's steel industry, shows how MITI, by negotiating on behalf of the firms and thereby preventing the foreign company from playing the Japanese companies off against one another, helped the firms get a good price for basic oxygen-furnace (BOF) technology.[31] Peck and Tamura argue that MITI played a key role in promoting the rapid diffusion of the liquid-oxygen process in steelmaking.[32] Kodama Fumio has found that loans from the government's Japan Development Bank (JDB) helped the auto industry borrow far beyond its normal borrowing capacity,[33] enabling it to expand to gain greater economies of scale than it would otherwise have been able to afford. And Imai Kenichi argues that cooperative R&D can be very beneficial to an industry by reducing the cost of R&D per individual firm and by institutionalizing the exchange of ideas among researchers in universities, government laboratories, and private companies.[34]

But there are also studies pointing out cases of government intervention that has obstructed technological advancement and efficiency. MITI's delaying Sony's acquisition of transistor technology by restricting Sony's use of foreign exchange is the first to come to mind.[35] Another commonly sighted failure of industrial policy is MITI's aborted attempt to consolidate the auto industry around Toyota and Nissan.[36] Excess capacity in Japan's steel industry in the early 1960s[37] and again in the 1980s is also cited as a negative by-product of industrial policy. There are both successes and failures in industrial policy; by the careful choice of a specific policy at a given point in time, an argument can be made to support either position. But such piecemeal approaches obfuscate understanding. We need to look at the full range of policies governing an industry over its development to ascertain whether policies were on the whole effective in that industry and under what conditions they have succeeded or failed. It is also necessary to consider the possibility that industrial policy may be a second-best solution—not perfect, but still better than having no policy at all.

This study focuses on the impact of a wide range of government policies on competition and performance in the computer industry from its infancy to the present. A secondary objective is to examine the policymaking process—the negotiation and compromise among several government ministries and corporations from which policies emerge. Concentrating on many policies over a period of three decades should provide a more balanced view of both the successes and failures in Japan's promotion of the computer industry and also present enough cases to suggest possible working hypotheses of why policies have been more successful in some cases than in others.

Some say the computer industry is not a representative case for analyzing the effectiveness of Japan's industrial policy. Peck and Tamura, for example, argue that promotion of computers has been far more extensive than other Japanese industries and that in no other case has there been a huge foreign company, like IBM, to contend with.[38] But the issue here is not how much Japan has promoted industries; it is the way in which the government promoted them and what the effects have been. The relatively extreme intervention in the computer case only gives us all the more opportunity to analyze effects and explore the possibilities of a government's shaping markets for competitive advantage. Moreover, most of the unique aspects of the computer industry work against the odds of successful development. IBM's dominance in computers, for example, was unparalleled in the steel, auto, or semiconductor cases. The incredible capital requirements for starting up in the computer business—to finance R&D and rent machines—also suggest that, if anything, it would be more difficult to nurture computers than other industries.

In evaluating the role of government policy in the rise of the Japanese computer industry, three important caveats must be recognized at the outset. First, even if the data suggest that Japan's industrial policy has significantly contributed to the development of the computer industry, Japan's economy as a whole may have suffered losses from this promotion due to social costs and other distortions in the allocation of resources; the resources poured into computers may have been more efficiently allocated to other industries. I think this highly unlikely. In any case, the question is not the focus of this study; it requires a separate macro analysis.

Second, even if Japan's industrial policy has helped the computer industry develop, it does not necessarily follow that such policies would be effective if applied to other industries under substantially different conditions or to other countries. Indeed, as this study suggests, there may be some conditions that are critical to successful industrial policies; the absence of the right conditions may help explain why France's efforts to promote the computer industry and Japan's efforts to promote petrochemicals have not succeeded.

Third, even if industrial policy contributes to the development of an industry in one nation, it does not necessarily follow that such policies are positive sum for the world economy as a whole. There are clearly potential cases of policies with beggar-thy-neighbor effects.

What follows is a detailed account of Japan's national strategy to develop a computer industry. There were four primary components to this strategy: protectionism, financial assistance, the establishment of a national-policy company to rent domestic computers, and cooperative R&D projects. Protectionism, by buffering Japanese firms from IBM's full market power, gave them the time to build up their technological and production expertise. Subsidies, loans, and loan guarantees gave the firms the working capital they needed to invest heavily in computers. The computer rental company, by carrying the burden of financing computer rentals, gave the firms their return on investment much earlier than they would have received it had they rented out their computers on their own. This up-front cash—interest-free loans—enabled them to invest heavily to improve their computers. The rental company also, by controlling the prices of the computers it rented out, limited price competition, thereby assuring the firms that their profits would not be reduced by cutthroat price wars. Cooperative R&D helped the companies get the biggest bang for their buck by reducing redundant R&D and sharing project results.

Chapter 2 shows how the government and the firms struggled, often through trial and error, to understand how best to encourage the industry without quashing the firms' initiative and making them totally dependent on the government. An innovative web of regulations on IBM along with several joint R&D projects set the groundwork for the industry. In Chapter 3, the single most important institution created to promote the industry—a computer-rental company called the Japan Electronic Computer Company (JECC)—is examined. By influencing supply, demand, and price, JECC created an artificial marketplace that favored domestic firms. Chapter 4 shows how the industry and the government, under intense pressure from the United States to open up the computer market, combined with spiraling oil prices, a sharply revalued yen, and a deafening blow from the giant IBM, joined forces in a sink-or-swim attempt to avoid the fate of General Electric and RCA—withdrawal from the computer business. Rebounding from the brink of bankruptcy with machines competitive with IBM in terms of hardware, the firms and the government set out to keep up with and, if possible, jump ahead of IBM. Chapter 5 details these efforts, up to the present, including the change in strategies resulting from the FBI's arrest of Hitachi engineers for stealing IBM technology.[39] The 6th and final chapter, through comparison of the various cases that unfold in the body of the text, evaluates the role of targeting policies in the development of Japan's computer industry and suggests some general conditions under which policies are likely to be most effective.

TWO

Changing Competition to Favor Domestic Firms,

1957–1969

In 1959, IBM rolled out what was to be the first of a series of revolutionary computers that would change the world in the ensuing decades. They used transistors, which made them faster, smaller, and more dependable than the glass-vacuum-tube computers common at the time. These machines, which made Japanese computers seem little better than abacuses, allowed ordinary firms to process huge amounts of information, boosting their productivity and competitiveness. Japanese users were eager to purchase these computers and thus flooded MITI's office with applications to import them. IBM's success pushed Japan to a critical juncture that would affect the long-term composition of the nation's economy: Should Japan allow the computers in to boost the nation's productivity or should it try to create a computer industry of its own?

The correct decision for Japan was not obvious. A couple of Japanese companies along with government labs and universities had researched computers in the 1950s, but their low-budget efforts were crude compared with those of U.S. firms, whose research projects were buttressed with ample sums from the Defense Department. It was also far from clear that Japan could succeed. A committee composed of people from the public and private sectors gathered in 1960 to discuss the issue. They quickly decided that a domestic computer industry was strategic for Japan's long-term economic interests.[1] Many firms had, by the late 1950s, already realized that their future businesses would involve computers. "The telecommunications and heavy-electrical-equipment makers felt that to survive they had to go into computers," explained Yoshioka Tadashi, a former MITI official intimately involved in promoting the industry.[2] "The firms wanted to go into computers, but they realized they could not do it alone, so they came to MITI and asked us for help," recalled Miyano Motoyuki, formerly of MITI.[3]

Although they realized that it would be difficult to compete with IBM, MITI felt that they should promote the industry. Computers certainly had the characteristics MITI considered important to the nation's long-term economic development: The industry had a high value-added component, required little natural raw materials or energy, used skilled labor, had substantial and expanding domestic and international markets, was sensitive to economies of scale, and was linked to many other industries—telecommunications, consumer electronics, heavy electrical machinery. The Japan Telegraph and Telephone Company (NTT), the telephone monopoly created in 1952, also supported the idea. NTT knew it would need computer technology; since by law it could not manufacture equipment, it would need private companies with the technological expertise to produce its equipment.[4] The major banks also saw computers as a potential growth area and were eager to see government backing;[5] "There was no question then but that the government should promote it," explained Okazaki Kōtarō of the Industrial Bank of Japan (IBJ).[6] The Ministry of Finance (MOF) was the only government actor reluctant to promote computers. "They were hesitant because they knew it would require a lot of money," recalled Kajiwara Yasushi of the IBJ, "but they were talked into it."[7] In this way, the government lobbied businesses; banks and firms lobbied the government; and MITI and NTT lobbied MOF. Gaining a consensus of all the major actors was critical to moving forward. "By forging a consensus, even if it failed, no specific person or group would be blamed."[8]

The idea of depending on foreign makers for computer technology and computers simply was not considered a viable option:[9]

There was a mood, then and even today, that we should use Japanese machines. It is hard to explain why. Japan was small, its population large, and it had few resources. But it was not only that. We were conscious of the fact that we were abhorred by the whole world because of World War II. We felt that, if something bad happened to Japan, no one would help us. So we thought that, even if domestic products were inferior, we should all use them. If we used a foreign product, others would whisper "Look what that company is doing" and we would be ostracized.

These are the words of Takeuchi Hiroshi, Managing Director of the Long-Term Credit Bank of Japan.[10]

The obstacles to building a viable computer industry were clear. IBM's domination of the Japanese and world computer markets, coupled with rapid technological change, made it nearly impossible for new firms to become competitive. Analysts believed a firm needed an estimated 10 to 15-percent share of the market to efficiently produce general-purpose computer systems.[11] Moreover, vast amounts of capital were required to invest in R&D and to finance computer rentals. Indeed, Japan had about as much a comparative advantage in supplying computers as she had in selling oil—none. Postwar Japan had a vast pool of cheap labor but only minimal amounts of capital and technology. The nation seemed destined to produce labor-intensive products in light industries like textiles or toys. Japanese corporations were anxious to invest in the new field, but could not afford to gamble on the industry without government support. The Japanese government decided to throw its weight behind the industry: Computers were given the ultimate accolade in Japan— they were designated a "strategic industry."

Japan seemed to have little to lose. By 1960, the country was in the midst of an economic explosion few would have dreamed possible a decade earlier. Many of the institutions, laws, and policies needed to foster computers—an agency to coordinate industrial policies, government investment banks, laws controlling foreign exchange and investment and imports—were already in place, having been used to promote such industries as steel and machine tools. With government help, the large, vertically integrated and diversified electronics companies that were already active in the consumer-electronics, telecommunications, and heavy-electronic-equipment industries were eager to gamble on this new technology.

MITI already had considerable power over the computer industry. The Extraordinary Measures Law for Promotion of the Electronics Industry, enacted in 1957, just two years before IBM put out its new computers, had already given the computer industry official backing as part of the larger electronics industry.[12] In that law, the government promised to "make efforts" to help firms get the funds to invest in modern plant and equipment; the law encouraged cooperation among firms to make production more efficient, and granted MITI, which had emerged after the war as the agency developing and coordinating industrial policy, the power to "advise" firms and penalize them for noncompliance. MITI could, for example, order companies to form a cartel, advising each company on how much of what product they should produce. The law also exempted the computer industry from the anti-monopoly law put in force by the U.S. Occupation. This law, and subsequent laws that extended its provisions to the present, symbolized the government's commitment to the industry and provided the legal basis for government subsidies, low-interest loans, and other aids to stimulate the industry.

The question was thus not whether to promote the industry but how. The committee decided that its first two tasks were to protect the market, which it did immediately by raising tariffs from 15 to 25 percent,[13] and to acquire IBM's basic patents for the Japanese makers. "There was infringement of IBM's patents, and, though it did not go as far as a lawsuit, IBM warned us many times," explained a former MITI official.[14] It is not surprising then that MITI concluded that Japanese companies could not even get off the ground in the field of computers without legal access to IBM's basic patents.[15]

IBM had been in Japan since 1925 selling its punch-card office machinery.[16] When its assets, confiscated during the war, were returned in 1949 by the U.S. Occupation, the company was re-established.[17] By moving in early, just one year before the Foreign Capital Law was enacted, IBM Japan avoided being forced by law to form a joint venture with a Japanese firm.[18] Still, various laws [19] prevented IBM from producing in Japan or repatriating earnings. In 1956, when it applied to MITI for permission to arrange with its parent, the IBM World Trade Corporation (WTC), to supply the necessary technology and capital to produce in Japan, MITI rejected the request.[20] MITI did not want to allow IBM to produce in Japan because that would make it much more difficult for the government to control IBM's sales. In January 1960, IBM tried again to transfer technology to IBM Japan; MITI again obstructed the transfer.[21] But, this time, MITI, desperately in need of IBM's basic patents, was ready to bargain.

IBM's J.W. Birkenstock flew to Japan to negotiate for permission to produce in Japan in exchange for opening up IBM patents to Japanese firms. To strengthen Japan's bargaining position, MITI represented the electronics firms in negotiations with IBM.[22] The government had done this before in steel, and the logic was simple: If each firm negotiated individually, IBM could raise the price of the patents by playing the firms off against one another; by representing all computer firms, MITI could negotiate from a position of strength.

Hiramatsu Morihiko of MITI told Birkenstock that IBM should make a 50–50 joint venture with a Japanese company in order to gain approval to produce in Japan and to repatriate profits overseas.[23] But IBM had some attractive bargaining chips of its own—ownership of a wide range of patents Japan would need in order to start building its computer industry. So Birkenstock did not budge; in fact he got tougher. He announced a more specific condition for handing over IBM patents: permission to manufacture in Japan its popular 1401 small computer, for which Japanese requests were flooding MITI's import-license office. Furious about the new condition, MITI abruptly broke off the negotiations.[24] Nonetheless, MITI knew that it was in a weaker position. MITI's Sabashi Shigeru finally agreed to allow IBM to set up a wholly owned subsidiary to produce in Japan, but politely warned IBM not to take advantage of Japan. "Japanese makers are mosquitoes, IBM is an elephant. I would appreciate it if IBM does not do anything to crush the mosquito under its feet."[25]

Sabashi wrangled a favorable deal for Japan: He not only got the patents; IBM also reduced the royalty it charged by 20 percent from what had originally been negotiated.[26] As a result, Japanese makers paid IBM a royalty of 5 percent of sales of systems and machines and 1 percent of sales of parts. Despite regulations restricting large transfers of foreign exchange, MITI allowed IBM Japan to repatriate 10 percent of sales as royalty in exchange for know-how and patents transferred from the parent firm to the subsidiary.[27] MITI made sure the technology from IBM was spread widely: 15 firms signed the 5-year contract. The contract was signed in December 1960 and was in effect from 1 January 1961 to 31 December 1965.[28] But, while the agreement on the patents and IBM's right to manufacture in Japan was made in 1960, the Japanese government did not allow IBM Japan to start production for two years—until 1963.[29]

Once the patents were obtained, 7 Japanese companies started producing computers legally on a commercial basis: Fujitsu, Hitachi, NEC, Toshiba, Mitsubishi Electric, Oki, and Matsushita. In order to speed up their business, most of the firms made technical agreements with foreign companies to gain manufacturing know-how and software. Fujitsu was then a tiny communications maker, heavily dependent on Japan Telegraph and Telephone (NTT), Japan's telecommunications monopoly. Fujitsu wanted to make a technical agreement with IBM, but IBM refused, saying that it had a worldwide policy of providing know-how only to its wholly owned subsidiaries. By the time IBM rejected Fujitsu's overtures, the most appropriate foreign partners had been taken, so Fujitsu decided to go it alone as Japan's only pure-blooded *(junketsu)* national computer firm. Fujitsu made the earliest and most substantial commitment to computers, and it was the only Japanese company that would stake its survival on its ability to make computers; today, computers constitute some 70 percent of its business, with telecommunications and semiconductors making up the remainder.

Nippon Electric Company (NEC), established in 1899 as a joint venture with Western Electric, was, like Fujitsu, heavily dependent on the government's telecommunications monopoly. After World War II, NEC, then backed by its industrial group—Sumitomo— went heavily into computers, semiconductors, and consumer electronics. It tied up with Honeywell in 1962 and, in a dramatic reversal, is today supplying Honeywell with computer technology and sophisticated computer products. Computers currently account for some 10–20 percent of its business. Hitachi, then a huge consumer-electronics and heavy-electrical-machinery maker, tied up with RCA in 1961; today computers account for some 10 percent of its business, with heavy industrial machinery, consumer electronics, telecommunications, and semiconductors making up the remainder.

Computers were but a small part of the sales of Toshiba and Mitsubishi, the two giant heavy-electric-equipment makers, and Oki, a small telecommunications maker. Toshiba, with turn-of-the-century ties with General Electric, tied up with GE in 1964 for computer technology; Mitsubishi Electric tied up with TRW in the early 1960s; and Oki Electric made a joint venture with Sperry Rand (UNIVAC) in 1963. Oki now depends on Unisys (recent merger of Sperry and Burroughs) for large and medium-scale computers, and primarily focuses on small computers, terminals, and other peripherals. Matsushita, then still a moderate-sized but fast-growing consumer-electronics maker, tried its hand at computers and had plans to tie-up with Philips of the Netherlands[30] but withdrew in 1964 because it was too risky and costly.[31] MITI had mixed feelings about these firms' collaborations with foreign companies:

> Our technology was way behind, so we [at MITI] were not against it, but we also did not approve it happily. In cases where the conditions were not good, we gave guidance to get the firms a better deal—on royalties, territory, and so on.[32]

The negotiations with IBM took place at a time when Japan was under increasing foreign pressure to liberalize its trade to conform to IMF, GATT, and OECD standards. In 1964, when Japan joined the OECD and changed to Article 11 status in GATT (no trade controls because of balance of payments deficiencies),[33] it officially committed itself to opening up its markets to foreign investment and imports. But this commitment, like many others that would follow, was only a formal *(tatemae)* promise aimed at gaining entrance to the club of advanced industrialized nations. In actuality *(honne)*, Japanese bureaucrats and business people had no intention of opening up their markets; to them that would have been tantamount to *harakiri* (suicide). Instead, covered by the facade of an open economy, bureaucrats set out to formulate new ways, preferably invisible to the foreign eye, to promote and protect strategic industries like computers.[34]

One such tactic was to closely supervise IBM Japan's activities by placing conditions on its production. Indeed, in spite of the computer makers' technical tie-ups with foreign companies, they still could not compete with IBM. The strings on IBM were significant:

> IBM had to release its patents to Japanese firms for a 5-percent royalty and had to export most of its production. As for computers for the domestic market, IBM had to follow MITI's guidelines; in this way, the type and number of IBM machines sold in the domestic market are restricted,[35]

explained MITI's Sabashi. Shiina Takeo, President of IBM Japan, recently confirmed that MITI had closely regulated the company's production.[36]

IBM Japan agreed to export a large proportion of its domestic production.[37] According to one source, IBM made a "gentleman's agreement" with MITI to export one-third of its production.[38] Another industry person explained that MITI might calculate that the Japanese market could absorb 40 percent of IBM Japan's production and then tell IBM to export the remaining 60 percent.[39] The domestic market grew faster than expected, however, and was able to absorb more of IBM's production. From 1965 through 1969, IBM Japan exported about 25 percent of its annual production.[40] MITI's Hiramatsu praised IBM's cooperation with the Japanese government: "Without using any political power, IBM is trying to form a loyal relationship with MITI."[41] MITI also controlled IBM Japan by regulating which computer models it could produce. MITI often refused or delayed permission on the grounds that it would negatively impact the domestic industry.

Hoping to get permission to produce its new 360 series in Japan, in October 1963 Birkenstock of IBM unilaterally lowered the royalties from 5 to 1 percent of sales for Japanese makers using its computer patents.[42] This move came just a month after an important Cabinet meeting reaffirmed a strong Buy-Japan policy: "In order to use foreign currency efficiently," the Cabinet argued, "the government will take the initiative in using domestic products. Let's also encourage the private sector to do so."[43]

IBM's offering was in vain. When it applied to MITI in mid-1964 for permission to produce models 20 and 40 of its 360 series, MITI officials stalled, complaining that the 360 series was far more advanced than domestic machines in technology, performance, quality, and price, and that the model 20 (small) and 40 (medium-sized) computers would compete directly with Japanese computers.[44]

IBM Japan's Chairman Inagaki made the matter public on 18 March 1965, hoping to get support elsewhere. He announced that

> if MITI does not approve this [IBM] plan to produce [the model 20 and 40 of the 360 series] in Japan, not only will users in the Japanese market have to import it, but also IBM World Trade Corporation will request that factories be established in other countries. Japan will suffer a loss of export [earnings].[45]

But this threat was not very effective. MITI did not allow IBM Japan to manufacture the 360 family series of computers until mid-1965, long after Fujitsu and NEC had introduced their "family series"—the Facom 230 and NEAC 2200 series—which started coming out in late 1964. Even when MITI did give approval, it required IBM to purchase parts locally.[46] And MITI's approval came only when it needed to renew the agreement for IBM's basic patents, which was to expire at the end of 1965. Even after the agreement was signed, the government delayed the start of IBM's production and even limited production volume.[47] It was not until February 1966 that production of the 360 series started in Japan.[48]

IBM's investment and procurement behavior was also a target of MITI control. When IBM tried to transfer funds to IBM Japan to construct a large factory, MITI used the Foreign Capital Law to limit the amount IBM could send.[49] In addition, MITI restricted the imports of parts, forcing IBM Japan to develop local suppliers.[50] MITI even used other foreign companies to battle IBM— to control foreign power with foreign power (*gaishi o motte, gaishi o seisuru*).[51] In 1958, Toshiba, Daiichi Bussan[52] and Sperry Rand established the Nihon Remington UNIVAC Co., which sold imported UNIVAC machines.[53] MITI required that the Japanese partners hold the majority of the shares so that, as a domestic firm, it could more easily be controlled by MITI.[54] The idea was to nurture UNIVAC as a strong competitor to IBM in order to avoid IBM domination of the Japanese market. "I felt that UNIVAC was used by MITI as an anti-IBM government policy," admitted a former executive of Nihon UNIVAC.[55]

MITI also used its powers to manipulate Texas Instruments (TI) for Japanese advantage. In early 1964, that U.S. semiconductor giant, which dominated about one-third of the world semiconductor market,[56] applied to create a wholly owned subsidiary in Japan. The application caused a shudder throughout the industry because it occurred at a time when the government, under severe pressure from the United States, was discussing capital liberalization.[57]

But U.S. pressure did not stop MITI from working in Japan's interest. MITI rejected the request.[58] Two and a half years later, MITI gave TI three conditions for entering Japan: creating a 50–50 joint venture with Sony; "voluntarily" adjusting the volume of its integrated-circuit (IC) production so that it would account for no more than 10 percent of Japan's total IC production for the first three years; and granting Japanese companies access to its patents for a reasonable price.[59] MITI's response came just one month before it started its first major public-private sector cooperative computer R&D project, a critical part of which was the development of ICs.[60] TI balked at MITI's conditions, in particular the joint-venture requirement. Ultimately, however, TI yielded to MITI's demands in order to gain a foothold in the Japanese market. MITI

approved a TI-Sony 50–50 joint venture in April 1968, and production started in 1969.[61] But the Japanese companies had already
gotten a critical jump. After beginning to make ICs only in 1966,
and with production volume in 1967 of only some 3 million chips
(equivalent to about one-tenth of TI's production),[62] production by
1968 was up to almost 20 million, more than a 6-fold increase in
just one year.[63] By delaying TI's entry and requiring that it join
hands with Sony, the government gave the Japanese semiconductor
firms, most of which were Japan's major computer and telecommunications companies, a crucial opportunity to build up economies of scale before encountering foreign competition. When Sperry
Rand decided it wanted to start producing in Japan rather than just
selling imported machines, similar restrictions forced it to make a
joint venture with Oki Electric in 1963 in order to get MITI permission to do so.

MITI's restrictions on foreign firms and technology were by no
means limited to the computer and semiconductor industries. The
Foreign Capital Law, for example, was used in several industries to
deter market entry. When Du Pont's patent on nylon expired in
1960, four new companies wanted to enter the market dominated
by two incumbent producers; MITI used the Foreign Capital Law
to delay for over a year the approval of the four firms' licensing
agreements with foreign companies. "With public authority stand-
ing at the gate, a would-be entrant's ability to clamber over the
economic barriers is no longer sufficient to assure his entry."[64]

Curbs on the activities of IBM, Sperry Rand, and TI were but
part of an elaborate network of protectionist measures buffering the
nascent computer industry. Tariffs were 25 percent,[65] and import
quotas were even more effective because they were easy to enforce;
to import a computer, it was necessary to receive an import license
from MITI.[66]

MITI used its authority over computer imports to prod Japanese
companies to "Buy Japanese." "Why do you have to use a foreign
computer?" was the greeting users faced when they came to MITI
to apply for a computer import.[67] "There were even cases where we
had to make it compulsory for them to change [their minds] from

a foreign to a domestic computer," recalled MITI's Hiramatsu Morihiko, whom the companies came to call "Devil Hiramatsu."[68] Yamamoto Shigeo, then head of Matsushita's data-processing division, recalled Hiramatsu's pressure tactics:

> We used one IBM and then our business expanded. When we went to MITI thinking we wanted to add one more [IBM], I was bawled out by Hiramatsu. He said he was sure that we must have some work for which we could use a domestic computer . . . so then we got a domestic computer, but it was not compatible with our IBM so it was a real hardship.[69]

An intentionally long import process also discouraged imports. Takahashi Shigeru of MITI's Agency of Industrial Science and Technology (AIST) gave as one reason for purchasing domestic machines that importing a computer could take as long as three years.[70]

Fujitsu Chairman Kobayashi Taiyū explained how MITI played an important role in stimulating the demand for domestic computers:

> Once Japanese companies like ours started to make computers, before we knew whether our computers would run or not, MITI was there helping us out by pressuring the auto and steel companies to use domestic computers.[71]

The government's decree also made use of the substantial impact that social pressure can have in a tightly knit, isolated society like that of Japan. "Once there was a consensus to use domestic computers, it was very difficult [due to social pressure] to use foreign products," recalled Takeuchi Hiroshi of the Long-Term Credit Bank.[72]

Some Japanese companies complained bitterly about government policies that forced them to use low-quality, unreliable domestic computers. MITI's pressure was particularly resented in the early 1960s because domestic machines were substantially inferior to their foreign counterparts. In 1961, 19 companies applied to import IBM's 1401 machine, explaining apologetically that they were sorry to apply for imports but that they did not want to be used as guinea pigs for the domestic computer makers.[73] Other firms criticized MITI policy, saying that domestic computers were "obstructions to the promotion of rationalization [efficiency]."[74] "There was huge

risk involved in buying Japanese computers," recalled Inose Hiroshi, former Dean of Tokyo University's Engineering Department.[75]
Government institutions were, of course, expected to purchase
domestic machines. "In principle, government offices are to use
Japanese computers," said Nakagawa Takashi of MITI. "As for private firms, it is okay if they want one foreign computer, but we
will never allow them to import more than one."[76] But firms in
growing industries such as steel, autos, and banking continued to
submit applications to MITI to import computers. Government institutions themselves eagerly sought IBM machines.[77] Even MITI
people asked to import IBMs.[78] Such purchases threatened to un-
dermine the policy. MITI's Hiramatsu went from official to official
lobbying against such applications. "We have to first show them
[Japanese users] that we will use Japanese computers."[79] "MITI
says it is outrageous for the Bank of Japan (BOJ) to use an IBM
machine," said a former BOJ official. So, when the bank moved to
upgrade its IBM, it paid lip service to domestic machines, sending
numerous statements to MITI in support of the policy.[80]

Some rebelled against the pressure. "It is crazy for you to pressure
NTT in its selection of a computer," an NTT official once warned
MITI's Nakagawa. "We will take you to court!"[81] NTT did not
succumb to MITI's pressure: As late as 1971, NTT was using 172
systems, 109 of which were foreign; of these, 75 were IBM.[82] NTT
favored foreign computers in the 1960s because, as the provider of
telephone services and other communications infrastructure to the
entire nation, it could not afford the substantial social costs inherent
in using inferior domestic computers. Even the Prime Minister's
office was using two IBM computers and only one domestic machine
as of 1970.[83]

Dependence on MOF for funds and interdependence with other
government agencies added to the difficulties MITI faced in implementing its policies. Instead of force, MITI adopted persuasion. In
cases where a foreign computer would greatly improve an agency's
efficiency, or, as in the case of NTT, make the nation's communications system more effective, MITI approved the import.

Even though MITI found it impossible to deny all import approvals, the process itself hindered imports. In 1982, 91 percent of all of the computers used by the government were domestic machines; when commercial users are included, the number drops to 56 percent.[84] This government favoritism towards domestic machines is all the more dramatic because the government tended to use large computers, where foreign firms were the most competitive.[85] Government favoritism provided an enormous market for domestic makers—a quarter of all computers purchased or rented during the 1960s.[86]

> Protectionism was one of the most important policies. The government created the computer market, first by making government labs buy domestic machines, then having national universities purchase them.[87]

The membership of the six major vertically integrated and diversified computer firms—Fujitsu, Hitachi, NEC, Mitsubishi, Toshiba, and Oki—in different *kinyū keiretsu* (industrial groups centered around a large bank) also facilitated government efforts to push a "Buy-Japan" policy. These groups, looser forms of the prewar zaibatsu that were dissolved by American Occupation authorities, are linked by buyer-supplier relationships, mutual shareholding, personnel exchanges, and ties to a major bank. Each member firm has independent management and is free to operate as it chooses. However, since the firms often own one another's shares, meet frequently, and share a common identity, they often purchase products from companies in their own group.

In a strict sense, these *keiretsu* often violate the anti-monopoly law the Occupation forces imposed to encourage a free market. Through a loose interpretation of the anti-monopoly law and encouragement of consolidations and mutual shareholding, the government promoted the resurgence of these industrial groupings after the war. In the computer industry as in others, the government used such groups to promote its goals. For example, when companies in the Mitsubishi group applied in 1961 to import over 30 IBM 1401 computers, MITI scolded the group: "There are too many applications to import IBM 1401s from the Mitsubishi group." MITI advised Mitsubishi officials either to use computers of other

Japanese companies or to make their own, "even if only for Mitsubishi group firms."[88] Mitsubishi chose to make its own machines.

While *keiretsu* firms have no legal obligation to purchase the computers of their affiliates, clearly there is an inclination to do so. As of 1968, about half the computers in use by firms in the major industrial groups were made by their *keiretsu*-group computer firm.[89]

Government protection of the domestic computer market, strengthened by the behavior of firms in Japan's *keiretsu*, helped shift demand to domestic machines and thereby handed domestic makers market share that, in a free market, would have been IBM's. Despite the inferiority of Japanese computers in comparison to their U.S. counterparts, dependence on imports dropped from 80 percent in 1959 to 20 percent by 1968;[90] purchases of foreign computers, including those made by IBM Japan, dropped from 93 percent in 1958 to 42.6 percent by 1969 (Table 1).[91] Nevertheless, foreign machines still dominated the more sophisticated large computer market at the end of the 1960s.[92]

Forcing Japanese companies to use inferior domestic machines in the 1960s clearly incurred substantial social costs. Yet these inefficiencies were a trade-off that was more than compensated for by rapid development in the long run; the industry avoided chronic inefficiencies in production and technological progress because domestic companies, though partially buffered from foreign firms, continued to compete amongst themselves. Indeed, the government promoted competition among several domestic firms. Moreover, the Japanese government, while limiting IBM's market share and subsidizing Japanese firms, used the threat of an unrestricted flood of IBM and UNIVAC computers to make domestic firms aware of the technological level they had to achieve to compete internationally. This threat, along with U.S. pressure to open up the computer market, made Japanese computer companies acutely aware that, without competitive machines, they could not survive in the long run. In short, protectionism bought time for the Japanese computer makers but offered no guarantees. The foreign threat and domestic competition continued to exert pressure upon them to make better products.

Table 1 Japanese and Foreign Shares of the Japanese Computer Market, 1958–1986 (units: billion yen; %) (Share of Annual Deliveries [Rental/Purchase] of General Purpose Computers)

	Year	1958	1959	1960	1961	1962	1963	1964	1965	1966	1967	1968	1969	1970	1971
JAPANESE	Amount	.07	.52	1.83	2.42	7.35	12.87	17.85	26.89	35.81	51.25	91.23	122.0	197.4	206
	Growth (%)	—	642.9	251.9	32.2	203.7	75.1	38.7	50.6	33.2	43.1	78.0	33.7	61.8	4.4
	Market Share (%)	6.9	21.5	27.3	18.2	33.2	29.7	42.8	52.2	53.6	47.2	56.5	57.4	59.7	58.8
FOREIGN (Primarily IBM)	Amount	.94	1.9	4.87	10.85	14.76	30.44	23.82	24.63	31.01	57.4	70.14	90.4	133.5	144.1
	Growth (%)	—	102.1	156.3	122.8	36	106.2	(−21.7)	3.4	25.9	85.1	22.2	28.9	47.7	7.9
	Market Share (%)	93.1	78.5	72.7	81.8	66.8	70.3	57.2	47.8	46.4	52.8	43.5	42.6	40.3	41.2
TOTAL	Amount	1.01	2.42	6.7	13.27	22.11	43.31	41.67	51.52	66.82	108.65	161.37	212.4	330.9	350.1
	Growth (%)	—	139.6	176.9	98.1	66.6	95.9	(−3.8)	23.6	29.7	62.6	48.5	31.6	55.8	5.8
	Market Share (%)	100	100	100	100	100	100	100	100	100	100	100	100	100	100

Year		1972	1973	1974	1975	1976	1977	1978	1979	1980	1981	1982	1983	1984	1985	1986
JAPANESE	Amount	222.7	271.4	310.3	342.7	415.1	713.5	794.8	909.8	1099.1	1350.2	1679.3	2090.4	2608.3	3054.5	3376
	Growth (%)	8.1	21.9	14.3	10.4	21.1	71.9	11.4	14.5	20.8	22.8	24.4	24.5	24.8	17.1	10.5
	Market Share (%)	53.2	51.4	48.4	55.8	56.7	66.4	67.2	69.6	72.5	72.2	74	74.4	74.6	74.4	76.7
FOREIGN (Primarily IBM)	Amount	196	256.9	330.6	271.3	316.4	361.1	387.1	398.1	416.9	519.8	588.7	719.8	890.2	1049.6	1027.
	Growth (%)	36	31.1	28.7	(−17.9)	16.6	14.1	7.2	2.8	4.7	24.7	13.3	22.3	23.7	17.9	(−2.2)
	Market Share (%)	46.8	48.6	51.6	44.2	43.3	33.6	32.8	30.4	27.5	27.8	26	25.6	25.4	25.6	23.3
TOTAL	Amount	418.7	528.3	640.9	614	731.5	1074.6	1181.9	1307.9	1516	1870	2268	2810.2	3498.5	4104.1	4403.0
	Growth (%)	19.6	26.2	21.3	(−4.2)	19.1	46.9	10	10.7	15.9	23.4	21.3	23.9	24.5	17.3	7.3
	Market Share (%)	100	100	100	100	100	100	100	100	100	100	100	100	100	100	100

Sources: JECC Kompyūtā Nōto, 1979, p. 10–11; Kompyūtopia, January 1981, 1983 and other January issues; Fujitsu no Gaikyō, 1987, p. 18.

Note: Some discrepancies may occur due to rounding.

Despite the importance of protectionism in offering a safe harbor for Japan's computer makers, it was not in itself enough to nurture an economically viable domestic industry. To encourage the firms to invest more heavily in computers, the government used a variety of subsidies, low-interest loans, tax benefits, and loan guarantees. This aid reduced the costs and risks of making computers while raising profit expectations. The measures assured the firms that, if they invested heavily to develop technologically advanced computers, they would have a good chance for a long-term return on their investment.

Contrary to the conclusions of some studies of Japan's industrial policy, this book shows that, at least in respect to computers, government monetary aid was significant, even compared to what the private sector itself was investing. In the 1960s, estimated government subsidies and tax benefits to the computer industry totaled $131.7 million (Appendix A), an amount equivalent to 46 percent of what the private sector itself invested in R&D and plant and equipment in the industry in that period ($288.6 million; Appendix B). If we include government loans of $410.3 million, total government aid was equivalent to 188 percent of what the firms were themselves investing. This does not include the benefit derived from government procurement of approximately one quarter of all domestic computers.

After World War II, several financial institutions were set up to funnel funds into industries deemed strategic, such as steel and chemicals. The Japan Development Bank (JDB), established in April 1951, supplied low-interest loans, primarily for investment in modern plant and equipment to government-designated industries. JDB loans, by signaling to private banks that the government was supporting an industry, induced those institutions to make loans to firms in that industry.[93] "If the JDB lends money to an industry, that means the government is backing it. Other banks will also lend money because they feel that MITI will rescue them if things really get into a pinch," explained Takeuchi Hiroshi, Managing Director of the Long-Term Credit Bank of Japan (LTCB).[94] The Japan Import-

Export Bank (JIEB),[95] established in 1950 to provide financing to stimulate exports, has also helped the vertically integrated computer companies by financing their exports of products ranging from consumer electronics to computer automated factories.

Two other quasi-government banks—the Industrial Bank of Japan (IBJ) and the LTCB—have channeled scarce resources into strategic industries such as computers. The LTCB, established in 1952 with 50 percent government ownership, later went private but continues to see itself as an institution of government policy.[96] "We get special privileges from the government," explained Takeuchi of the LTCB. "To get these privileges, we must cooperate with government policy."[97]

The IBJ, established in 1902 as a special bank under government supervision, was transformed into a private bank in 1950 by the U.S. Occupation. But Japanese still consider the IBJ a close ally of MITI and its objectives.[98] "We were a national bank until 1950," explained Inaba Masahiro of the IBJ; "because of this historical relationship our way of thinking is close to that of the government."[99] Unlike the United States, where the Glass-Steagall Act prohibits bank ownership of corporate shares, Japanese banks such as the LTCB and IBJ are each allowed to hold up to 5 percent of a company's shares, and such holdings tend to identify them as government-policy banks.[100] They have been key suppliers of capital both directly to Japan's computer companies[101] and for setting up various MITI-sponsored institutions to promote the industry's growth.

While the quasi-public banks helped guide funds into specific industries, this relationship was reinforced by more direct financial controls. MOF oversees the Bank of Japan (BOJ), "the single tap through which virtually the entire Japanese monetary and credit supply must flow."[102] The BOJ lends money to the 13 city banks, which in turn lend money to firms at low interest rates set by the government. Low interest rates created excess demand for loans and thereby gave MOF the power to allocate credit through its control over the BOJ.[103] "Few scholars dispute that MOF used 'administrative guidance'[104] to direct credit to specific industries or even specific firms in need of funds for expansion of their productive capacities," argues Kozo Yamamura, an economist at the University of Washington.[105]

One of the most powerful sources of capital for industrial development in Japan is the Fiscal Investment and Loan Program (FILP), a huge discretionary "second budget" separate from the general account budget.[106] This budget, first established in 1953 when MOF pooled the postal-savings accounts, national pensions, and various other accounts, is made annually by MITI and MOF bureaucrats, with little interference from outside interest groups. As of 1988, this postal-savings-account system alone had deposits of over 120 trillion yen ($894 billion), making it the largest financial institution in the world.[107]

These institutions—the government-policy banks and the postal-savings system—provided the government with the funds it needed to target computers. The government has tried to get the most clout out of each yen of financial aid by using it to influence firms' decisions at the margin—by granting firms just enough assistance to encourage them to make a given investment, but no more, and by tying the aid to specific investments. For basic R&D considered to at best have long-term prospects for commercialization, the government has footed the entire bill.[108] For R&D that can be commercialized immediately, the government grants subsidies to cover about half a project's total cost. These subsidies are actually "conditional loans" *(hojokin)* which, at least in theory, must be repaid, depending on the success of the project.[109] In short, as the content of an R&D project moves from the basic R&D stage to the commercialization stage, the government grants less aid and the form of aid generally changes from full payment, to subsidies, to low-interest loans, and finally to loan guarantees.

The government has also offered tax incentives to induce firms to invest more in modern equipment and R&D. Various tax policies reduced Japanese corporations' effective tax rate between 1950 and 1975 from 42 percent on average to 20 percent.[110] Companies also received tax breaks to encourage specific activities like R&D. If a firm's expenditures on R&D in any year exceeded its R&D expenditures in any previous year, 25 percent of the excess was allowed as a tax credit. The credit was increased to 50 percent for the portion of the excess above 15 percent of the amount spent in the previous peak year. The credit was limited to 10 percent of the company's taxable-income tax.[111]

Not until the 1970s and 1980s would the government make more extensive use of tailor-made tax policies to promote computers. In the 1960s, only one such measure—the computer buyback reserve—was used. Enacted in 1968, it allowed firms to put 15 percent of the revenue received from a computer sale into a tax-free reserve to be used when the user traded in the computer. To prevent IBM Japan from benefiting from this measure, it was allowed only for companies renting through joint-venture rental firms.

If Japan's banks, postal-savings system, and tax policies played a key role in financing the industry's development, so did its national phone company—NTT. A government monopoly up until April 1985, then partially privatized, but still under government control, NTT pumped huge, but relatively invisible, amounts of money into the computer industry. "NTT's financial support was critical to the firms' survival,"[112] explained Maeda Norihiko, a former high-level MITI official who participated in developing and implementing MITI's computer industry policies.

Set up by U.S. Occupation authorities in 1952 as an independent entity under the jurisdiction of the Ministry of Post and Telecommunications (MPT), NTT is one of the biggest corporations in the world today. NTT has been able to use its financial muscle to fund R&D by NEC, Hitachi, Oki, and Fujitsu—the four computer firms that also have large telecommunications divisions—and to purchase their products at prices higher than normal. Indeed, NTT is referred to as the *doru bako* (dollar box) helping these firms survive.[113] Its high quality standards have also pressured domestic makers to pour resources into quality control. Fujitsu's Tajiri Yasushi argued that

NTT has probably been the greatest help to Fujitsu's business. Because of the profitability of doing business with NTT, it was more important [than MITI] for private industry. Our business with NTT has always been based on NTT purchasing the product, and we have always made a profit on business with NTT.[114]

NTT got its first break into the industry in the late 1960s when the line dividing the fields of computers and data communications started to blur. By funneling profits from its telephone operations into data-communications R&D, most of which was consigned to Fujitsu, Hitachi, and NEC—the same three firms that MITI consistently promoted—NTT acted as a patron to the infant industry. While the firms clearly fit into NTT's strategy, NTT was also a key component of the companies' own corporate strategies.

MITI initially opposed NTT's entry into what was considered MITI territory, but the Ministry and its arch rival, MPT, which supervises NTT, squared away their differences in order to achieve a higher national objective: opposing foreign firms and promoting the development of a strong domestic computer/data communications industry.

MITI needed NTT's resources to finance its computer strategy because the tight-fisted MOF was not always willing to provide the funds. NTT was flush with funds from high-priced telephone installations and services and, as an "independent" entity, had abundant cash with which to subsidize computers for use in data-communications systems.

The Japanese government saw a strategic role for NTT in computers. Makino Yasuo, a high-level MPT official, explained in parliamentary proceedings: NTT "has substantial organizational, technological, and financial power. We think that one major way to fully utilize and enlarge this [our resources] is to promote Japan's on-line information processing."[115] When opposition-party members complained in parliamentary committees that NTT was subsidizing its data-communications division with profits from telephone operations rather than using the profits to alleviate the shortage of telephones,[116] MPT Minister Ide Ichitarō replied that, while in principle NTT wanted its data-communications division to be self-supporting, it was still, at that time (1971), in the red.[117]

Not only could NTT dip into profits from other divisions to

invest heavily in data communications; it also received a variety of consignment fees and low-interest loans from the government annually. For example, from 1964–1971, NTT received a total of 157 billion yen ($436.1 million) in low-interest loans[118] from the FILP budget, largely composed of citizens' savings in post-office accounts, and a total of 504.7 billion yen ($1.4 billion) in consignment fees from the general budget.[119] Toda Iwao, head of NTT's Communications and Information Processing Laboratory, explained further how NTT was able to build up its financial resources:

> When NTT was established [in 1952], the first president was a very great man; he said that, "without money, we cannot do any business," so he created a bond system whereby people who wanted to have a phone had to buy a bond for 100,000 yen [then about $278] from NTT. Then NTT would return the money after ten years. This was a system of getting money in advance, so NTT got a lot of money in advance and invested it in telecommunications equipment and R&D. As demand increased, so did the [up-front bond] money; of course, users also paid a monthly fee.[120]

Didn't consumers complain about this requirement of 100,000 yen, an enormous amount of money in a war-devastated nation? "They made it a law . . . that's why I said the first president was great," replied Toda.[121] Indeed, Japan was not as concerned with whether the average Japanese could afford a telephone as with getting the funds to build a competitive industry.

NTT's dependence on private companies for all its equipment and much of its R&D gave those firms in the "NTT family" a guarantee of substantial R&D grants and heavy procurement of their products. NEC's President Kobayashi Kōji, said:

> If we are to start doing an on-line information service, it will take a substantial amount of money, so if a large firm like NTT does not start it for us, . . . it cannot be done . . . so I want NTT to put all its power into it for us and invest in it. I look forward to NTT's doing the same as America's Department of Defense.[122]

"If you look at the projects done by U.S. businesses and the Pentagon, it is exactly the same thing as the projects between Fujitsu and NTT," explained one Fujitsu manager.[123] Indeed, firms in the so-called NTT family, such as Fujitsu, NEC, and Hitachi, not only got NTT to finance a substantial portion of their research; they also, by manufacturing equipment for NTT, were essentially guaranteed a large share of NTT's procurement, which totaled approximately $13.3 billion from 1965 to 1975.[124] As of 1968, 70 percent of all NTT purchases were from Fujitsu, NEC, Oki, and Hitachi.[125] NTT bought 60 percent of each of these firms' telecommunications production.[126] By concentrating its resources on a few vertically integrated and diversified companies, the NTT helped them gain the economies of scale and technological expertise needed to compete with IBM, yet still left the firms to compete with one another in taking these gains to the marketplace for commercial products as rapidly and efficiently as possible. "NTT is the most important player in the computer industry."[127]

The amounts NTT spent on computers for use in its communications network were substantial: 170 billion yen ($472.2 million) over the five-year period starting in 1968,[128] with the bulk going to support the development and procurement of machines made by Fujitsu, Hitachi, and NEC.

While NTT and MITI provided substantial financial backing to the industry in the 1960s, the amounts would be even higher in the 1970s, though would never reach the level of the U.S. government's support for R&D. Yet, financial support in the 1960s was indispensable to the firms' technological advancement and improvement in production: Including loans, it was some 188 percent of what the firms were investing themselves in computers at that time. Moreover, it acted as a lever to encourage the private sector to commit some of its own scarce capital and human resources to computer development. This government financial aid, together with profits from other divisions, enabled the computer makers to stay afloat in the 1960s, when most were losing substantial amounts of money; even the best off—Fujitsu—did not turn a profit in computers until about 1966.

> In the 1960s, Japanese companies almost gave us their computers. They wanted us to work with them and give them feedback to improve their systems. If we wanted new software, they would give it to us for free. They were losing money, but they looked at it over the long term.[129]

explained Tokyo University's Inose. It is hard to imagine that they could have practiced business this way if not for the substantial financial backing provided by the Japanese government.

Protectionism and financial assistance prepared the ground and planted the seeds for a computer industry. But this alone by no means guaranteed a good crop. The industry required a healthy market environment in which to grow. The government, by persuading the computer firms to specialize, helped them build up the economies of scale and technological expertise necessary to compete with a giant like IBM.

Government attempts to influence how many firms operated in the computer industry and which firms conducted what type of R&D were aimed at promoting more efficient production, R&D, and sales—what the Japanese call *gōrika* (rationalization). While *gōrika* would involve pressures for mergers and other drastic measures in the early 1970s, in the 1960s it primarily manifested itself in cooperative R&D projects organized and sponsored by MITI and NTT. "Cooperative" R&D conjures up images of members of different firms working together on the same problem. While this did occur, it was rare. For the most part, tasks were assigned to different companies. In some cases, the firms divided up the work and gave one another access to the resulting patents; in other cases, the firms split into groups to take different approaches to the same problem, while agreeing to share results. In general, R&D projects have encouraged NEC, Fujitsu, and Hitachi to concentrate their efforts on mainframes, memory devices, and integrated circuits; and Oki, Mitsubishi, and Toshiba on peripheral equipment and small computers for specialized uses. It is no coincidence that the former three firms are today Japan's major makers of mainframes, the latter three of peripheral equipment and small, specialized computers.

The first cooperative R&D project sponsored by the government—the FONTAC project—was aimed at helping the firms compete with IBM's second generation 1401 machine, for which Japanese companies had been flooding MITI's office with import applications. Half the cost of this 26-month project, which started in September 1962, was covered by a 350-million-yen ($972,000) subsidy.[130] The project, which attempted to create a prototype machine to counter IBM's second-generation computers, was largely a failure.

The three major telecommunications firms—Fujitsu, NEC, and Oki—were selected to work on the project: Fujitsu developed the main processor, NEC and Oki the peripheral equipment. When the project was completed in late 1964, the parts of the prototype machine made by the different firms did not connect properly: "The FONTAC machine did not run." [131] To add salt to the wound, IBM's new, more sophisticated 360-series computers, announced a few months before the project was even completed, made the FONTAC obsolete. Nonetheless, the firms gained valuable R&D experience: Fujitsu, after working another year on its FONTAC processor, used it in its second generation FACOM-230-50 computer (1965), [132] which, despite being outdated, was the most sophisticated domestic machine available at the time. Moreover, FONTAC, as the first joint government–private-sector effort in computers, set a precedent and model for cooperative research projects that is still followed today.

The failure of the FONTAC project put in stark relief for the government the need to commit greater financial and human resources to the industry. But the real blow was IBM's introduction in 1964 of the 360 series—a third-generation machine superior to anything in existence. Soon after IBM's announcement, Matsushita Electric Co., known for paying closer attention than other Japanese firms to short-term profits, withdrew from the industry and instead focused its attention on consumer electronics. Explaining the withdrawal, President Matsushita Konosuke said that seven companies were too many; "about three firms would be appropriate for the computer industry." [133]

IBM's new 360 family of computers represented a quantum leap in technology. Using integrated circuits rather than less sophisticated semiconductors, large core memories with fast access times, multiprogramming which allowed many programs to run simultaneously, and a new disk memory that allowed the machine to store far more information in secondary memory than ever dreamed possible, these computers were faster, smaller, and substantially cheaper, given their processing speed, than the machines in use at that time. In response, Fujitsu added ICs to upgrade its 230-50 computer and created a 230 family of machines. The other makers turned to the American firms with which they had technology agreements for help to counter IBM's 360 series.[134] The fruits of these efforts were hailed as "competitive" machines when they came out in 1968; but they were at best competitive with only the very earliest IBM 360 machines, and thus were three to four years behind; their software was inferior as was their overall reliability and quality.[135] Nonetheless, due to strong protectionist policies, they sold well and helped increase the Japanese makers' share of the market (Table 1).

But MITI and the makers knew that the introduction of IBM's 360 series meant they were falling further behind. Jolted by the announcement, MITI turned to its Electronics Industry Deliberation Council to chart out a course to shore up the industry. A computer-policy division was established in the Council, and Fujitsu's President, Okuda Kanjirō, was appointed to head it.[136] In its March 1966 report to MITI on "Policies for the Strengthening of the International Competitiveness of the Computer Industry," the Council proposed that, as of 1968, "a majority of computers in use [installed base] in Japan [must] be domestic models. Moreover, two-thirds of these domestic models [must] be developed in Japan."[137]

To attain this goal, the report urged that several steps be taken: that the firms standardize their products, form a production cartel for input-output devices, and put more effort into software development. It also urged that the government allow faster depreciation of computers to decrease computer users' tax burden. A national program to promote cooperative R&D between the public and private sectors was another of several key recommendations, most of which were implemented in the following decade.

The National Research and Development Program, more commonly known as the "Large-Scale" or *Ōgata* Project, was formed in MITI's Agency for Industrial Science and Technology (AIST) in 1966. For this program, committees of people from government, academia, and business select research topics deemed strategic to the nation's long-term development, such as technologies to solve energy and social-welfare problems or computer technologies too costly and risky for the private sector to develop alone. The research projects are fully funded by the government, and the work consigned to private companies. By the early 1980s over 20 projects had been undertaken in the program.[138]

The "Super High-Performance Computer Project" *(Chōkō Seinō Denshikeisanki)*, a 12-billion-yen ($33.33 million) effort that concentrated the entire Japanese computer industry on the development of one system—the prototype of a machine superior to IBM's 360 series[139]—was one of the program's first projects. The Electrotechnical Laboratory (ETL) inside AIST supervised the project, which started in 1966. Of the 12 billion yen, 9.9 billion was consigned to the firms; the remainder was used by the AIST Lab and to administer the project.[140] Research on hardware and software was divided: 47 percent of the total 9.9 billion yen consigned to the firms went to a software firm created specifically for the projects—the Japan Software Company.[141]

Twelve billion yen ($33.33 million) in government aid may seem to be a meager amount today, but it was a relatively large amount for the six computer firms, which together only invested 11.2 billion yen ($31.11 million) in R&D related to computers between 1961 and 1965.[142] Fujitsu's FACOM-230-60 and NEC's NEAC-2200-700 machines, both of which sold very well, each cost an estimated 2–3 billion yen ($5.56–$8.33 million) to develop,[143] only a fraction of the consignment payment granted for this project.

The government, in October 1967, made a general plan of the computer system it wanted developed and invited the three top mainframe companies to submit proposals for the machine. As in subsequent R&D projects, MITI wanted to set a very high technological goal, whereas the firms wanted a lower goal that could be commercialized more quickly.[144] The firms submitted their proposals, and Hitachi emerged victorious in late 1968, thereby becoming the leader responsible for creating the final prototype.[145] Ultimately, they extended the project a year because, mid-project, IBM introduced a machine using a metal-oxide semiconductor (MOS) design memory; in response, the project members decided to switch their efforts from the less sophisticated core-design memory they had planned to a more advanced MOS memory.[146]

Hitachi, Fujitsu, and NEC were assigned research on mainframes and integrated circuits. With significantly larger market shares than the other three domestic makers, the market had already "picked" them as the strongest companies. The government tried to further buttress these companies by alloting them the most sophisticated research—the mainframe and ICs—in this and later projects.

The government encouraged these three companies to form a research cooperative along with a new software firm, the Japan Software Company, which would develop the project software. Toshiba, Mitsubishi, and Oki Electric were consigned work on peripheral equipment such as optical character recognition, Chinese character display, and graphic cathode tube (CRT) displays. By being prohibited from joining the research cooperative and being consigned peripheral equipment, these latter companies were gently nudged towards the less technologically sophisticated computer products and away from computer mainframes. Without the tax benefits and access to the know-how resulting from the joint mainframe research, these companies had little chance of succeeding in the development of large computers.

This project represented the makers' first shot at creating a sophisticated computer without help from their foreign partners; developing integrated circuits, memories, secondary storage systems, and a series of compatible machines were all new to them. They achieved most of their specific hardware goals,[147] but they were defeated in their overly ambitious goal of making the world's most advanced computer. "Though not a commercial success, the project was very important to the industry for R&D," explained Tokyo University's Inose, who participated in the project.[148] Though the Japanese were advancing technologically, in the marketplace they continued to fall further behind.

Not all the project goals were reached. According to AIST's final evaluation in February 1973, some specific technical goals, such as those for pipeline operations and letter-recognition devices, were not fully achieved.[149] But the cooperative endeavor helped the industry move forward technologically in several strategic areas. Of paramount importance were advances in the development of ICs, which made it possible to make powerful computers much smaller in size.[150] Development of a more sophisticated main memory cut central processing unit (CPU) idle time substantially, allowing the user to get more computing done per yen spent.[151] The project's standardization of the firms' input-output interface[152] facilitated the firms' inroads into peripherals in the 1970s. Cooperation on standards allowed the firms to focus their efforts on making a smaller range of high-quality products; no longer did each firm have to make every type of device necessary for their systems. This also reduced the risks for the consumer; even if a company went out of business, the user knew that the now defunct firm's products could be plugged into other companies' machines.

Thus, despite the inability to achieve all its over-ambitious targets for computer hardware, the project spurred the industry to make technological headway in integrated circuits and high-speed memories; had Japanese firms not been able to offer these advances in their products, it would have been difficult to persuade computer users to buy domestic machines. Would the firms have been able to make such advances on their own without the project? "They could have done it, but time-wise they would have been very late; one of the main purposes of the project was to help them make the advances as fast as possible," explained a former MITI official.[153] Kuwahara Yutaka of Hitachi's Central Laboratory agreed: "National projects [like the super high-performance-computer project] help us do things earlier rather than later."[154] Aiso Hideo, then a MITI laboratory researcher working on the project and later a professor of Keio University who heads both the fifth-generation and supercomputer projects, argued, "It would have been very difficult for a firm to do it alone; also, [without the project], Hitachi would have gone along with RCA [then its technical partner] and would not have developed its own technology."[155]

As financier of the project, the government owned the resulting patents but offered them to participating firms at low prices.[156] The patents were also made available to other companies to accelerate diffusion of the new technologies, although outsiders did not have the advantage of know-how gained in the project. The cartel-like division of labor, coupled with sharing the resulting patents, reduced redundant investment and allowed the industry as a whole to develop a system prototype that no one firm alone had enough resources to do.

NEC and Hitachi used the project's new technological advances in a subsequent NTT project; [157] and Hitachi also used the mainframe technology in commercializing its 8700 model soon after the project ended. [158] The 8700, though not competitive with the IBMs of the time, sold well, in part due to government procurement, "Buy-Japan" pressure on the private sector, and the tendency of *keiretsu* firms to buy from their group computer company. Indeed, about a year before the Super High-Performance Computer Project was completed, IBM introduced its 370 series, a technological leap ahead of its 360 series.

Key advances in hardware notwithstanding, the project completely failed in the area of software. The joint-venture software firm—the Japan Software Co.—that MITI encouraged NEC, Fujitsu, Hitachi, and the Industrial Bank of Japan (IBJ) to create turned out to be nothing short of a fiasco. [159] The Japan Software Co. was created to develop the software for the project but, insulated from the market forces that would require it to keep in touch with consumer demand and managed by people having little knowledge of software technology or trends, it was never able to attain its goals. Having been guaranteed government subsidies for the 6-year project, the shareholder firms had little motivation to worry about whether the company was competitive in the marketplace. The company was doomed from the start because of inappropriate management and the fact that the subsidies were not tied to performance; these problems were further exacerbated by the fact that the project software represented the nation's first attempt to develop operating-system software; the software for the earlier FONTAC project had been farmed out to a U.S. company. [160]

The shareholder companies started squabbling early on. Each wanted to prevent the other from dominating management of the *kokusaku gaisha* (national-policy company.) To solve the problem, the committee in charge of preparing for the company's establishment decided the joint venture should have a few engineers from each computer company, with the remaining engineers and the chairman to be selected from a group of "neutral" people. But, while the officers of the Japan Software Co. may have been "neutral" to the firms, they had a distinct government tilt: [161] The President, Kitadai Seiya, was a former vice-president of Japan's central bank; several officials from MITI's Small and Medium Business Enterprise Bureau retired and "descended from heaven" *(amakudari)* into the board of Japan Software; [162] other board members came from various ministries and the IBJ. [163] Would Japan Software have had a better chance at success if it had been run by a businessman familiar with software technology? "It would have done better perhaps, but even businessmen [in Japan] did not know about software. The Japan Software Co. was too premature," [164] explained Professor Inose.

These managers, from the top echelons of Japan's business and government institutions, viewed the company as a prestigious national effort that should be placed above the nitty-gritty of private software firms.

> Japan Software is an elite company. It must always be one step ahead of the private software companies. Thus, work for the private sector should be left to general software companies. . . . Just because they say that in the future the large-scale [super high-performance computer] project work will taper off does not mean that it is necessary for Japan Software to be reduced so low as to do business in the same arena as the private software companies. [165]

Japan Software had a tall order to fill: to develop a "common language" that would enable any program to be used on any NEC, Fujitsu, or Hitachi machine. [166] The idea sounded attractive: If the three mainframe makers could use the same software, they could sharply reduce their costs. But the idea proved technologically infeasible for Japan's inexperienced software technicians. Moreover, the intimate relationship of software to hardware and design specifications made it difficult to reverse engineer U.S. software as they had done for hardware. The Japanese language served only to further exacerbate their deficiencies.

Consequently, the technical goals for project software were very vague, and the company, despite a 3-billion-yen subsidy,[167] was not able to come close to achieving them. In its final evaluation of the results, MITI's AIST stated that the common language could not even be evaluated;[168] the attempt to create a common language ended in humbling defeat. The upshot: The company was dissolved in December 1972, just five months after the project ended; it had not developed enough outside orders to survive once the project subsidies stopped. Indeed, the project work accounted for an overwhelming share—77 percent—of the firm's total sales of 3.9 billion yen between 1966 and 1971.[169] As long as the project was in process, the firm was financially sound, but, when the project ended, orders plunged, leaving it with accumulated debts of 342 million yen ($950,000).[170]

Japan Software's inability to make sophisticated software was one reason why it was not able to attract outside orders. But the company was as capable in simpler software as other Japanese software companies and could have gotten such orders had it not been for its policy of setting prices some 10 percent higher than the market price.[171] While some software houses responded to this price leadership by raising their prices, the subcontractors of the computer firms did not, which left the national-policy company at a competitive disadvantage in attracting new business. MITI did not make it clear to the managers that the firm had to succeed in the marketplace to survive.[172] "The government was too easy on Japan Software. Its prices were very high. MITI did not have a good plan for the company to survive over the long term," explained Yamamoto of JIPDEC.[173] Aiso added, "They did not have to compete with other firms [as long as the project subsidies lasted] so they could do whatever they wanted."[174]

Other market factors out of management's control also contributed to the company's demise. IBM, yielding to U.S. antitrust policy, unbundled its software and hardware prices in the early 1970s, thereby allowing companies the option of pursuing an IBM-com-

patible strategy—making hardware like IBM's that could run on
IBM software. Two of the three computer makers in the Japan Software Co.—Fujitsu and Hitachi—decided to go IBM-compatible,
thereby reducing their need for a joint-venture software company
that would, because of NEC's participation, also develop non-IBM
compatible software. A second factor—the soaring cost of software
development as a proportion of a system's total cost—further exacerbated doubts about the company's long-term usefulness. OECD
data suggest that software accounted for about 5–10 percent of the
cost of a computer in the U.S. in the 1950s but increased to 50
percent in the late 1960s and 70 percent in the early 1970s.[175] As
this trend progressed, the makers decided that they did not want to
have an increasingly important part of their computer systems produced outside their firms; they wanted to keep their hands directly
involved in the software business.[176]

Labor-union problems provided a convenient excuse for MITI and
the computer firms to abandon the floundering company. Software
engineers, working overtime to reach the project goals, demanded
better wages in exchange.[177] But these pleas fell on deaf ears, since
the company was already in a tight financial bind. Ultimately, these
demands by the union's so-called "Communist" members gave the
firm a bad reputation; people in the industry, saying Japan Software
had serious problems with product development because of the union-management struggle, started ordering software from other firms.[178]

Fujitsu's Naitō Tsugio took over the presidency of Japan Software
in late 1971 to try to solve the union problem among others. But
Fujitsu's grip immediately turned the other shareholder firms—NEC
and Hitachi—away from the company, further exacerbating the
plunge in Japan Software's sales.[179] Then MITI and Fujitsu set out
to bankrupt the firm: Fujitsu started its own software company and
enticed top Japan Software engineers to work for it;[180] MITI threatened to give software contracts for other national projects to firms
other than Japan Software because of its union problems. In a letter
from Japan Software Managing Director Sonobe Tatsurō to the Industrial Bank of Japan (IBJ) in May 1972, Sonobe expressed his
opposition to rejuvenating the staggering software firm because most

of the union members were Communists and because of MITI's concerns about the firms:

> Now MITI is showing great hesitation about consigning the software for the second large-scale project [pattern project] [to Japan Software] because of the Communists dominating the union . . . MITI is requesting that we get rid of them.[181]

The Japan Software Co. fiasco illustrates the limitations of industrial policies when they target vague goals in areas where few have any expertise and when they are not structured in ways that require firms to become more competitive over time. The national-policy company was created in a protective cocoon, with no incentives to compete, so, at the end of the project when the firm was thrust out into the real world, market competition destroyed it.

Before the Super High-Performance Computer Project ended, precipitating the bankruptcy of the Japan Software Co., a new government actor had already jumped into the computer-data communications field to help shore up the domestic industry. NTT made its first entrance onto the computer-industry stage in 1968 when it announced a cooperative research project to develop a large-scale high-performance computer. The entry of NTT, with its enormous financial resources, procurement power, and research experience, was to have a profound impact on the long-term development of the industry. Even a former MITI man admitted that "NTT is one of the major forces backing up Japan's electronics industry; the roots of Japan's electronics industry are in NTT."[182]

Some felt that, by going into the field of computers and data communications, NTT was stepping into MITI's territory.[183] Ministerial squabbles over turf between MITI and the Ministry of Post and Telecommunication (MPT), which oversees NTT, are not uncommon. Nonetheless, they overcame their differences because of their fundamental agreement on a strategic national goal: to promote the development of a strong domestic computer-data communications industry free from foreign invaders. Actually, cooperation for the national good was not rare between the two institutions despite deep feelings of competition. In the late 1950s, when NTT and MITI were both experimenting with computers, leaders of both institutions got together and decided that NTT's Electrical Communications Laboratory (ECL) would develop a parametron-based [184] computer and MITI's Electrotechnical Laboratory (ETL) a transistor-based computer. "They divided it up that way so that, if one failed, at least the other might succeed," recalled Toda Iwao, the head of NTT's Communications and Information Processing Laboratory. [185]

Despite disagreements, MITI and MPT worked together to revise the Public Electric Communications Law to allow NTT legal entry into the field of data communications and services, which was not legal when NTT initially started its Dendenkosha [NTT] Information-Processing System (DIPS-1) Project in 1968. The motivation for the alliance was simple: to get the vertically integrated and diversified domestic electronics firms into communications services quickly in order to prevent its takeover by foreign firms when the market would inevitably, due to U.S. pressure, have to be opened. Honoki Minoru, director of NTT's data-communications division, explained NTT's motivation:

> In the background of NTT's having to go into data communications aggressively was, frankly, a view of this as a policy to counter IBM. If our computer makers had only been a bit stronger, it would have been okay for NTT not to do the DIPS Project, but five or six years ago, our national [computer] technology and IBM's were on different levels. Because of this, NTT had to take the lead and do it [develop computers for use in data communications]. Also, in regards to the liberalization of communications circuits, the situation was the same. The reason we hesitated for many years was because we were waiting until domestic technology caught up to that [IBM's] level. [186]

MPT Minister Ide Ichitarō also emphasized the importance of cooperation between MITI and MPT in nurturing an information society: "Both ministries will continue to promote appropriate policies, on which we are currently cooperating, for the development of a sound information society." [187]

In its first project—the DIPS-1 Project—NTT invested 30 billion yen ($83.33 million) to commercialize the results of MITI's

Super High-Performance Computer Project into a machine that NTT could use to offer on-line data communications services. NTT's project was not, as some claimed at the time, redundant with MITI's Super High-Performance Computer Project, which was aimed only at making a prototype.[188] Rather it used the MITI project's intermediate results on the design and production of LSIs and memory devices, the same input-output interface standard, and improved upon the compiler, which had not been completely successful in the MITI project, to develop a usable machine.[189] The same three firms that worked on the mainframe in MITI's Super High-Performance Computer Project developed the DIPS-1 system; MITI and NTT hoped that this would promote standardization among the nation's top three mainframe makers. To prevent one firm from dominating the field, NTT promoted competition among the three firms in the development of a DIPS machine; each firm studied logic design, production design, and production separately, and each made its own version of the DIPS-1 machine.[190] "If we cooperate with only one company, the technology will accumulate and stop there; we like to have a few firms compete because it speeds up development," explained Toda of NTT.[191]

The DIPS-1 Project achieved the bulk of its goals,[192] the most important of which were standardization and the development of a reliable large-scale computer system for use in its communications network. In contrast to MITI's project, the DIPS-1 Project targeted goals that were realistic in terms of computing speed and memory capacity, reflecting NTT's need for a usable machine to offer data-communications services as soon as possible.

The firm's DIPS-1 machines, sold exclusively to NTT since that was the only market for them, were available starting in August 1972. The machines were used to support a network of public data-communications services—the DEMOS-E and DRESS services[193]—to users throughout the nation. But only 22 DIPS-1-based systems were ever installed.[194] Indeed, NTT needed only a limited number; furthermore, just before the DIPS-1 machines hit the market, IBM announced a far more advanced series—the 370 series. It would take refinement of the results in a subsequent NTT effort—the DIPS-11

Project—to counter the IBM-370. Nevertheless, by developing a sophisticated domestic machine, even if it was not top class, the Japanese firms were able to get their foot in the telecommunications market and to gain the experience necessary for further advances.

> The DIPS Project was indispensable; it is most important in NTT projects to polish our front line of technology. We did not expect just to develop machines to sell to NTT; we gained good technology that we could use in later commercial machines. We like to be a business success, but technical success is of primary importance.[195]

Without DIPS, argued Professor Aiso, NTT could have started providing communications services only by using foreign computers.[196] Gaining a foothold through this project was thus of critical importance to warding off the foreign threat.

In the infant stage of the computer industry, the government rigged the market in favor of domestic firms. But it did so in a way that continuously forced domestic firms to produce better products. Protection, for example, was provided to prevent complete foreign domination. Yet UNIVAC and IBM imports along with IBM Japan production were allowed in limited quantities to remind firms of the technological gap they had to reduce in order to survive. Financial aid was tied to specific objectives to encourage the firms to do more R&D and to invest in the computers and computer components the government regarded as strategic to the industry's growth.

Pushing the technologically unsophisticated companies to invest in computers was one of the government's most difficult tasks in the 1960s. The firms lagged far behind IBM, and IBM's domination of the world market made the idea of competing frightening. They wanted to be in the computer business but were skeptical. It was up to the government to alter competition enough to persuade firms that investment in computers could be profitable in the long term, but not to protect them so much that they would get fat and inefficient. This was no easy task; it was thus inevitable that, in the 1960s, the government and the companies would go through a process of trial and error in an attempt to find a reasonable balance between government direction and the firms' individual corporate strategies on the one hand, and between helping the firms and pressuring them to advance on the other.

The R&D projects were a major way that MITI and NTT tried to cut overall costs and risks for the companies by directing them towards specific market segments. The FONTAC Project set a precedent for joint government–private-sector projects; its inability to produce a workable prototype showed the difficulties of this type of project. But Japan did not really get serious until IBM's 360 machines came out. The Super High-Performance Computer Project, backed by substantially more funds and government involvement than the FONTAC Project, helped the firms counter IBM's 360 series by concentrating their efforts on ICs, memories, and standardization. NTT's entry into the field of computers with the DIPS-1 Project supplied the industry with a much-needed injection of government money and support and resulted in the commercialization of a third-generation machine that could be used in NTT's telecommunications system. The failure of the Japan Software Co. highlighted the ineffectiveness of industrial policies that target vague goals and that do not require firms to become gradually competitive to survive. This failure led to greater software efforts by the government and industry in the 1970s.

While the government provided a variety of assistance to the industry in the 1960s, it by no means guaranteed long-term support for each firm; future assistance was contingent on a firm's success in the marketplace. As for the R&D projects, it was clear that the government was planning to support the industry over the long run, but failure of a firm to commercialize the results of one project jeopardized its chances for joining the next project.

The ability of the private sector and the government to reduce the technological gap with IBM to just four years by the early 1970s was in large part due to the selective protectionism, subsidization, and R&D cartels of the 1960s. But of at least equal importance was a short-staffed, hardly known, national-policy computer-rental company called the Japan Electronic Computer Co. that MITI and the firms created in the early 1960s. Without this institution's carrying the burden of financing rentals, the computer makers would not have been able to focus their efforts on improving their technology and production capabilities. To this innovative institution we now turn.

THREE

Increasing Supply and Demand: The Japan Electronic Computer Company

The Japan Electronic Computer Co. (JECC) has no sales division, only a few hundred employees, and at best earns profits of $1 to $2 million a year; it is not surprising that few Japanese have ever heard of it. Yet, this quasi-private computer-rental company has played a critical role in the development of a modern Japanese computer industry. To the all-star team of Japanese computer companies that jointly own JECC—Fujitsu, Hitachi, NEC, Toshiba, Mitsubishi, and Oki—the rental company is a conduit for a generous flow of subsidized government loans; between 1961 and 1981 the Japanese government poured some $2 billion in low-interest loans into JECC to help the company purchase computers from the member firms and rent them to the public at competitive rates.[1] With these funds, JECC rented some 65 percent of all domestic computers rented or sold in the 1960s, 30 percent in the 1970s, and 11 percent in the early 1980s. Through JECC, the fledgling computer makers received private bank loans to which they otherwise would not have had access.[2] For MITI, which placed many of its retired officials in top management spots at JECC, the public corporation provided an arena from which to steer the computer industry through turbulent waters. Through JECC, MITI quelled price wars, rationalized development efforts, and spurred the sales of domestic computers. With the strategy and government backing of a public corporation, and the profit, loss, and product constraints of a private company, JECC maintained a strategic balance between subsidizing the firms and pressuring them to make better computers.

JECC, which was created by MITI to promote the development of an economically viable computer industry, has been the most important single institution spurring the industry's development. Analysis of how it was established and how it influenced the demand, supply, price, and technological sophistication of domestic computers offers new insight into the ways in which state intervention can spur rather than stifle industrial development.

The creation of JECC was not the result of superior insight into the market mechanism and industrial development on the part of Japanese bureaucrats. Instead, it was the outcome of a dialectic between the opposing forces of a government's desire to control and the private sector's desire to be independent. Negotiations over JECC's establishment and operations show that the process of reaching consensus in Japan is not always as smooth as commonly believed— that the development of Japan's targeted industries has been the result of a complex interaction of public and private forces.

In 1960, when government and business leaders decided to promote a domestic computer industry, MITI proposed the creation of JECC as a "national-policy company" that would plan computer production, rent out computers, research large-scale computers, and promote programming. JECC would allot the development of parts of large-scale computers—mainframes, terminals, peripherals—to different firms, which would create prototypes. After purchasing the prototypes, JECC would commercialize them.[3] JECC would function as an institution of central planning for the industry. "In the early 1960s, the [Japanese] computer makers were really like babies walking in tottering steps; we felt we had to do something to help them. JECC was suggested as one way to help them," explained one former MITI official.[4]

MITI's idea seemed to make sense: By avoiding redundant research and gaining scales of production, Japan would be better positioned to stand up to IBM. To cement the ties between the national-policy firm and the private companies, MITI called for joint capitalization of JECC—half government, half private sector—and recommended that the private sector contribute engineers and the government long-term low-interest loans to the national-policy company. As it turned out, the Japanese companies fiercely resisted MITI's move, pointing to the deleterious impact the plan would have on competition. Kozakabashi Shōjirō, a section chief at Toshiba, complained:

> The plan for a national-policy company is aimed at promoting the development of [our backward] computer industry; but the kind of cooperative work [proposed by MITI] would only nip the bud of the free development that has already started.[5]

To counter MITI's proposal, NEC President Kobayashi Kōji suggested that each firm manufacture its own computers but that the government purchase and resell them.[6] Other industry people recommended that the JDB lend money to each firm to set up its own rental system. For the companies, the ideal was an independent industry receiving subsidies through low-interest government loans and guaranteed government purchases. But MOF, with tight control over the nation's purse strings, balked at the idea of supplying the enormous amount of funds necessary to maintain a national computer monopoly, and was even more opposed to giving separate grants to each company.[7] As a compromise of the MITI, MOF and private-sector proposals, JECC was established as a centralized but private joint-venture computer-rental company capitalized by seven firms.[8] While the government could use JECC to coordinate prices and influence the types of machines the makers produced, it would, in exchange, offer low-interest loans to JECC to enable it to purchase computers from the private companies that joined JECC. The companies were left to compete in researching, commercializing, and marketing their computer products.

The JECC system worked in the following way. After a user made an agreement with a computer maker for a specific machine at a monthly fee set in consultation with JECC, the user signed a rental agreement with JECC, which then purchased the computer from the maker and rented it to the user. Users were required to keep a computer for at least 15 months, after which they could trade it in for a new one at no penalty. When a computer was traded in, the maker had to buy it back from JECC at the remaining book value (Figure 1).

While marketing the computers was primarily the responsibility of the individual makers, JECC buttressed their efforts substantially by advertising itself as a renter of domestic machines at low monthly fees and by publishing extensively the benefits of using computers. Moreover, JECC's management of the rental system took a huge administrative burden off the shoulders of each individual computer maker.

Only seven companies joined JECC despite the fact that fifteen companies originally contracted with IBM for its basic patents.[9] A MITI committee of people from government, industry, and academia had concluded that success in the computer industry would require access to vast amounts of capital, amounts that only the seven large, experienced electric and telecommunications firms would be capable of generating.[10] MITI believed that the computer industry could support only a few profitable firms—that "excessive" competition would lead to redundant investment and cutthroat pricing, and thereby discourage firms from investing. Not surprisingly, the firms that joined JECC are Japan's primary computer makers today; the one exception is Matsushita, which withdrew from the computer industry in 1964 after IBM announced a new, technologically advanced series of computers.

Strategic industry decisions were made by a committee of industry people, academics, and bureaucrats, with expertise in diverse areas such as policymaking, business, and computer technology. This committee recommended that JECC initially focus on low-priced small computers in order to avoid direct competitive clashes with IBM. This strategy not only allowed the Japanese makers to capture a niche that IBM was more willing to relinquish but also focused the industry's scarce resources on the smallest and simplest machines; technological expertise and scale economies gained in these products would give them a foothold from which gradually to ex-

Figure 1 The JECC Rental System

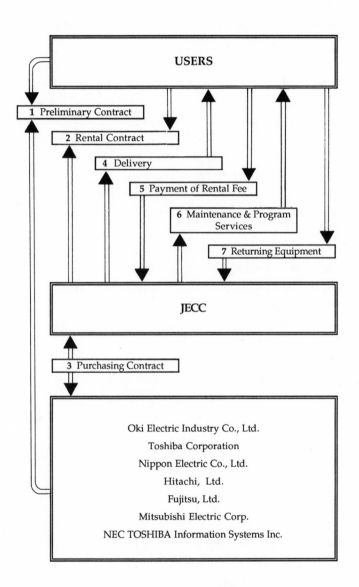

USERS

1 Preliminary Contract

2 Rental Contract

4 Delivery

5 Payment of Rental Fee

6 Maintenance & Program Services

7 Returning Equipment

JECC

3 Purchasing Contract

Oki Electric Industry Co., Ltd.
Toshiba Corporation
Nippon Electric Co., Ltd.
Hitachi, Ltd.
Fujitsu, Ltd.
Mitsubishi Electric Corp.
NEC TOSHIBA Information Systems Inc.

Source: JECC annual financial report, 1979

pand upscale. This approach contrasted sharply with that of the French, who focused on top-of-the-line, technologically sophisticated machines that failed to appeal to a broader market. From the beginning, the Japanese were interested in a marketable computer, not a national status symbol.

There were three key prices that set the parameters of this artificial market. First, the monthly rental fee was important because it was the basis of competition between domestic and foreign makers. Second, the price for which JECC bought a computer from the maker was critical because it determined the firm's revenue. Lastly, the book value of computers was important because the makers had to buy back from JECC at remaining book value machines that had been traded in; the method of depreciation—which determined the book value remaining after a given rental period—had a direct impact on the firms' cash flow.

There was no debate over how to set the first price—the monthly rental fee; MITI, JECC, and the computer makers agreed that it had to be set substantially lower than IBM's in order to be competitive. Indeed, even though their production costs were substantially higher and production scale far lower than IBM's, the Japanese makers had to rent their machines at prices some 40 percent lower than comparable IBMs in order to attract customers.[11]

But the other two prices were open to negotiation. Giving the makers their return on investment in advance by purchasing their machines and renting them to the public was JECC's primary method of subsidizing the industry; but the price for which JECC purchased machines from the makers and the price at which the makers would have to buy back from JECC machines that were traded in would determine how large that subsidy would actually be.

The computer makers naturally wanted to sell their machines to JECC for as high a price as possible—as much as 50 times the monthly rental fee—in order to get more up-front cash; but, for JECC, the higher the price, the more money it would need to borrow. MITI, concerned with JECC's survival as an institution, and MOF, concerned with JECC's annual requirements for low-interest loans, fought to keep prices at a level that would subsidize the firms without bankrupting JECC. They finally settled on 44, a level similar to IBM's at the time.[12] Later, however, when IBM cut its sales prices to only 25–30 times the monthly fee to attract more computer sales than rentals, JECC continued to purchase Japanese computers for a costlier 44 times the monthly fee; thus, the makers have continued to receive huge amounts of up-front cash through the JECC system at a time when, in a free market, they would have been forced to slash prices to compete with IBM. The computer makers naturally enjoyed this favorable multiplier, but it squeezed JECC's profits, forcing the government to continue supplying low-interest loans to the rental company. A JECC official explained that JECC's profits were intentionally kept low because the computer makers—JECC's shareholders—preferred that JECC buy their machines at high prices to supply them with more cash in advance.[13]

While, as a national-policy company, JECC could funnel substantial subsidies in the form of up-front cash to the makers, its responsibilities as a private corporation required that it post at least a meager profit and repay its loans on schedule. Thus, while JECC purchased the makers' machines at high prices, when users traded the machines in, the makers had to buy them back at the remaining book value—the value of the machine after depreciation; in effect the firms received up-front cash which they then had to pay back when their machines were traded in; the system penalized firms whose machines were returned after a short rental period.

In order to minimize this "buyback" book value, the companies tried to persuade JECC to use the accelerated depreciation method; under this method, in comparison with the slower straight-line method, JECC would depreciate (expense) more in the early years, thereby reducing the book value remaining when a user traded in the computer two or three years later. The government balked: While faster depreciation would decrease the book value for which firms had to buy back machines, it would also push JECC into the red, especially in the early years, because depreciation is expensed. MITI and MOF wanted JECC to depend as much as possible on private banks for loans; in fact they wanted to shift the entire burden of renting computers to the private sector as soon as the market allowed. If JECC ran at a loss, the ministries reasoned, private banks would be reluctant to grant it loans. To prevent JECC from running at a loss, the government decided that JECC would use the slower, straight-line method of depreciation (6 years) and that any potential losses would have to be borne by the makers themselves.[14]

Thus, although JECC subsidized the industry with substantial up-front cash and low-interest loans, the constraints on it as a private corporation would not allow it to use a depreciation method that would favor the firms at the risk of bankrupting itself. These private-sector constraints—JECC's depreciation and trade-in practices—put considerable pressure on the firms. By allowing users to trade in machines after 15 months, JECC pressured the makers continuously to offer improved computers, lest their competitors take away their customers; but offering new models every 15 months inevitably made existing models obsolete before a sufficient return had been made on them to cover costs, let alone to provide a profit. There was only one way the companies could alleviate this vicious circle: If models were offered that made major improvements on existing machines, users would be more likely to keep domestic machines for longer than the average 2.5 years;[15] this would allow the firms to introduce fewer models at a slower pace, thereby enabling them to receive a greater return on a given model before it became obsolete. By having JECC function like a private company in terms of depreciation and trade-in practices, the government forced the makers early on to confront a perennial problem in the computer industry: how to manage the pace at which they introduced technologically advanced computers in order to be profitable in the long run. This tension between technological advancement and profit runs like a thread through the history of computer development: Firms constantly have to evaluate whether to delay the introduction of new advanced machines until they get a better return on their existing ones.

Through its control over JECC, the government was able to shape the parameters of the emerging domestic computer market. With JECC renting computers for low monthly fees, the percentage of domestic machines rented and the overall supply and demand for

Table 2 Percentage of Foreign and Japanese Computers Rented
and Bought, 1957–1969 (%)

	1957	1958	1959	1960	1961	1962	1963
Japanese Computers							
Rented				3.7	27.8	45.8	55.4
Bought	100.0	100.0	100.0	96.3	72.2	54.2	44.6
Foreign Computers							
Rented		53.0	75.7	62.0	71.0	63.8	84.2
Bought	100.0	47.0	24.3	38.0	29.0	36.2	15.8

	1964	1965	1966	1967	1968	1969
Japanese Computers						
Rented	65.3	77.6	78.4	76.5	69.5	71.7
Bought	34.7	22.4	21.6	23.5	30.5	28.3
Foreign Computers						
Rented	89.9	82.6	75.9	82.8	73.6	77.8
Bought	10.1	17.4	24.1	17.2	26.4	22.2

Source: Denshi Kōgyō Nenkan, 1970–1971, p. 180.

domestic machines surged. Before JECC was created, only 4 percent of domestic machines were rented; this jumped to 46 percent one year after its establishment and to 78 percent by 1965 (Table 2).[16] The growth rate of the market for domestic computers far outstripped that of IBM and other foreign makers, despite the fact that Japanese computers were considered substantially inferior to their Western counterparts until the mid-1970s. With overall growth of 67 percent in computer purchases from 1961 to 1962, domestic makers enjoyed a 203 percent jump from 2.4 billion yen to 7.3 billion yen ($20.4 million), while foreign firms increased only 36 percent from 10.8 billion yen to 14.8 billion yen ($41 million). By 1965, the Japanese firms overtook foreign firms in market share, increasing sales 51 percent to gain a 52.2-percent share of the domestic market; that same year the sales of foreign firms grew a mere 3.4 percent, decreasing their market share to 47.8 percent (see Table 1).[17]

JECC had a very big effect in reducing our need for capital; if there had not been a JECC in the 1960s and 1970s, we [Fujitsu] could not have expanded our scale of production; in that sense JECC played a very big role.[18]

In addition to stimulating the demand for and supply of domestic computers, JECC acted as a conduit of vast, but relatively invisible, government funds to the firms. This financing freed the computer makers from having to take on the large loans they would have needed to rent out machines themselves and also supplied them with an immediate return on investment. Had the firms run their own rental systems, they would not only have had to provide financing for computer users but would also have received their return on a machine in meager payments spread over 44 months. Receiving the money for a sale immediately from JECC had a dramatic impact on their cash flow. For example, when Fujitsu sold $63.6 million worth of computers to JECC in 1969, it received the total amount immediately from JECC; had it rented out its machines on its own, Fujitsu would have received only $17.3 million (12/44) in 1969 and been stuck with financing the remaining $46.3 million. This vital up-front cash enabled the makers to concentrate their efforts and resources on production, quality, technology, and cost.

It is impossible to calculate definitively the importance of JECC to the firms. Nonetheless, we can estimate the benefit during the 1961–1969 period by calculating the subsidies implicit in low-interest JDB loans and in receiving an early return on investment. The subsidy implicit in low-interest JDB loans is the difference between the interest JECC paid on JDB loans and the estimate of what the firms would have had to pay if they had borrowed the money at the prime rate from private financial institutions. This subsidy amounted to 2.03 billion yen ($5.64 million) during the period from 1961 to 1969 (Appendix C).

The benefit of receiving their return on investment immediately under the JECC system can be estimated by comparing the firms' cash flow in the 1960s under the JECC rental system—217.3 billion yen (Table 3)—with the hypothetical cash flow they would

Table 3 Firms' Estimated Cash Flow under JECC, 1961–1969
(unit: billion yen)

	1961	1962	1963	1964	1965
Sales to JECC[1]	1.10	3.20	5.90	11.70	20.80
Computer Trade-Ins[2] (depreciated amount)	(0)	(.047)	(.462)	(1.176)	(2.734)
Estimated Cash Flow Under JECC	1.10	3.15	5.44	10.52	18.10

	1966	1967	1968	1969	Total
Sales to JECC[1]	26.90	36.80	66.60	82.50	
Computer Trade-Ins[2] (depreciated amount)	(5.168)	(7.389)	(8.880)	(12.354)	
Estimated Cash Flow Under JECC	21.730	29.41	57.72	70.15	217.30[1]

Sources:
1. *JECC Kompyūtā Nōto,* 1972, p. 255.
2. *Zaikai Kansoku,* May 1969, pp. 81, 84.
   Under the JECC system, the firms had to buy back computers that were traded in at their book (depreciated) value.
3. $603.6 million at 360 yen to the dollar.
   Some discrepancies may occur due to rounding.

have had under their own rental system—120.3 billion yen (Table 4). JECC thus plowed an additional 97.01 billion yen ($269.47 million) in up-front cash to the makers (Table 5). In the 1960s, this up-front cash, which was essentially an interest-free loan, constituted an 8.1-billion-yen ($22.5 million) subsidy; this is what the firms would have had to pay in interest if they had borrowed the up-front cash from private banks at the prime rate (Table 6). By giving the makers up-front cash, JECC made it possible for them to invest heavily to improve their computers. Indeed, if they had rented out their own computers, receiving a cash flow of 120.3 billion yen, it would have been extremely difficult, if not impossible, to invest the 103.9 billion yen they plowed into R&D and

Table 4 Hypothetical Cash Flow under Firms' Own Rental System, 1961–1969 (unit: billion yen)

	1961	1962	1963	1964	1965	1966	1967	1968	1969	Total
Expected Rental Income[1]	.300	.300	.300	.200						
Reduced Income due to Trade-Ins[2]	(0)									
E.R.I.		.873	.873	.873	.582					
R.I.		(−.047)								
E.R.I.			1.609	1.609	1.609	1.073				
R.I.			(−.462)							
E.R.I.				3.190	3.190	3.190	2.127			
R.I.				(−1.176)						
E.R.I.					5.670	5.670	5.670	3.780		
R.I.					(−2.734)					

E.R.I.					7.336	7.336	7.336	4.890	
R.I.					(−5.168)				
E.R.I.						10.040	10.040	10.040	
R.I.						(−7.389)			
E.R.I.							18.160	18.160	
R.I.							(−8.88)		
E.R.I.								22.500	
R.I.								(−12.354)	
Estimated Cash Flow under Own Rental System	.300	1.130	2.320	4.700	8.320	12.100	17.800	30.440	43.200	120.300[3]

Notes:

1. Expected Rental Income (E.R.I.). JECC's rental fee equals 1/44 of the sales price. This model assumes that the firms would also rent in the same way and thus receive their rental income over 44 months.

2. The firms' flow of expected income over 44 months will be reduced by an amount equivalent to the remaining book value of the traded-in machines. This assumes that the firms will use the same type and period of depreciation as JECC.

3. 120.3 billion yen equals $334.2 million at 360 yen to the dollar.

   Some discrepancies may occur due to rounding.

Table 5   Estimated Benefit of Up-Front Cash through JECC, 1961–1969 (unit: billion yen)

	1961	1962	1963	1964	1965
Firms' Estimated Cash Flow under JECC	1.10	3.15	5.44	10.52	18.10
Firms' Estimated Cash Flow under Own Rental System	0.30	1.13	2.32	4.70	8.32
Up-front Cash through JECC	0.80	2.02	3.12	5.82	9.78
	1966	1967	1968	1969	Total
Firms' Estimated Cash Flow under JECC	21.73	29.41	57.72	70.15	217.3
Firms' Estimated Cash Flow under Own Rental System	12.10	17.80	30.44	43.20	120.3
Up-front Cash through JECC	9.63	11.61	27.28	26.95	97.01[1]

Note: 1. $269.47 million at 360 yen to the dollar.
      Some discrepancies may occur due to rounding.

plant and equipment during the 1960s.[19] Had they done so, they would have only had 16.4 billion yen ($45.6 million) remaining to cover production and overhead costs.

> In order to compete in the marketplace against IBM's rental system, we needed a finance mechanism so that we could recover the development and manufacturing cost [of producing computers] as soon as possible; in that regard JECC was a great help to Fujitsu.[20]

The crux of the issue, however, is whether the firms could have obtained enough loans from private sources to finance their own rentals and, if they could have, whether they would have been willing to invest such exorbitant sums in the risky computer business. While impossible to prove, the evidence suggests that it is highly unlikely that, with the possible exception of Hitachi, they would have been able to acquire sufficient loans. "We could not have borrowed the money from banks for the purpose of renting computers," explained Tajiri of Fujitsu.[21] Even JECC, with strong government backing, was not able to attract adequate loans from the private sector. To assure JECC access to capital, MITI and the JDB established a system of "cooperative financing" *(kyōchō yūshi);* under this system, which was used to promote other strategic industries, representatives of the government, JECC, and the JDB met several times annually with a group of banks to negotiate loans adequate for JECC to rent out domestic computers. The major functions of the *kyōchō yūshi* system were to diversify risk and provide a stable supply of loans.[22] In the early 1960s, private sources were willing only to match JDB loans; later, the burden has been approximately 40 percent on the JDB, 60 percent on private sources.[23] A high-

Table 6   Estimated Subsidy Implicit in Receiving Return in
Advance—an Interest-Free Loan—through JECC,
1961–1969 (unit: billion yen)

	1961	1962	1963	1964	1965
Up-Front Cash (Interest-Free Loan)	0.80	2.02	3.12	5.82	9.78
Prime Rate (%)	8.70	8.70	8.70	8.70	8.70
Implicit Subsidy	0.07	0.18	0.27	0.51	0.85

	1966	1967	1968	1969	Total
Up-Front Cash (Interest-Free Loan)	9.63	11.61	27.28	26.95	97.01
Prime Rate (%)	8.40	8.20	8.20	8.20	
Implicit Subsidy	0.81	0.95	2.24	2.21	8.10[1]

Source: Prime rate data are from *Economic Statistics Annual,* Research and Statistics Department, The Bank of Japan.

Note: 1. 8.1 billion yen equals $22.5 million at 360 yen to the dollar.
　　　Some discrepancies may occur due to rounding.

level JDB official said in an interview that the JDB guaranteed loans that private financial institutions made to JECC in the 1960s.[24] But, even with this guarantee, private banks were willing only to maintain—not substantially increase—their level of loans to JECC when the market boomed in the late 1960s and early 1970s; as a result, JECC was forced to search overseas for the funds needed to support computer rentals.

Since a JDB guarantee was needed to induce private banks to lend to the government-backed JECC in the 1960s, it is highly unlikely that private banks would have made the huge loans the computer firms needed, especially since such loans would have tightly pinched the makers' balance sheets and income statements. To rent out their own machines in the 1960s, the firms would have needed at least 140.42 billion yen—the amount JECC borrowed from 1961 to 1969 (Table 7). But the industry invested only 103.9 billion yen in plant and equipment and R&D during this period;[25] they would have had to more than double their investment in order to rent out their own computers. Could the firms have borrowed that much money, and, even if they could, would they have been willing to invest it in a computer-rental system?

Fujitsu, for example, whose machines accounted for 25 percent of JECC's purchases from 1961 to 1969, would have had to borrow about 25 percent as much as JECC borrowed to finance the rentals of its machines; it would have needed an extra 35.1 billion yen, thereby more than doubling its long-term loans of 29.34 billion yen in this period, and pushing up its already high debt-equity ratio.[26]

It is not only improbable that the firms could have borrowed enough money, but also that they would have decided to enter the risky computer business. Indeed, JECC manipulated the market to make firms view entry as profitable in the long run. Even with JECC, most of the firms' computer divisions were in the red until the late 1960s;[27] without JECC, and the government backing it provided, they would have lost even more money. Had they entered, they, like RCA and GE of the United States, would have been under considerable financial pressure to withdraw from the risky business. They had little knowledge and experience in the

Table 7 New Loans to JECC, 1961–1969 (unit: million yen)

	1961	1962	1963	1964	1965
Total Loans	800	1,600	3,141	5,268	14,643
JDB	400	800	1,500	2,500	5,500
City banks	400	800	1,303	2,181	5,143
Trusts			338	587	1,700
Life insurance					1,250
Others					1,050
Mutual S&L					
Foreign					

	1966	1967	1968	1969	Total
Total Loans	22,392	20,604	28,132	43,840	140,420
JDB	8,000	6,000	8,000	18,000	
City banks	8,442	7,324	10,056	12,573	
Trusts	2,700	2,800	3,660	3,656	
Life Insurance	2,500	2,950	3,930	3,890	
Others	750	450	1,030	900	
Mutual S&L			650	1,050	
Foreign		1,080	806	3,771	

Source: JECC 10 Nenshi pp. 50–51, 59.

field, and their computers were far inferior to their foreign counter-parts. Who would lend money to firms operating in such a risky environment, and what firms would be willing to invest their scarce resources in such a losing venture?

JECC's financial backing was vital to the industry's development. But the national-policy rental company also buttressed the industry in other ways. In consultation with MITI and the computer makers, JECC set computer rental prices to prevent domestic price competition. The makers already had to sell at a loss to compete with IBM; the last thing the government and the industry wanted was for prices to be further whittled away by price competition among domestic makers.

In addition to setting the prices of domestic computers, JECC also required that all rental machines have its approval.[28] Since both JECC and the computer makers were interested in renting out the type of computers that users desired, market demand and production costs were the primary determinants of the machines that JECC approved. Nonetheless, JECC did use its discretion at times to pressure the makers to produce certain types of machines before market demand and production costs warranted such a strategy. For example, as the firms became competitive in small machines, JECC shifted its support from the rental of small computers to medium and large-scale ones, thereby encouraging the makers to increase their efforts to produce larger, more sophisticated machines.

JECC also used its discretion to compel the makers to manufacture computer parts locally rather than to import parts from foreign firms with which they had technology agreements and then assemble them domestically. Initially, JECC was willing to rent the computers of companies having at least 51 percent Japanese equity; however, in April 1968, MITI shifted the criteria from equity to local content, requiring that JECC rent out only computers having at least 90 percent domestic content.[29] JECC warned the makers that it would not rent imitations of their foreign affiliates' computers—the makers had to make "large design changes"; the firms balked, complaining that it would be too difficult to meet these requirements.[30] But MITI did not budge. Consequently, firms were not able to register some of their computers with JECC; Oki, for example, delayed applying to JECC for its OUK-9000 series until it could raise the local content, and JECC deferred approval of 10 Hitachi machines until 90 percent of their content was domestic.[31] The new local-content requirement gave Fujitsu, which did not have a technological cooperation agreement with a foreign firm, a competitive advantage and handicapped Oki, which depended on its 51–49 percent joint venture with Sperry Rand for UNIVAC computers.

JECC thus worked in various ways to influence competition in the emerging computer market. As a public corporation, it subsidized the companies; yet, as a private firm that needed to survive the demands of the marketplace, it pressured the computer makers to advance technologically and cut costs. Its dual public-private objectives forced a balance: JECC gave enough assistance to allow domestic firms to make the investment necessary to become competitive but did not shelter them to the extent that they could afford to become fat and inefficient. JECC influenced firms' decisions at the margin.

Maintaining this delicate balance was no simple task. In the late 1960s, JECC confronted its first serious conflict between supporting the industry on the one hand, and pressuring them to advance on the other. The conflict started when the firms, in response to IBM's introduction of a new advanced series of computers, were pressured to introduce new models earlier than they would have liked. Introducing new models inevitably meant having to buy back the machines customers traded in for the new models; this resulted in a deluge of trade-ins that threatened to destroy the industry. The ratio of the value of machines that the firms had to buy back to their new sales reached dangerous levels in the late 1960s: 24.3 percent in 1966, 30.8 percent in 1967, and 23.1 percent in 1968.[32] As the situation reached crisis proportions, MITI, JECC, and the makers responded with various strategies to help the firms curtail their buy-back burden. In 1967, JECC decreased the book value of traded-in computers by shortening the economic life of its computers for depreciation purposes from 6 years to 5 years and 4 months; to counterbalance the negative impact of this on JECC's profits, the government cut the JDB interest rate on loans to JECC from 8.2 percent to 7.5 percent.[33]

The makers also tried to drum up customers for used computers, most of which remained in inventory after having been traded in;[34] but Japanese users insisted on renting new machines. The government and the makers also tried to encourage firms to purchase rather than rent small computers. To do so, they established an installment payment system for small computers worth up to 50 million yen in 1966. MITI negotiated with the Industrial Bank of Japan and the Long-Term Credit Bank on behalf of the firms and persuaded each to lend 3 billion yen ($8.33 million) a year to finance the system.[35] But this endeavor proved to be futile. Begun on 1

October 1966, the system's first sale was not until the 17th, and that was of a Fujitsu computer to Fujitsu itself![36] This failure underlined the necessity for a rental system; with technology changing rapidly, users were not willing to purchase computers, even if they could make payments over several years.

The government also established a "Reserve for Computer Buyback Losses" in 1968, which allowed computer firms to place 10 percent of the sales price of a computer they sold into a tax-free reserve to cushion themselves against losses incurred when their computers were traded in. In cases when computers were traded in after only 2 or 3 years of use, causing the firms to incur a loss, they were allowed to deduct this loss from the reserve fund, thereby mitigating its effects. Money remaining in the reserve had to be added back to income after 5 years. By permitting the companies to put aside money in a tax-free reserve, this system allowed them to take a tax write-off sooner rather than later, and thereby provided them with additional up-front cash.[37] For 1968 and 1969, this resulted in decreased tax revenues for the government (up-front cash for the firms) of 3.7 billion yen ($10.28 million).[38]

The buyback problem would not have reached crisis proportions had the government simply poured vast sums into the industry to help the firms cope. But it did not. MOF was not willing to allocate to JECC the vast extra sums necessary to support the booming market. Ironically, JECC's success in stimulating the supply and demand for computers meant that JECC had to buy an ever increasing number of computers to maintain rentals of 65 percent of the nation's machines. This could not go on forever. While JECC's raison d'être was to purchase machines from the makers and rent them to users, the industry's explosive growth, far greater than expected, ultimately stretched JECC's financial resources to the limit. Indeed, according to its original plan, which assumed that the industry would be able to carry most of the burden of rentals in the late 1960s, JECC was to maintain but not increase its financial support of the industry after 1965.[39] A JECC official explained, however, that it became clear to the government early on that the industry would need more long-term assistance because of the high costs and risks of operating in the industry.[40] To get the extra funds necessary to continue purchasing an ever increasing number of computers from the makers, JECC was forced to scrounge around the world for funds. Unable to obtain sufficient loans, JECC gradually went into debt to the computer companies in the late 1960s. This debt reached 43.4 billion yen at the end of fiscal 1969.[41]

The firms, struggling to cope with the flood of computers that had been traded in, were furious that JECC could not pay them immediately for their computers. Takara Yoshimitsu, then Vice-President of Fujitsu, said:

> After the war, there were broad promotion policies taken to promote basic industries such as shipping and steel; the computer industry is the nucleus of the 1970s. It is a private industry. If the government does not give us more money, we will be controlled by foreign capital. . . . If they'd only give us money, we'd export or consolidate our firms. But first we must settle the problem of money.[42]

Similarly, NEC President Kobayashi Kōji argued, "Without army provisions [JDB money] we cannot fight the foreign makers."[43] Katō Teruyoshi of NEC pleaded for the government to supply JECC with more funds: "We beg you to make your greatest efforts to assist us with funds."[44]

It is not surprising that the firms complained; it was clearly not to their advantage to have JECC owe them money. But the debt was only temporary, brought on by a sudden sharp increase in the demand for new computers. Rather than having JECC close up shop, MITI decided to have the companies bear the burden until it could gather the funds necessary to alleviate the difficulty. Even though the firms were not, temporarily, receiving up-front cash in a tangible form, they still received the "benefit" of JECC on paper and knew that it would ultimately be translated into cash.

Having the firms bear the burden of JECC's cash crisis marked the beginning of the government's move to force the firms to shoulder more of the burden of financing rentals. Indeed, not only did the government not yield to the firms' demands that JECC immediately pay off its debt; it also pressured the companies further, demanding that they increase their equity in JECC by 33 percent in 1967. "But what was JECC established for?" asked the firms.[45] Nevertheless, they finally agreed to contribute more capital. Ultimately, the JDB did substantially boost its loans to JECC to help relieve the national-policy company's financial bind; in 1969, it lent 18 billion yen, more than double its 1968 amount (8 billion yen); in 1970, it increased its loans to JECC by 28 percent; and in 1971 it lent 41 billion yen, 78 percent more than it had lent in 1970 (Tables 7 and 8). An increasingly larger proportion of the JDB budget went to JECC when the crisis became severe in 1969, and the JDB also started to guarantee loans from overseas banks.[46] By the end of 1970, the JDB was guaranteeing a total of 4 billion yen ($11.11 million) in foreign-currency loans for JECC.[47] This increase in JDB assistance, however, by no means kept up with the rapidly expanding market for domestic machines.

Despite these efforts by both the firms and the government, the firms were still burdened with heavy buybacks and JECC was still strapped for cash at the end of the 1960s. The government, unwilling to inject JECC with a massive dose of money, had taken a stance: it was willing to help the computer makers help themselves, but not to grant JECC the huge loans it would need to continue financing rentals of the majority of domestic machines. The government started gradually to dismantle parts of the artificial market it had so carefully constructed. If the firms were to become internationally competitive, they would have to commit more of their own resources. The future of both the national-policy company and the industry it had helped nurture were on the line.

Table 8 JDB Loans to JECC, 1970–1981 (unit: billion yen)

1970	1971	1972	1973	1974	1975
23	41	20	11.5	32.5	46

1976	1977	1978	1979	1980	1981
43	35.5	53.5	45	46	44

Source: JECC Kompyūtā Nōto annual; and documents without titles given to me by the JDB.

As the government gradually withdrew, in relative terms, its financing of computer rentals through JECC in the early 1970s, the proportion of domestic rentals financed by JECC plummeted from an average of 65 percent in the 1960s to 30 percent in the 1970s, and 11 percent by the early 1980s.[48] By gradually weaning computer makers from their addiction to the JECC system, the government helped alleviate both JECC's financial crisis and the makers' buyback burden. Indeed, the buyback problem stemmed in part from a fundamental flaw in the JECC system: By giving the firms their return in advance, JECC made them vulnerable to plummeting profits in periods when heavy trade-ins were coupled with slow market growth. If a company rented out its own computers rather than selling them to a firm like JECC, it could establish a stable flow of revenue that would not fluctuate much, even in periods of sluggish growth or heavy trade-ins. By giving the makers little option but to decrease their dependency on JECC, the government not only started to shift the burden to the computer makers; it also helped them stabilize their revenue and profits.

MITI and the Ministry of Finance (MOF) also started to demand more of the firms in exchange for the benefits of JECC. In the early 1970s, for example, they demanded that the six firms team up in three groups in exchange for JDB loans to JECC. MOF officials argued that the government should not give so much money to support one firm like JECC when there were "six makers selfishly competing with one another."[49] In exchange for consolidating into three groups for a cooperative R&D project, the government helped shore up JECC in the early 1970s, lending 41 billion yen in 1971, 11.5 billion yen in 1973, 46 billion yen in 1975, and 53.5 billion yen in 1978 (Table 8).

Most of the government's efforts, however, were aimed at helping the makers decrease their dependence on JECC. In 1970, for example, the government had JECC stop renting small computers, based on the rationale that the makers could afford to rent out, or users to buy, inexpensive small computers; scarce government funds were to be used to support the rentals of the machines that were the least competitive with IBM—medium and large-scale computers.

Two new tax measures prodded users to purchase rather than rent machines. One, enacted in 1970, allowed computer buyers to depreciate 20 percent of the cost of the computer in the first year. With the legal lifetime of a computer set at 6 years, the declining balance depreciation method allowed a firm to depreciate 31.9 percent of a computer in the first year. By combining this with the 20-percent special depreciation, users could depreciate over 50 percent of the cost of a new computer in the first year.[50] This 20-percent allowance was raised in 1972 to 25 percent of the cost in the first year, which, together with the allowable declining balance method, meant that a user could depreciate almost 60 percent of the cost of a computer in the first year.[51] The other new tax measure, passed in 1972, cut by one-third the fixed-asset tax applied to computers so as to encourage purchases over rentals. Like the special depreciation measures, this one also targeted medium and large-scale computers.[52]

The buyback-loss reserve, created by the government in 1968 to allow the firms to put 10 percent of their computer sales revenues into a tax-free reserve, was increased to 15 percent of their computer sales revenues in 1970 and to 20 percent in 1972. From 1971, this reserve was allowed for any Japanese firm renting out computers, not just for JECC; foreign companies with Japanese operations, such as IBM Japan or Burroughs Japan, were categorized as foreign firms and thus were not eligible for the benefits of this tax measure, which resulted in 56 billion yen ($205.55 million) in decreased government tax revenues (up-front cash flow to the makers) from 1970 through 1981.[53]

In addition, from 1973 the government provided subsidies so that Chamber of Commerce offices could buy computers that had been traded in. This subsidy, which totaled 2.71 billion yen ($10.35 million) from 1973 to 1980, helped cut the makers' load by providing them with a market for their used machines.[54]

Despite these efforts, trade-ins continued to destabilize the makers' income: In years of heavy sales to JECC, income surged, but, in slow-growth years when trade-ins were high, it plummeted. The cash flow under JECC from 1970 to 1981 was more volatile than it

Table 9   Firms' Estimated Cash Flow under JECC, 1970–1981
(unit: billion yen)

	1970	1971	1972	1973	1974	1975
Sales to JECC	92.2	87.4	89.2	101.4	124.4	126.4
Trade-Ins (Depreciated[1] Amount)	(16.9)	(26.0)	(42.4)	(52.5)	(46.9)	(43.1)
Estimated Cash Flow Under JECC	75.3	61.4	46.8	48.9	77.5	83.3

	1976	1977	1978	1979	1980	1981	Total
Sales to JECC	134.1	134.2	130.6	143.5	177.7	184.2	1,525.3
Trade-Ins (Depreciated[1] Amount)	(62.2)	(67.4)	(63.3)	(75.4)	(74.6)	(78.0)	(648.7)
Estimated Cash Flow under JECC	71.9	66.8	67.3	68.1	103.1	106.2	876.6[2]

Notes:
1. For 1970–1981, only data on undepreciated trade-ins are available. To estimate the depreciated amount, I use JECC's straight-line method of depreciation. In 1970, JECC depreciated at 17.3% a year, in 1971 at 17.4%, and from 1972 on at 18%. I assume that trade-ins in 1970 and 1971 were traded in after 3 years of use on average, and that trade-ins from 1972–1981 were traded in after an average of 2½ years.
2. $3.57 billion dollars using 360 yen to the dollar for 1970, 300 for 1971–1976, and 200 for 1977–1981.
   Some discrepancies may occur due to rounding.

would have been under their own rental system (Tables 9, 10, 11); indeed, while it takes substantial capital to start a rental system, once in operation, the system supplies a stable flow of revenue that in some years can equal or even exceed that under a system like JECC, in which the firms sell their machines to a rental firm.

Although the cash flow was somewhat volatile, up-front cash through the system continued to be substantial in the 1970s—some 141.82 billion yen ($565.62 million); but it was small relative to

Table 10 Hypothetical Cash Flow under Firms' Own Rental System 1970–1981 (unit: billion yen)

	1970	1971	1972	1973	1974	1975	1976	1977	1978	1979	1980	1981	Total
Expected Rental Income (E.R.I.)	6.69*												
Reduced Income due to Trade-Ins (R.I.)													
E.R.I.	18.16*	12.12*											
E.R.I.	22.50*	22.50*	15.00*										
E.R.I.	25.15	25.15	25.15	16.80									
R.I.	(−16.90)												
E.R.I.		23.84	23.84	23.84	16.0								
R.I.		(−26.00)											
E.R.I.			24.40	24.40	24.40	16.24							
R.I.			(−42.40)										
E.R.I.				27.60	27.60	27.60	18.40						
R.I.				(−52.5)									
E.R.I.					34.00	34.00	34.00	22.60					
R.I.					(−46.90)								

E.R.I.						34.80	34.80	34.80	23.00				
R.I.						(−43.10)							
E.R.I.						36.60	36.60	36.60	36.60	24.40			
R.I.						(−62.20)							
E.R.I.								36.60	36.60	36.60	24.40		
R.I.								(−67.40)					
E.R.I.									36.00	36.00	36.00	24.00	
R.I.									(−63.30)				
E.R.I.										39.10	39.10	39.10	
R.I.										(−75.40)			
E.R.I.											48.00	48.00	
R.I.											(−74.60)		
E.R.I.												50.40	
R.I.												(−78.00)	
Total hypothetical cash flow	55.60	57.61	45.99	40.14	55.10	69.54	61.60	63.20	68.90	60.70	72.90	83.50	734.78[1]

Notes:

*denotes income flow from computers rented in the late 1960s.

1. $3.00 billion dollars using 360 yen to the dollar for 1970, 300 for 1971–1976, and 200 for 1977–1981.

Some discrepancies may occur due to rounding.

Table 11 Estimated Benefit of Up-Front Cash through JECC,
1970–1981 (unit: billion yen)

	1970	1971	1972	1973	1974	1975
Firms' Estimated Cash Flow under JECC	75.30	61.40	46.80	48.90	77.50	83.30
Firms' Estimated Cash Flow under Own Rental System	55.60	57.61	45.99	40.14	55.10	69.54
Up-Front Cash through JECC	19.70	3.79	0.81	8.76	22.40	13.76

	1976	1977	1978	1979	1980	1981	Total
Firms' Estimated Cash Flow under JECC	71.90	66.80	67.30	68.10	103.10	106.20	876.60
Firms' Estimated Cash Flow under Own Rental System	61.60	63.20	68.90	60.70	72.90	83.50	734.78
Up-Front Cash through JECC	10.30	3.60	(−1.60)	7.40	30.20	22.70	141.82[1]

Note:
1. $565.62 million using 360 yen to the dollar for 1970, 300 for 1971–1976, and 200 for 1977–1981.
Some discrepancies may occur due to rounding.

what the makers had received in the earlier period; moreover, in 1978 they would have actually received more under their own hypothetical rental system than under JECC (Table 11).

One might suspect that, with diminished up-front cash, the firms would have been better off switching to their own rental system in the 1970s; but they would not have been. Indeed, the benefit of 141.82 billion yen in up-front cash under the JECC system is calculated on the assumption that the firms started their system in 1961 and built it up over the decade to a stable system in the 1970s. It would not have been to the firms' advantage to start a rental system in 1970. A comparison of their cash flow under JECC from 1970 to 1975—393.2 billion yen (Table 9)—with an estimate of what it would have been if they had set up their own rental system in 1970—227 billion yen (Table 12)—shows that the firms still received a decidedly higher flow of up-front cash under JECC— 166.19 billion yen or $503.6 million dollars. This underscores the heavy load on a firm in the first few years of setting up a rental system.

The firms did not, however, face the all-or-nothing option of going through JECC or through their own rental system. JECC was still willing to finance a substantial, though reduced, share of rentals; the firms thus took a route midway, relying on JECC for some

Table 12　Hypothetical Cash Flow if Firms Switched from JECC to Their Own Rental System from 1970 (unit: billion yen)

	1970	1971	1972	1973	1974	1975	Totals
Income	25.15	25.15	25.15	16.80			
(Trade-Ins)	(−16.90)						
		23.84	23.84	23.84	16.00		
		(−26.00)					
			24.40	24.40	24.40	16.24	
			(−42.40)				
				27.60	27.60	27.60	
				(−52.50)			
					34.00	34.00	
					(−46.90)		
						34.80	
						(−43.10)	
Estimated Cash Flow under Own Rental System from 1970 (B).	8.25	22.99	30.99	40.14	55.10	69.54	227.01
Estimated Cash Flow if continue through JECC (A)	75.30	61.40	46.80	48.90	77.50	83.30	393.20
Estimated Up-Front Cash through JECC (A)−(B)	67.05	38.41	15.81	8.76	22.40	13.76	166.19[1]

Note:
1. $503.6 million dollars at 330 yen to the dollar.
　Some discrepancies may occur due to rounding.

rentals and renting out some machines on their own. With the exception of Hitachi, the makers continued to rely on JECC to rent out some 40 percent of their computers in the early 1970s and 19 percent in the late 1970s and early 1980s.[55] Hitachi, the only maker with access to the enormous amount of capital necessary to set up a rental system, started to rent out its own computers in the early 1970s, drastically curtailing its dependence on JECC.[56] The objective of Hitachi's dramatic shift, according to Nakamura Noboru, a board member of Hitachi, was to establish a steady flow of revenue so that, even in recessions and periods of excessive trade-ins, they would still earn income in their computer division; they felt it was better to receive profits as they earned them rather than in advance.[57]

This decision was not without substantial cost. The injection of a massive dose of capital into Hitachi's rental system caused heavy losses in Hitachi's computer division. Mita Katsushige, Senior Managing Director of Hitachi, explained that, when Hitachi started the rental system, computer-division expenses had to be paid with profits from other consumer-electronics divisions: "A large deficit occurred (in computers), but, looking from the outside, no one knew because it was covered by other profits."[58]

The other firms did not have Hitachi's prerogative; they did not have numerous profitable divisions from which to siphon profits into computers; moreover, computers accounted for a far greater proportion of their total business than the 7 percent it accounted for in Hitachi's sales. In 1973, for example, just as Hitachi's system got into full swing, the firm plowed 60 billion yen ($181.82 million) into rentals.[59] In that same year, Fujitsu, a much smaller firm, had after-tax profits of only 10.7 billion yen; it simply could not afford to plow some 60 billion yen into financing rentals.[60]

> Hitachi could do it because for them the computer business was only 10 to 20 percent of their business, and they had the finances to do it; but, in the case of Fujitsu, the computer business was 50 to 60 percent of our business in the 1970s; to finance the computer-rental business was too much.[61]

Indeed, acquiring loans to rent out all their machines would have tightly pinched the makers' balance sheets and income statements.

JECC borrowed approximately 982 billion yen between 1970 and 1981.[62] In comparison, the Japanese makers invested a total of 1.2 trillion yen ($5.2 billion) in plant and equipment and R&D during this period;[63] they would thus have needed almost double the amount of funds to rent out their own machines. It is unlikely that they could have acquired such loans, especially in the early 1970s when money was tight, JECC was struggling to obtain enough loans, and the computer industry teetered on the brink of bankruptcy. For example, Fujitsu, Japan's largest computer maker, had long-term loans of 128.1 billion yen from 1970 to 1981, and Fujitsu computers accounted for 39.5 percent of JECC purchases during that period.[64] Thus, if Fujitsu had wanted to set up its own rental system it would have had to borrow about 387.9 billion yen, equivalent to 39.5 percent of what JECC borrowed during that period; it would have had to more than triple its long-term loans in the 1970s, increasing its already high debt-equity ratio.

Despite the makers' decreased reliance on JECC in the 1970s, the rental firms still played a key role in stimulating the demand and supply of domestic machines. An average of 30 percent of all domestic machines sold or rented during the period 1970–1981 still went through JECC.[65] The financial benefits from JECC, though diminished, were still vital to the industry: JECC funneled some 141.82 billion yen ($565.62 million) in up-front cash—interest-free loans—to the makers from 1970 to 1981 (Table 11). Had the companies borrowed an equivalent amount from a bank at the prime rate, it would have cost them 12.73 billion yen ($50.77 million) in interest (Table 13). The makers also received a subsidy of 37.27 billion yen ($160.33 million) implicit in JDB low-interest loans to JECC during this period (Appendix C). Thus, although the percentage of domestic machines that JECC rented decreased sharply in the late 1970s and 1980s, JECC continued to rent, in absolute terms, many computers, thereby injecting into the firms a huge dose of interest-free loans to keep their operations afloat as they invested heavily to compete with IBM. "Even though the relative amount of computers [rented through JECC] has decreased, the absolute amount is still very big. JECC still plays an important role," explained Oketani Kisaburō of Fujitsu.[66]

Table 13 Estimated Subsidy Implicit in Receiving Return in
Advance—An Interest-Free Loan—through JECC,
1970–1981 (unit: billion yen)

	1970	1971	1972	1973	1974	1975
Up-Front Cash (Interest-Free Loan)	19.70	3.79	0.81	8.76	22.40	13.76
Prime Rate (%)	8.50	8.20	8.00	8.30	9.40	9.70
Implicit Subsidy (Interest Saved)	1.67	0.31	0.06	0.73	2.11	1.34

	1976	1977	1978	1979	1980	1981	Total
Up-Front Cash (Interest-Free Loan)	10.30	3.60	(−1.60)	7.40	30.20	22.70	141.82
Prime Rate (%)	9.20	8.20	7.10	7.70	9.50	8.50	
Implicit Subsidy (Interest Saved)	0.95	0.30	(−0.11)	0.57	2.87	1.93	12.73[1]

Sources: Prime-rate data are from *Economic Statistics Annual*, The Bank of Japan.
Note:
1. $50.77 million dollars using 360 yen to the dollar for 1970, 300 yen for 1971–1976, and 200 for 1977–1981.
Some discrepancies may occur due to rounding.

JECC also took on other functions over the years so that, while no longer necessary for the industry's survival in the 1980s, it still plays an important role. JECC publishes several of the most authoritative surveys and analyses of the industry; it is also being used to rent out software programs; its board, composed of top MITI and JDB officials and the chairmen of the shareholder computer firms, remains a critical forum for government-business interaction and inter-firm linkages.

JECC, one of the many public-policy companies created by the Japanese bureaucracy to pursue its objectives, was the most important single institution the government used to target computers. The corporate form is particularly well suited to this purpose: As a public-policy company, it can provide financial backing; as a private corporation, it can demand that firms in the targeted industry make better products and cut costs in exchange for government aid; moreover, as an institution separate from its parent ministry, its subsidies are largely invisible to the public eye.

By creating an artificial market that made the firms view entry as profitable in the long run, the government was able to encourage firms to invest heavily to win a Japanese chunk of the rapidly expanding computer market. JECC provided vital ingredients—substantial up-front cash and management of a price cartel—to the fledgling industry. Contrary to what one might expect, JECC did not become a dumping ground for machines the makers could not sell elsewhere. Indeed, JECC was allowed to purchase only computers that users specifically asked to rent. If no one asked to rent a firm's computers, JECC never purchased them; thus, the companies that had the best machines received the most benefit through JECC. Responsible to both the public and private sector, JECC was able to intervene in the marketplace to spur the industry's development without sapping the individual companies' initiative and making them dependent on the government over the long term.

JECC did not operate in a vacuum. Its impact on the supply of and demand for domestic computers was contingent on MITI's broader protectionist policies. Its pressure on the firms to make technological advances was influenced by government aid for R&D. In the early 1970s, just as JECC and the makers faced their biggest challenge to keep the rental system solvent, the makers were also under fire from other quarters—especially foreign ones. By the early 1970s, IBM and the U.S. government threatened to destroy all the advances that JECC and the makers had so diligently made.

FOUR

Strength Through Concentration, 1970–1975

In spite of MITI and the computer makers' valiant efforts, by the early 1970s the Japanese computer industry was teetering on the brink of ruin. The flood of computer trade-ins that plagued the industry starting in the late 1960s seemed trivial compared to the threat the infant industry now faced. In 1970, IBM announced a new, greatly advanced series of computers—the 370 series—several times as powerful as the computers in use at the time. IBM suddenly seemed unbeatable. The challenge came at a time of national turmoil. What had been a smooth-running engine spurting unprecedented rates of economic growth started to encounter its first major problems. The concurrence of these events provided the basis for change.

In the late 1960s and early 1970s, citizens, long silent about the impact of the nation's "growth-at-any-cost" policies on their environment, started demanding a halt to the widespread industrial pollution that was poisoning people, of which the Minamata case of mercury poisoning was only the most publicized. In 1970, the famous "Pollution Diet" passed many stringent laws aimed at reducing pollution.[1] In 1971, Japan was shaken by the so-called "Nixon shocks"—a unilateral decision to unlink the dollar's tie to gold, which, by leading to a 17-percent revaluation of the yen, reduced the competitiveness of Japan's products. Moreover, the Nixon administration, under Kissinger's advice, was pressing Japan to limit its exports of textiles to the United States and to open up its markets, including computers, to foreign imports.

Japan saw itself confronted with some fundamental questions regarding its economic future. How was a poor island nation with few natural resources going to survive? Allowing a free flow of imports was tantamount to inviting the United States to occupy Japanese industry as it had done in Europe, they argued. The unrestrained entry of foreign products and companies would be nothing less than the coming of Commodore Perry's black ships, which forced Japan to open itself to Western trade in the 1850s.

These problems were exaggerated, as Japan was wont to do. But the concerns were real and they led to a major shift in policy. Having focused on major capital-intensive industries like steel and chemicals in the 1950s and 1960s, Japan, by the 1970s, began to see its real future in high-technology industries. The shift would in one blow ease the pollution problems, reduce dependence on energy-intensive industries, and provide more appropriate jobs for Japan's increasingly educated labor force. Based on a consensus of business leaders, bureaucrats, and academics formalized in MITI's 1971 Report on "Industrial Policies in the 1970s," the national strategy was redirected to promote "knowledge-intensive" industries.

The cornerstone of the shift towards knowledge-intensive industries was the computer industry. The computer industry was not only a promising market in itself, as demonstrated by its rapid growth in recent years; it was also becoming evident that it would play a prominent role in the competitiveness of Japan's machine-tool, telecommunications, semiconductor, and consumer-electronics industries. IBM's challenge to the computer industry with its announcement of the new 370 series in 1970 was potentially far more devastating in this context. Soon after the announcement, RCA and GE, the American electronics giants, withdrew from the computer business. The Japanese were particularly stunned because they were still struggling in the Super High-Performance Computer Project to develop a computer competitive with IBM's previous generation of computers.

Japan would turn to its full repertoire of industrial-policy tools to counter IBM. But foreign pressure for an open computer market gave Japan little time to act. The very thought of a free inflow of U.S. high-technology products sent Japan's computer makers and MITI bureaucrats scurrying for a defensive strategy. The computer industry was now a sacred cow. Turning this industry over to the forces of a free market would have to be delayed as long as possible. While few agreed on how to make the industry strong enough to survive a foreign attack, there was unanimous agreement that the black ships had to be held at bay long enough for the Japanese to get ready for battle.

> We at MITI worried a lot. We felt it [the pressure to open Japan's computer industry] was a major crisis—that if we liberalized computers, IBM would come charging in . . . We told users to forbear for just a bit longer because we thought Japanese makers would be able to make them [computers competitive to IBM]. People in the computer industry were against liberalization, but we knew that, given the international situation, we had to open up the market.[2]

Unlike the 1960s, when MITI could openly flaunt high tariffs, small quotas, and laws controlling foreign exchange and investment to hold off IBM, MITI now had to learn to be more subtle. Foreign nations were still waiting for the market opening Japan had promised in 1964 when it joined the OECD and was officially proclaimed a developed nation in GATT. MITI's efforts to stall the liberalization of the domestic computer market met some heavy obstacles. In the textile talks between Prime Minister Satō Eisaku and President Richard Nixon in 1969, Nixon made a series of demands, including that Japan's markets be opened to U.S. high-technology goods. As part of the negotiations, Nixon had promised to return Okinawa, which the United States had occupied since World War II, in exchange for what he thought was a promise from Satō to control the exports of textiles.[3] Owing to opposition from both MITI and the textile industry, Satō was not able to control textile exports, embarrassing and infuriating President Nixon and Henry Kissinger. In 1971, as negotiations on textiles and high-tech products continued, Satō, anxious about whether Okinawa would actually be returned, made the unusual move of circumventing all negotiations then taking place on trade and capital liberalization and publicly ordering MITI to include computers among the list of items to be liberalized.[4] Satō's announcement was opposed by MITI Minister Tanaka Kakuei and Foreign Minister Fukuda Takeo. The weight of the bureaucratic machinery would water down Satō's hopeful promises. Still, the threat provided the crisis atmosphere MITI needed to reorganize the industry in the way it had long wanted to.

It was a question of coordinating the demands of the business community with Satō's requirements and MITI's own desires. Keidanren, Japan's largest and most powerful business association, strongly opposed Satō's proposal, as did the Japanese computer makers. They asked that liberalization of mainframes be put off until April 1977, that they receive subsidies to strengthen their firms before the market opened, and that the interest rate on JDB loans to JECC be reduced to 3.5 percent.[5]

In the subsequent compromise, business and MITI got much of what they wanted. Prime Minister Satō Eisaku came out virtually empty-handed. The decision was made to liberalize the industry a full 4 years later—at the end of 1975. That was 16 months earlier than the computer makers had requested, but a far cry from what Satō had planned. Even so, the race was on. Within 4 years, foreign companies would be able to build factories to produce computers in Japan and imports could flow in freely, hindered only by low tariffs. There was little time to make important changes.

> The summer of 1971 [when the decision was made to liberalize the computer market at the end of 1975] was a very long, hot summer when, like some 100 years earlier when the black ships commanded by Perry woke up our tranquil sleep, the doors to our country's computer industry were pried open.[6]

MITI and the makers immediately began discussing countermeasures. Having agreed to decrease its tariffs gradually and eliminate quotas on computers, MITI had to create new tools—the more invisible the better—to protect the domestic market. With the 1957 law targeting electronics and computers about to expire, MITI seized the opportunity to extend the law with new amendments granting MITI further powers to control foreign firms. While the 1957 law gave MITI the power to call for cooperative efforts to rationalize the industry, the new provision authorized MITI to "warn" firms outside the cooperative group if their production had a negative impact on the effectiveness of the cooperation or if the outsider tried to start or increase production in the area in which the cooperation was occurring. Miyazawa Kiichi, then MITI Minister, told the Diet that the new 1971 law would be used to control foreign computer firms if they became a disturbance to the domestic industry: "If possible, we should be broad-minded towards foreign firms because it is to our country's benefit; however, if a foreign firm becomes the cause of disturbances, we could use . . . this [the 1971] law."[7]

Another potent tool to obstruct foreign entry was the stranglehold NTT, the telephone company, had over the emerging field of data-communications services. NTT monopolized data-communications services and access to all the telecommunications wires linking the nation that had to be tapped in order to offer services. Not only did NTT rarely purchase foreign computers; it also set standards. Any equipment that was tied to its lines had to have its approval. This requirement often impeded the activities of foreign firms. Akazawa Shōichi, then head of MITI's Heavy Industries Bureau and later Vice President of Fujitsu, explained MITI's and NTT's stance:

> As for dealing with the entry of foreign firms [into the data-communications services industry], we will take a cautious attitude. Domestic firms will be promoted. We should take a passive attitude [towards allowing foreign entry] until Japanese firms can compete with foreign firms.[8]

Once again, MITI and the Ministry of Post and Telecommunications (MPT), which oversaw NTT, worked together to delay foreign entry so as to buy more time for domestic firms to improve their products.

These protectionist laws acted as an effective deterrent. Foreign firms, IBM in particular, were well aware of what MITI could do if they grew too fast. A 1974 MITI Report issued an ominous warning to IBM:

In cases where a large firm abuses its economic power, it is necessary to maintain fair market competition through use of the anti-monopoly law in order to strengthen the foundation of our nation's computer industry's development. . . . If by some chance the share of domestic computers falls suddenly after liberalization, in cases where there is the danger that serious damage will be done to the domestic industry, we will have to study the possibility of invoking the use of safeguards and emergency tariffs based on GATT Article 19.[9]

Translated, Japan would not let itself be bullied by IBM.

As potent as these laws were, they were but a minor portion of the array of tools MITI had to protect local firms from foreign invaders. IBM still needed to receive MITI permission to produce new models in Japan. Up through the late 1960s, IBM Japan was limited to producing only its 360-20 and 360-40 models.[10] But IBM had a card to play: Japanese firms' access to IBM patents expired at the end of 1970 and would have to be renewed if the firms were to continue to make computers.

IBM tried to use this trump card in negotiations with MITI and the firms over the patent renewals, putting a new condition on the bargaining table. IBM wanted to broaden the "cross-licensing" part of the contract to include patents that the Japanese firms held in conjunction with third parties, such as NTT or MITI's Agency for Industrial Science and Technology (AIST). IBM complained that, since the Japanese makers were able to supply NTT with IBM patents, it was only fair that IBM should have access to the patents resulting from joint projects of the firms with NTT or AIST.[11] Naturally, MITI, NTT, and the firms were not keen on this idea. IBM tried to play tough but knew that permission from MITI to start producing its 370-135 computer in Japan was contingent on its renewing the patent contract. If IBM did not give the Japanese firms access to its patents, MITI could shut down IBM Japan's activities by cutting off its ability to take money in or out of the country through the Foreign Exchange Control Law.[12]

In the end, they "compromised," but the cards were stacked against IBM. The Japanese companies were able to renew their contract for IBM's patents and even received a 40-percent reduction in the royalty fee.[13] Access to Japanese patents held in conjunction with third parties would be decided on a case-by-case basis; if IBM wanted access to such a patent, it was to tell the involved parties and they would discuss it.[14] This compromise allowed IBM to save face despite defeat. IBM was granted access to these patents held with third parties only more than a decade later.[15]

IBM could have held out longer in the negotiations because, without IBM patents, the Japanese could not legally manufacture computers. But IBM gave in, in part because it still did not view the Japanese makers as a threat.[16] Meanwhile, it continued to make fat profits in the fast expanding Japanese market. Moreover, bogged down in antitrust concerns at home, IBM did not want to create problems on another front, an area which, incidentally, was making up an increasing share of IBM's sales.

That IBM yielded on the patent issue was not lost on MITI officials. Soon after, they gave IBM the green light to manufacture some of its new systems in Japan,[17] but they delayed until the late 1970s IBM's request to produce a few machines that MITI felt would have directly competed with Fujitsu and Hitachi computers.[18]

In addition to tying IBM's arms behind its back and using laws to constrain the activities of foreign firms, MITI still continued, in the early 1970s, to regulate imports through the more conventional tariffs and quotas. But international pressure did gradually help hammer down Japan's tariffs and eliminate its quotas. Tariffs on mainframes, for example, were cut from 15 to 13.5 percent for members of GATT in 1972. Tariffs on peripherals, which had been raised from 15 to 25 percent in 1970[19] when the Japanese makers decided to move into peripherals, were reduced slightly to 22.5 percent for members of GATT in 1972.[20] Formal quotas on computers ended in 1972 and on peripherals in 1971.[21] But imports of mainframes and peripherals did not increase as dramatically as expected after the quotas were lifted (Table 14); even without quotas, other formal and informal protectionist measures remained.

Notwithstanding official moves towards opening up the market, foreign companies still faced various obstacles, many of them inherent in Japan's network of business connections rather than direct

Table 14 Import of Computer Systems, 1962–1975
(unit: million yen)

	Main Units	Peripheral Equipment	Sub Total	Parts	Total	Increase (%)
1962	8,017	5,786	13,803	835	14,638	67.4
1963	14,807	5,600	20,407	1,157	21,564	47.3
1964	15,679	8,773	24,452	2,751	27,203	26.2
1965	8,493	10,457	18,950	3,517	22,467	△ 17.4
1966	6,182	10,641	16,823	7,674	24,497	9.0
1967	7,792	24,693	32,485	9,847	42,332	72.8
1968	8,613	28,923	37,536	9,097	46,633	10.2
1969	14,774	34,030	48,804	12,358	61,162	31.2
1970	22,718	51,551	74,269	21,525	95,794	56.6
1971	21,659	48,873	70,532	22,904	93,436	△ 2.5
1972	23,437	38,221	61,658	27,432	89,090	△ 4.7
1973	32,469	49,564	82,033	25,461	107,494	20.7
1974	48,609	65,436	114,045	30,787	144,832	34.7
1975	45,504	51,870	97,374	33,285	130,659	△ 9.8

Source: Ministry of Finance

Note: △ = decrease.

results of explicit government policies. For example, when a special U.S. trade representative complained in 1972 that JECC protected Japanese makers, a Japanese government official replied: "Foreign capital is not excluded from JECC. If the shareholders agree on it, it is possible for foreign firms to become shareholders."[22] Of course the Japanese computer makers, who own JECC's shares, would never accept a foreign maker as a member.

But American persistence did result in some concessions. Taya Hiroaki, an official of the Electronics Policy Division of MITI's Heavy Industry Bureau, said that, at the Hakone Conference on Japan-U.S. Trade Problems in July 1972, "The Americans made us promise that we would tolerate an increase in the foreign share of the computer market up to a 50-percent share."[23] Government procurement still remained an important tool for protecting the market: The government purchased or rented approximately 20 percent of domestic firms' computers in the first half of the 1970s.[24]

Despite these various protectionist tactics, IBM's introduction of the 370 series coupled with the "window of opportunity" that U.S. pressure helped pry open for foreign computers in the early 1970s contributed to a plunge in the market share of domestic makers from 60 percent in 1970 to 48 percent in 1974 (Table 1).

The Japanese makers needed more time to prepare for foreign competition. They also needed money. A recession caused by the revaluations of the yen and the sharp rise in oil prices caused by the Arab oil cartel made private banks reluctant to plow funds into an industry under the threat of obliteration by a foreign giant; without government funds, the industry would be destroyed.

The consensus to channel large amounts of money into the computer industry was not developed overnight. It occurred incrementally as the government and firms realized just how serious their plight was. While MITI undoubtedly intended to continue offering aid to the industry, the push for large amounts of aid—far greater than that given in the 1960s—did not occur until the government made the decision in 1971 to open up the computer market at the end of 1975. Tanaka Kakuei, then MITI Minister, took responsibility for arranging financial assistance for the industry. In 1971, Tanaka requested a special 165.5-billion-yen ($502-million) account (*tokubetsu kaikei*) to funnel aid into specific areas such as mainframe R&D and JECC;[25] these funds were to be acquired from tariffs on computers.[26] One very important string would be attached to the aid: It was contingent on the six firms' reorganizing into three groups.[27]

But MITI was not able to keep its promise of $502 million in aid. The Ministry of Finance (MOF) found it politically impossible to approve such a large amount of aid for just one industry; MOF kept delaying approval of the "special account," and in the end it was never approved.[28] Nor was the industry's request for a decrease in the JDB interest rate to 3.5 percent ever implemented. Instead, MOF approved a mixture of subsidies and low-interest loans totaling 119 billion yen ($360.6 million), somewhat less than the 165.5 billion yen MITI had originally promised.[29] In this case as in others, MOF tried to limit the funds MITI was able to get for the industry; clearly, "government policy" was the outcome not only of government-business negotiations, but also ministry-ministry negotiations.

But MOF's approval of a smaller aid package for the specific categories Tanaka outlined in his request for special funds belies the true financial backing the government was funneling into the industry during that period. Indeed, total subsidies and tax benefits to the industry in the first half of the 1970s reached an estimated $632.42 million (208.7 billion yen). Coupled with huge loans of $1.244 billion (410.6 billion yen), this aid helped the firms make the heavy investment necessary to combat the IBM 370. This $1.877 billion (619.3 billion yen) in total aid in this 6-year period was 168.33 percent of what the firms were investing themselves in R&D and plant and equipment during that period ($1.115 billion or 367.9 billion yen). Considering only subsidies and tax benefits, it was equivalent to 56.73 percent (Appendix D and E).

Opposition party members complained in parliamentary meetings that the government was favoring the computer industry over others in this period of tight money.[30] The complaint was justified: Government subsidization[31] of high-technology industries was the only category that increased as a percentage of total subsidies from 1972 to 1975; subsidies were slashed for the shipping and coal industries and small and medium enterprises; those for agriculture were kept the same.[32] These complaints made it all the more important for the government to develop less visible means for promoting the industry.

One such means was a seemingly "private" system, whereby the government purchased bonds from the IBJ, LTCB, and Japan Real Estate Bank, in exchange for their agreeing to use the funds to give low-interest loans to the industry.[33] "The Japan Development Bank is not allowed to lend money for working capital, so, to loan the money, the government has to go through a bank like the IBJ or to create a new institution," explained Takeuchi of the LTCB.[34] The long-term loans to Fujitsu, NEC, and Hitachi from these three banks between 1969 and 1977, for example, totaled 101.09 billion yen ($306.33 million)[35] (Table 15). In addition, the IBJ made very large short-term loans to the firms, especially Fujitsu and Hitachi. While the firms had to repay the short-term loans within the year, they always received another larger loan immediately. In effect, in the first half of the 1970s, these two firms together had on average a short-term loan of some 23.5 billion yen ($78.3 million) from the IBJ every year.[36]

The JDB and the Import-Export Bank also funneled money to these three firms through JECC and other MITI-orchestrated institutional arrangements, and granted them low-interest loans of some 76.32 billion yen ($245.87 million), ostensibly for investment in plant and equipment in the period from 1969 to 1977 (Table 15). While these loans were not given entirely for the support of the computer industry, they undoubtedly padded the firms' cash holdings, allowing them to channel more funds into computers.

A comparison of the estimated annual government assistance received by Fujitsu, Japan's largest computer firm, with its annual profits and estimated investment in R&D and equipment in fiscal year 1975 provides a rough index of the relative importance of government aid to Fujitsu's capacity to invest in computers. The following estimate errs on the conservative side and includes only the most obvious, easily quantifiable benefits. In fiscal year 1975, Fujitsu received $34.83 million in government subsidies and tax benefits,[37] equivalent to 39 percent of what Fujitsu invested in R&D and plant and equipment in the computer industry that year.[38] Including low-interest loans of $95.95 million to Fujitsu that same year,[39] total government aid to Fujitsu was $8 million greater than the total of Fujitsu's investment in R&D and plant and equipment and its profits that year.[40] During this risky period in 1975, just before the computer market was to be opened and when the Japanese economy was sluggish following the oil shock, this type and amount of aid undoubtedly had a critical impact on Fujitsu's investment and product-strategy decisions.

Infusions of cash and protection from foreign competition en-

Table 15 Total Long-Term Loans to Fujitsu, Hitachi, and NEC from the IBJ, LTCB, JREB, JDB, and JIEB, 1969–1977 (Units: billion yen; million dollars)

	1969	1970	1971	1972	1973	1974	1975	1976	1977
Industrial Bank of Japan (IBJ)	8.26	9.60	10.00	3.15	4.80	13.00	6.70	8.10	8.30
Long-Term Credit Bank of Japan (LTCB)	1.70	2.10	2.44	1.80	2.30	1.73	1.00	2.60	2.20
Japan Real Estate Bank (JREB)	0.75	1.24	1.60	1.02	1.14	1.50	.80	1.65	1.61
Japan Development Bank (JDB)	0.30	1.32	2.60	1.32	1.65	3.00	2.40	1.90	1.70
Japan Import-Export Bank (JIEB)	5.30	5.84	5.50	6.10	5.60	5.20	3.35	16.14	7.10
Exchange Rate (Yen to one Dollar)	360	360	330	330	300	300	300	300	270
TOTAL	16.31 ($45.3)	20.10 ($55.8)	22.14 ($67.1)	13.39 ($40.6)	15.49 ($51.7)	24.43 ($81.4)	14.25 ($47.5)	30.39 ($101.3)	20.91 ($77.4)

Source: Company Financial Reports
Note: Some discrepancies may occur due to rounding.

abled the Japanese industry to survive at least in the short term, despite IBM's announcement of a revolutionary computer series. But, without more advanced computers, pressure would mount on MITI to withdraw its support for a domestic computer industry and instead to use foreign machines to help boost the competitiveness of Japanese industries. The government felt it was imperative to consolidate the industry into fewer firms. "It would have been impossible to survive in severe competition with IBM in the late 1960s and early 1970s. The situation was very clear," explained Amaya Naohiro, a former high-level MITI official.[41]

The only way the industry could compete with IBM was by gaining economies of scale in R&D and production; this could, in part, be achieved by limiting competition among domestic makers. "Scale was the problem. It was too small, which raised their costs. They had to work together to strengthen themselves," explained Miyano Motoyuki, formerly of MITI.[42] To reduce redundancy and encourage specialization, MITI proposed the reorganization (*saihensei*) of the industry. This was by no means MITI's first attempt to encourage cooperation and oligopolization of an industry. In the late 1960s, it was obsessed with increasing concentration (*sangyō no shūyakka*) to prevent a foreign invasion; MITI had unsuccessfully pressured small auto companies to merge with Nissan or Toyota; in steel, MITI succeeded in pressuring Yawata and Fuji to merge, creating the largest steel company in the world—New Japan Steel—in 1970.[43]

Government pressure on the computer companies to merge began in the early 1970s. Komiyayama Shigeshiro, MITI's Industrial Policy Vice-Minister advised the Parliament:

Six [computer] companies in Japan is definitely too many. . . . We should use administrative guidance to make two or three firms, not six, to unify and to effectively use our engineers and thereby contribute to the development of Japanese computers.[44]

The Ministry of Finance (MOF), controller of the purse strings, also pushed for consolidation. "If we are going to promote the computer industry, six firms should not be selfishly competing; we should reduce the industry to about three firms in order to gain international competitiveness,"[45] prodded one MOF official.

But it became clear to MITI and MOF that the firms would not be willing to merge. Indeed, in spite of the unity implied by the concept of Japan Inc., Japanese companies are fiercely independent. Lifetime employment engenders deep pride in the company, and close ties with subcontractors, main banks, and other *keiretsu* member firms make mergers and acquisitions substantially more difficult than in the United States. In the computer case, ties with different foreign firms only exacerbated the problem.

> Because the [computer] makers other than Fujitsu each had a foreign maker behind them, it was rather difficult to reorganize. In other industries, reorganization has meant mergers of companies, but, due to the special characteristics of the computer industry, it [reorganization] means business cooperation at the technology level,[46]

acknowledged Akazawa Shōichi, then head of MITI's heavy industry bureau and later a Vice-President of Fujitsu. Based on this realization, MITI moved to encourage the firms to gain the same benefits of a merger through cooperation, a process called *taisei seibi* or *kōzō kaizen.* Through temporary cooperation, economies of scale in production and R&D could be acquired without the potential negative effects of mergers.

While the computer companies rebuffed the government's overtures for mergers in the late 1960s, the introduction of IBM's 370 series in 1970, the decision to open up the computer market by the end of 1975,[47] and IBM's announcement that, as of March 1972, it would decrease by 3–9 percent the sales prices and rental fees for its 370 series machines, made the firms pause to contemplate the wisdom of braving the turbulent waters alone. Yoshioka Tadashi, formerly of MITI, recalled:

> Everyone felt that we had to do something fast; none of the firms very strongly rejected the idea of consolidating into three groups. It was like a marriage; everyone wondered whether it would go well or not. There were very heated discussions, and I heard there were even cases when people threw ash trays and such things in anger. But once the discussions proceeded, everyone decided to do it, and the six firms formed three groups.[48]

The firms were really in no position to reject the idea. Their profits were plunging,[49] and, after a decade of pushing back the

Table 16 Share of World Computer Market, 1971 (unit: installed base—%)

U.S. Firms		European Firms		Japanese Firms	
IBM	62.1	ICL (Britain)	2.6	Fujitsu	1.1
Honeywell	8.5	Siemens (W. Germ.)	0.8	NEC	0.9
Sperry Rand	5.0	CII (France)	0.1	Hitachi	0.8
Burroughs	4.0	Philips (Holland)	0.2	Toshiba	0.3
Control Data	3.4	Telefunken (W. Germ.)	0.1	Oki	0.2
RCA	2.0	Others	0.3	Others (mostly	
NCR	1.9			Mitsubishi)	0.1
Others	5.6				
Total of U.S. firms	92.5	Total of European firms	4.1	Total of Japanese firms	3.4

Source: Asahi Shimbun, 6 March 1973.

foreign share of the Japanese computer market, they had stalled in 1971 and watched their market share gradually slide (see Table 1). Unless the Japanese firms could shore up their domestic and world market shares, there were doubts that they could survive (Table 16). The final impetus for the restructuring of the market into three groups was MITI's promise that, in exchange, it would fund an R&D project—the New Series Project—to develop a line of computers to combat IBM's new 370 series. The firms in each group would combine their computer efforts to develop a series of computers of a size and type agreed upon with the government; while no one firm had the resources to develop a full line of machines to counter IBM, by dividing up the market, they could as an industry supply a full line.

The firms reluctantly agreed. "MITI, like a teacher at an elementary school athletics meet, waved the flag and the students followed," explained Fujitsu's Tajiri.[50] Fujitsu joined with Hitachi, NEC with Toshiba, and Mitsubishi with Oki.

> Fujitsu and Hitachi's Vice-Presidents were good friends; I heard that they went golfing and decided at that time to do it [join together]. Mitsubishi and Toshiba were competitors in heavy machinery equipment, and NEC's group—Sumitomo—and Mitsubishi's [the Mitsubishi group] would not work, so Mitsubishi was left with Oki; and Toshiba and NEC were left— they had a common connection with Honeywell.[51]

Kiyomiya Hiro, Fujitsu's Vice-President, had to explain to his employees the company's decision to cooperate as well as compete with their arch rival Hitachi:

Frankly speaking, if we do not do this, we cannot confront our American competitors. For example, if Japanese makers in the domestic market did not cooperate and only competed, before we knew it, we would be taken over by the American firms; there is a danger that every maker would be dealt a fatal blow. On the other hand, if we only cooperate and do not compete at all, we will all slide into stagnant waters, which also would be bad. The British and French computer industries are examples of this. Thus, using cooperative relations during the early stages of development as a base, we will then compete on commercializing the product; as a whole, we must oppose the threat posed by foreign capital. Thus we will cooperate on R&D, but in sales and production we will compete fiercely as we have in the past . . . I would like all of you to understand the meaning of this cooperation, and I beg you to work hard so that this cooperation will have true significance . . . Finally, I would like to add that in the background of this move is the earnest guidance of MITI and the deep understanding of NTT. In regards to the big problem created by the decision to liberalize the computer industry in 3 years, both NTT and MITI have been serious and forward-looking in considering what form our computer industry should take in order to oppose the giant power of American capital.[52]

Fujitsu and Hitachi concentrated on developing large IBM-compatible machines; NEC and Toshiba focused their efforts primarily on medium and small-scale Honeywell-compatible machines; and Mitsubishi and Oki worked on small computers for specialized uses such as factory control.[53] The New Series machines were to be developed by 1975 or 1976—leaving a mere 4 to 5 years for development and commercialization.

The government granted subsidies of 70.3 billion yen ($235.5 million) to cover half the cost of the New Series Project.[54] The Fujitsu-Hitachi group was favored: They received approximately 45 percent of the subsidies, the NEC-Toshiba group 40 percent, and Mitsubishi and Oki 15 percent.[55] These groups faced a task of ominous proportions. The IBM 370 had 2 to 5 times the cost-performance of the IBM 360, a larger main memory capacity, a high-speed large-capacity file, and a channel with higher ability to transmit data and better reliability.[56] Major advances in ICs, memory devices, and mainframe architecture made for a tall order.

Fujitsu and Hitachi were the first group to announce their cooperation—on 22 October 1971. As the two strongest firms, theirs was the most important group. They agreed to go IBM-compatible—to make computers that could run on IBM software and be plugged into IBM machines. Taking an IBM-compatible strategy was possible only because, in 1970, IBM, under antitrust pressure, had unbundled—begun to sell separately—its software and hardware. To counter the flood of imports that were expected with liberalization, the government wanted at least these two firms to be able to compete head-on with IBM.

> From MITI's standpoint, because IBM dominated some 60 percent of the worldwide computer market, at least one of the groups had to be IBM-compatible so that they could sell in the Japanese and international market.[57]

Although Fujitsu's Tajiri argued that the decision for the Fujitsu-Hitachi group to go IBM-compatible was the companies' decision, a Hitachi manager said that MITI pressured them to adopt that strategy.[58]

They agreed to develop an "M-series" of 4 large computers—2 computers each, and to standardize their mainframe architecture, software, and the interfaces of their input-output device to make their machines compatible. Fujitsu was in charge of making the largest and smallest models—the M-190 and M-160—and Hitachi the two middle models—the M-180 and M-170. By making the machines for the most part compatible, a customer who had software for the smaller Fujitsu M-series machine would be able to upgrade to the larger Hitachi M-series machine without worrying about needing new software. As they were members of the same research association, patents resulting from the project would be open to both firms, although there would be no obligation to share hardware know-how. In consultation with MITI and NTT, Fujitsu and Hitachi agreed to make their "M-series" machine so that it would meet the requirements of a project NTT was about to start—the DIPS-11 Project—to improve upon its DIPS-1 machines.

The partnership of Hitachi and Fujitsu was filled with problems from the start. Each having a 15-percent share of the domestic market, they were relatively strong, and each had too much pride to subordinate itself to the other. Thus, while Toshiba took a back seat to NEC, and Oki to Mitsubishi, Fujitsu and Hitachi demanded "cooperation between equals." Neither of the firms was enthusiastic about the cooperation, yet they wanted the subsidies and felt that some type of cooperation, however loose, was necessary if they were to come out rapidly with a full series to counter IBM. Fujitsu's Kiyomiya explained their love-hate relationship: "While above the desk we were shaking hands, below it we were kicking . . . with one hand we were shaking hands and with the other hand hitting each other."[59]

The difficulties Fujitsu and Hitachi had in cooperating were rooted in the market. As longtime rivals with several computer series that competed directly with one another, it was difficult to cooperate on one computer series while still in competition on others.[60] For example, in mid-1973, Fujitsu introduced a FACOM 230-8 series of machines to function as a bridge between its FACOM 5 and new M-series machines. With this introduction, Fujitsu was reluctant to push rapid sales of the M-series machines because it would make its 230-8 series obsolete and thereby trigger massive trade-ins with attendant losses. Fujitsu had kept this new series of computers a secret from Hitachi until the day before it was announced, infuriating Hitachi when it was unveiled.[61] Hitachi was particularly vulnerable because it did not have a bridge machine to compete with Fujitsu's and was thus in a rush to get its M-series models out.

This was not the only flare-up between the two competing allies. Fujitsu made a strategic decision that would boost its competitiveness in the marketplace but make cooperation with Hitachi increasingly difficult. Against MITI's advice, Fujitsu decided to invest in Amdahl Corp., the mainframe maker started by one of IBM's top engineers, Gene Amdahl. Amdahl, who had designed the IBM-360 series, set out in the early 1970s to make an IBM-370-compatible computer. When Amdahl ran into financial difficulties in 1972, Fujitsu bailed it out. From late 1972 through 1976, Fujitsu put a total of $54 million in capital and loans into Amdahl.[62] In return, Fujitsu gained access to Amdahl's technology and ultimately produced its own 370-compatible series of computers.[63] While Fujitsu's attempt to purchase a large portion of Fairchild of the United States in early 1987 would provoke an uproar, the more strategic takeover of Amdahl occurred with hardly a whisper.

Joining forces with Amdahl was the outgrowth of Fujitsu's decision to go IBM-compatible. The decision was not made easily. Fujitsu's Kobayashi recalled that some employees were strongly opposed to the idea of Fujitsu, which had been using its own technology, imitating IBM's.[64] While MITI was pleased that Fujitsu was going IBM-compatible, it was by no means thrilled with the idea of Fujitsu, the only domestic maker with "pure national technology" *(jun kokusan gijutsu)*, tying up with a foreign firm. In particular, MITI felt that the timing was bad, as the domestic firms were regrouping to gain strength to counter IBM after liberalization.[65] After Fujitsu assured MITI however, that it would not become totally dependent on Amdahl for technology, MITI approved the cooperation.[66] The tie-up is a clear case of MITI's not getting its way when its strategy directly countered that of the firm.

When Fujitsu's President Ikeda Toshio talked with Gene Amdahl in 1970 about the possibility of teaming up, Ikeda explained that Fujitsu would have to find other companies willing to cooperatively finance the collaboration because Fujitsu expected it to require at least 10 billion yen ($30.3 million).[67] After several trips to Silicon Valley for negotiations, Ikeda, on the plane back to Tokyo, bubbled with enthusiasm to his assistant, Matsuo Noboru:

> If this goes well, it will be incredible! First, the IBM-compatible route would, without fail, be successful. Next, we would have NTT use the system [M series] for us. And third, we'd approach Hitachi and say that they could also make the same machine.[68]

Ikeda was fully confident that Hitachi and NTT would fit neatly into his strategy. But Hitachi, while initially showing interest in joining the Amdahl-Fujitsu group, declined the offer after studying the Amdahl plan: Hitachi felt it was impossible to meet the plan's goals.[69] Actually, Hitachi had little reason to team up with Amdahl and Fujitsu. Unlike Fujitsu, it did not need the collaboration in order to go IBM-compatible. Through its long cooperation with RCA, Hitachi already had some information on building IBM-compatible machines.[70]

In addition to trying to get Hitachi to fit into its strategy, Fujitsu also turned to NTT, the telecommunications and computer giant, and asked if it would use the Amdahl-type machine in its vast computer networks. NTT officials replied that, while it was all right for Fujitsu to use Amdahl technology, the computer's architecture had to be made according to NTT's standards.[71] Still, Fujitsu based its decision to tie up with Amdahl in part on an assumption that NTT, with whom it was cooperating in a separate computer project, would use Fujitsu's Amdahl-type M-series machines in its data-communications systems.[72] Indeed, the fact that Fujitsu operated in both the computer and telecommunications markets increased the probability that a return on its investment in Amdahl could be made rapidly. Fujitsu thus not only fit into NTT's strategy for developing a world-class data-communications industry; NTT, because of its huge procurement budget, also made Fujitsu's strategy of allying with Amdahl financially feasible. Their ability and willingness to coordinate their respective strategies was undoubtedly facilitated by Fujitsu's having long been NTT's favorite child.

Fujitsu needed to depend on NTT to purchase many of its machines in order to get a return on the heavy investment it put into Amdahl. Indeed, the major incentive for Fujitsu's asking Hitachi to team up with Amdahl was to have a partner to help finance the venture. With Hitachi unwilling, Fujitsu was strapped. Without heavy infusions of government aid, Fujitsu would have had grave difficulties making its hefty investment in Amdahl. Fujitsu received approximately 15.8 billion yen ($47.88 million) in subsidies for the New Series Project from 1972 to 1976,[73] the period in which Fujitsu lent and invested a total of 17.82 billion yen ($54 million) in Amdahl.[74] In this same period, Fujitsu also received approximately 8.063 billion yen ($24.43 million) in direct subsidies and

92.09 billion yen ($279.1 million) in loans through JECC.[75] With its after-tax profits plunging from 13.7 billion yen ($41.51 million) in 1972 to 6.7 billion yen ($20.3 million) in 1976,[76] it is unlikely that Fujitsu could have afforded the Amdahl investment without heavy government financial support.

Despite the headaches and huge sums of money involved, the investment in Amdahl brought a good return. When others in Fujitsu squabbled about the expense, Ikeda reminded them: "The fact is that, if we did not cooperate with Amdahl, it would have been impossible for our company's computers to have taken an internationally compatible [IBM-compatible] course."[77] Indeed, teamwork with Amdahl was a critical ingredient in Fujitsu's ability to develop the sophisticated upper-end models of the M-series. Chairman Kobayashi acknowledged this when he explained that Japanese computer makers were able to survive the shock of IBM's 370 series because MITI got the firms together for subsidized cooperative R&D, and because, in the case of Fujitsu, it cooperated with Amdahl.[78] He says that Amdahl designed the machine (which became Fujitsu's M-190) so that LSIs would be used throughout, whereas other computers of the time used LSIs only in some parts of the machine.[79] Moreover, he admits that the reason Fujitsu was not caught in the FBI's "IBM Sting Case" in 1982 was because it did not have to steal IBM information; it received it through Amdahl.[80] The Fujitsu-Amdahl tie-up is a clear case of a corporate strategy decision, completely unrelated to and in fact opposed to government policy, having a critical impact on the firm's competitiveness.

Sales of the M-series rejuvenated Fujitsu and Hitachi. While in 1976 and 1977 installations of IBM's 370 in Japan were still high, they tapered off and in some cases decreased sharply by 1978 and 1979 when the full line of the M-series was out (Table 17). Many new buyers turned to the M-series, which on average were priced 15–20 percent lower than comparative IBM machines.[81] Sales of the Fujitsu-produced Amdahl V470 series, better than Fujitsu ever imagined, also helped fill Fujitsu's pockets.[82] The success of the Fujitsu-Amdahl collaboration got under the skin of IBM Chairman Frank Cary. In the summer of 1976, Cary invited Eugene White, then President of Amdahl Corporation, to IBM's headquarters to ask him why he was cooperating with Fujitsu and to advise that he restrain from acting in ways that endangered America.[83]

The project called for only 4 M-series machines, but early on

Table 17 Installations of New Series and IBM-370 Series
Computers, 1976–1979
(unit: cumulative number of computers)

	First Year on Market	1976	1977	1978	1979
FUJITSU					
M-130	1978			8	103
M-140	1978			12	79
M-160S	1978			20	51
M-160II	1976		11	37	64
M-180II	1977		2	9	21
M-190	1976	1	10	17	15
M-200	1978				2
HITACHI					
M-150	1977			55	88
M-160	1975	5	38	85	110
M-170	1976	1	20	43	85
M-180	1976	4	8	11	26
IBM JAPAN					
3031	1978				44
3032	1978				22
3033	1978			5	33
370-115	1974	83	107	116	108
370-125	1073	79	85	78	75
370-135	1972	197	170	65	45
370-145	1972	69	75	35	25
370-155	1971	24	17	10	5
370-138	1977		21	122	132
370-148	1977		14	76	63
370-158	1973	212	217	220	180
370-168	1973	40	52	64	60

Source: Kompyūtopia, January 1980, pp. 16–17.

Fujitsu and Hitachi, responding to competitive pressures, each introduced an additional machine to attract customers to their own models.[84] While this did increase competition more than MITI had hoped, the new models helped Fujitsu and Hitachi offer a more complete series of machines to compete against the IBM-370. Indeed, the market took over from where the project ended.[85] Market segmentation by government policy, at least in this case, had at best a temporary effect. But it was important; by dividing up the market, MITI could at least be assured that the industry would make the designated models.[86] If they filled out their lines later, all the better.

Given the market environment within which Fujitsu and Hitachi were competing, the success of their cooperative efforts was destined to be limited. While their M-series machines were not completely compatible—taking a software application that runs on a Fujitsu machine requires minor changes to run it on a Hitachi machine[87]—they did standardize their mainframe architecture.[88]

> It is a good thing that Fujitsu and Hitachi had the same architecture because this meant that, from the users' point of view, either of them could be purchased; without government intervention, Hitachi and Fujitsu probably would have had different kinds of architecture,[89]

explained Hitachi's Kuwahara. Indeed, standardization assured potential users that, if one of the two firms stopped making computers, their machines and software could still be used on and in conjunction with the other's computers. Along with standardizing their architecture, government financing of the project also helped the firms survive. "It [the subsidies for the project] was big money back in the 1970s," conceded Fujitsu's Tajiri.[90]

Indeed, the Fujitsu and Hitachi group machines played a crucial role in Japan's ability to counter IBM's 370 series (Table 18). They were the most important machines of the New Series Project because they competed with IBM's large-scale computers, a market segment that, up until this project came to fruition, had been almost completely dominated by IBM; while refinements have been made over the years, the M-series today remains the mainstay of Fujitsu's and Hitachi's offerings.

Table 18 General Comparison of New Series Machines with
IBM-370 Series
(comparison based on technical specifications)
( ) date machines were first delivered on market

IBM 370 Series	Fujitsu-Hitachi "M" Series	NEC-Toshiba "ACOS 77" Series	Mitsubishi-Oki "Cosmo" Series
IBM 3033 (1978)	M-190 (F) (1976)	ACOS-900 (1978)	
168 (1973)		ACOS-800 (1978)	
	M-180 (H) (1976)		
	M-180 II (F) (1977)	ACOS-700 (1975)	
	M-170 (H) (1976)		
158 (1973)			COSMO-900 (1977)
	M-160 (F) (1976)		
		ACOS-600 (1975)	
145 (1971)	M-160 II (H) (1975)	ACOS-500 (1976)	COSMO 700 (1975)
138 (1976)	M-150 (H) (1977)		
135 (1972)	M-140 (F) (1977)	ACOS-400 (1975)	
	M-130 (F) (1978)		
125 (1973)		ACOS-300 (1975)	
			COSMO 500 (1976)
115 (1974)		ACOS-200 (1975)	COSMO 300 (1976)

Source: Based on specifications of computers given in Jōhō Sangyō Shimbunsha, *Jōhō Sangyō Benran.*
Dates first delivered on the market are from *JECC Kompyūtā Nōto,* 1979, p. 411.

While Fujitsu and Hitachi ended up going their own ways technologically, technical cooperation between NEC and Toshiba went
quite smoothly; the two still work together today. It was natural
for NEC and Toshiba to fuse their efforts, since they both had ties
to Honeywell. NEC had collaborated with Honeywell since the early
1960s, and Toshiba, which had a technological agreement with
GE, was thrust into Honeywell's arms when GE, withdrawing from
computers, sold its computer division to Honeywell. The two firms
were initially reluctant to cooperate because they had similar lines
of computers;[91] but that was precisely MITI's motive—to decrease
competition between the firms to help each gain greater economies

of scale.[92] Combined, the alliance had 20 percent of the computer market; nevertheless, they faced stiff competition from the Fujitsu-Hitachi group and IBM Japan, both of which had a 30-percent share. NEC, which had a profitable computer division, sat in the driver's seat, while Toshiba, saddled with a computer division in the red, took the back seat.

Their agreement, announced in November 1971, quelled rumors that MITI was pressuring both companies to leave the computer industry.[93] Toshiba and NEC would henceforth collaborate in researching and producing a series of 8 computers ranging from small to large (Table 18). Each company was responsible for R&D and production of different computers;[94] software and peripherals were also developed according to this same division of labor. Their new series of computers would be made compatible with each of their current machines, and they would sell each other's machines.[95] They also agreed to supply one another with products that the other did not make.[96]

To coordinate their sales activities, they created a joint-venture company—NEC-Toshiba Information Systems, Inc. (NTIS) in March 1974; NEC supplied 60 percent of the capital and Toshiba the remainder.[97] The need for a *chōsei kikan*—an institution to coordinate their efforts—became necessary so as to minimize the problems arising from their being both competitors and allies. Indeed, despite the accord on selling each other's computers, in reality, Toshiba tended to sell only Toshiba's ACOS machines and NEC its own ACOS machines.[98] By setting up NTIS to function as a sales company for their cooperatively developed ACOS series, the alliance was able to overcome this problem.[99]

Their collaboration resulted in a competitive series of small to large computers. But, like the Fujitsu-Hitachi group, NEC and Toshiba did not succeed without help from a foreign hand—Honeywell. Indeed, the software and hardware of NEC and Toshiba's ACOS-77 series were remarkably similar to Honeywell's 60 series.[100] Honeywell spent an estimated 100 billion yen developing its 60 series;[101] thus NEC and Toshiba were able to save a substantial amount of money by borrowing heavily from the Honeywell system. Indeed, they spent only approximately 56 billion yen,[102] half of it covered by government subsidies.

The ACOS-77 Series of small and medium-size computers came out as scheduled in 1975, but their large machines[103] did not hit the market until 1978. The reason for the delay was that Honeywell had not yet finished its large machines.[104] NEC's ACOS machines sold well, especially the lower-end computers, which did not compete heavily with Fujitsu and Hitachi;[105] but Toshiba's models did not sell well, and, by the 1980s, Toshiba, no longer willing to bear the high cost of producing mainframe computers, a small fraction of their total business, decided to drop out of mainframes. Toshiba merged its mainframe computer sales force into NTIS, its joint venture with NEC, and funneled its own efforts into small business computers and minicomputers.[106]

Contrary to MITI's expectations, the ACOS series was largely the result of foreign, not indigenous Japanese, technology, but the project did attain some of MITI's key objectives. It consolidated these two players, gave them the time and money to improve their hardware manufacturing capabilities, and helped them survive the IBM threat of the early 1970s. If NEC had not been able to continue investing heavily in computers, NEC would not have improved upon Honeywell technology to the extent that today, in a dramatic reversal, it is the primary supplier of mainframe technology and machines to Honeywell.[107] In 1987, Honeywell spun off its computer division into a joint venture with NEC and France's Machine Bull. NEC is the primary supplier of technology to the new venture.

While the New Series Project was critical in pressuring Fujitsu and Hitachi and NEC and Toshiba to collaborate, for Mitsubishi and Oki it merely reinforced a relationship that had already started to gel in 1970. Soon after IBM announced the 370 series in 1970, these two firms started to forge links so as to steel themselves for the battle. Mitsubishi had tied up with TRW in the early 1960s but, by the 1970s, TRW was bowing out of the business. Mitsubishi responded by making a technical agreement with Xerox on the one hand, and creating ties with Oki and Sperry Rand's UNIVAC on the other. Mitsubishi joined the Oki-UNIVAC group in early

1970 when it struck an accord with their joint venture, Oki UNI-VAC, and Sperry Rand's Japan sales office, Japan UNIVAC, to coordinate their production and sales of computers and peripherals. Oki UNIVAC subcontracted part of its computer and peripheral production to Mitsubishi; in return Mitsubishi sold imported UNI-VAC machines and Oki UNIVAC machines to the Mitsubishi industrial group.[108] Mitsubishi and Oki agreed that they would depend on Japan UNIVAC for large-scale machines rather than trying to make such machines themselves.[109] Because of its intricate ties with Sperry Rand, this group was referred to derogatorily as the "half-breed combine" *(konketsu rengō)*.[110]

Their cooperation for the New Series Project was announced in November 1971 on the same day that NEC and Toshiba publicized their decision to join forces. With a combined share of only 15 percent of the Japanese market, it is not surprising that this group would have the most symbiotic alliance of the three. They were to cooperatively develop the COSMO series—4 small and medium-scale general-purpose computers that could also be used for industrial-control purposes.[111] To strengthen their ties, each bought 1 million shares of the other's stock,[112] a common practice in Japan, and, in 1972, Mitsubishi contributed capital to Oki UNIVAC.[113] They planned to sell their New Series machines under the COSMO-OKITAC and COSMO-MELCOM (Mitsubishi) brands.[114]

As planned, the Mitsubishi-Oki group did develop a 4-machine series,[115] but their machines were not great successes in the marketplace. Oki, in fact, did not manufacture the machines it helped develop, a decision that would haunt it later when, partly because of this failure, MITI dropped it from the next government project.[116]

Mitsubishi's machines sold moderately well. As of June 1979, there were 41 of Mitsubishi's COSMO MELCOM-300 machines installed, 80 of the 500, 48 of the 700, and 5 of the 900;[117] installations of comparable IBM-370 models that same year were 108, 75, 25, and 180 respectively (Tables 17 and 18). The project helped Oki and Mitsubishi survive temporarily, but it only delayed their ultimate withdrawal from the mainframe market.

The project subsidies, the market segmentation, and the standardization of Fujitsu's and Hitachi's architectures were critical to enabling Fujitsu, Hitachi, and NEC to make a strong comeback against IBM. But, beyond that, the technological advances made in the New Series Project were the result of market forces—especially alliances with foreign firms—not of government policies. This case stands out as a clear example of the business sector's successfully lobbying the government for subsidies; but, in exchange, Fujitsu and Hitachi standardized their architectures, NEC and Toshiba consolidated their computer lines, and they all temporarily segmented the market so that, at minimum, they would as an industry be able to counter rapidly IBM's full line of 370 machines. The project helped bring the makers neck-and-neck with IBM in hardware by the mid-1970s, a feat reflected in their rising market share from 1975 onward (Table 1).

The project made the difference between the industry's success and imminent failure. Kobayashi Taiyū, Fujitsu Chairman, explained that the Japanese makers were able to stay in the market after IBM shocked the industry with the 370 series "because MITI started providing research grants and made different companies get together for cooperative development of new machines; for the first time, Japanese makers were ready for battle."[118] "Without the project, the companies would not have decided to develop a computer to counter IBM's 370; they could not have survived," explained Maeda.[119]

The subsidies and market segmentation, along with continued protection and help from JECC, reduced the costs and risks of remaining in the industry. Indeed, the creation of an attractive market environment, one in which the firms felt that, if they invested heavily, they would realize profits in the long run, was necessary for the industry's survival. But the effectiveness of this national strategy was contingent on the firms' willingness to put their own resources on the line. Unlike their U.S. counterparts, GE and RCA, the Japanese firms were willing to accept low, even negative, returns in the short run. The vertically integrated and diversified computer makers saw computers not only as a strategic business in itself, but also as the key to advances in their other businesses. "Computers and electronic circuits are leading-edge technologies. As you pull up the leading edge, its skirts broaden and impact all Mitsubishi products and improve them," explained Ota Hideo, a Mitsubishi manager.[120] "The Japanese feel computers not only are important as an industry but also lead the technical growth of all other industries. They won't drop out of the computer business, even if they're losing money," agreed Yamauchi Ichizo, a security analyst with Nomura Securities.[121]

Meanwhile, as the firms were working on their New Series Project machines, some were also working with NTT in its DIPS-11 project, which started in August 1973. In this effort, NTT provided Fujitsu, Hitachi, and NEC with a total of 5 billion yen ($15.15 million) to develop large-scale computers for use in NTT's telecommunications system.[122] Largely redundant with MITI's New Series Project, this effort funneled to the three top computer and telecommunications companies money that MITI was not able to squeeze out of the Diet. NTT's Toda Iwao explained: "To cut costs we made an effort to make them [the New Series and DIPS-11 machines] have a common base. If we had not done it that way [overlapping the projects], we would have all lost money."[123] NTT gave each of the three companies the assignment to develop a computer of different scale and performance.[124] NTT required that the new machines be compatible with the DIPS-1 machines so that they could be added easily to the communications network.

NTT's objective was undoubtedly to shore up the industry before liberalization. Yonezawa Shigeru, NTT's President, warned in 1973 that the DIPS-1 machines were becoming obsolete and needed to be upgraded: "When the imports of computers are liberalized, IBM [and] other foreign makers will start selling their machines."[125] Honoki Minoru, director of NTT's data-communications division, was also concerned with keeping the foreign invaders at bay:

Due to coordination between MITI and the Ministry of Post and Telecommunications (MPT), and, following national policy, we are steadily progressing towards the completion of a large-scale, high-performance computer that will be able to sufficiently counter foreign computers in the future.[126]

The firms achieved their goals.[127] The machines were fundamentally the same as their New Series Project machines, although some parts had to be reworked to make them fit into NTT's data-communications systems.[128] NTT ordered 30 DIPS-11 systems, 10 each from Fujitsu, Hitachi, and NEC.[129]

While the New Series and DIPS-11 Projects focused on countering IBM's 370 series, Japan Inc. was busy working on projects to improve on foreign technology by adding sophisticated graphics and pattern-recognition capabilities. Because of the slow, arduous process involved in typing information in Japanese onto a computer, Japan was particularily interested in developing ways for computers to recognize vocal and written patterns. If they could develop technologies that could read handwritten or spoken Japanese into a computer, Japanese companies' efficiency could be boosted sharply over the long term. MITI believed the firms could gain a competitive advantage in the Japanese market by offering sophisticated Japanese language systems, something IBM and other foreign makers were not investing in. To this end, MITI proposed the Pattern Information Processing Project (PIPS)[130]—to develop a prototype pattern-recognition system.

MITI's exotic proposal did not excite the Japanese makers. Few believed they could find commercial applications for the proposed research.[131] But MITI was determined. By paying for the project's entire cost, it was able to induce the firms to participate. Originally scheduled for 8 years at a cost of 35 billion yen, the project actually lasted 10 years—from 1971 to 1980—and cost less than originally budgeted—22 billion yen ($66.67 million).[132]

The major computer makers were assigned the development of 6 different sub-systems of a total prototype system. Toshiba was in charge of 2 systems, one to recognize printed characters and another to recognize various shades ranging from white to black. Fujitsu was in charge of the handwritten-character-recognition system, Hitachi the object-recognition system, Mitsubishi the color chart, and NEC the voice-pattern-recognition system. After the system prototypes were complete, the Electrotechnical Lab in AIST and the firms put the sub-systems together to form a total system.[133]

While the companies achieved most of the specific technical goals of their respective sub-systems,[134] the industry and even AIST itself viewed the project as largely a failure.[135] This is no surprise: When the project ended in 1980, substantial research was still needed to make useful systems. For example, the voice-recognition prototype could identify words if they were pronounced separately, but what was really needed was a system that could recognize words spoken continuously—without unnatural pauses between them. The companies' predictions proved correct: Few of the technologies were used in products soon after the project ended.[136]

> The pattern project was extremely farsighted. . . . It was challenging almost to the impossible . . . there were too many hasty expectations of the results, so the more people expected, the more they were disappointed.[137]

Nevertheless, some of the project's results have been commercialized. Toshiba used its PIPS results to make a machine the post office uses to read the addresses on letters, another machine that recognizes counterfeit money, and a voice-recognition machine that can recognize bank-account numbers over the phone and tell the caller the account's balance.[138] Fujitsu has made several products using the results, including engineering workstations using high resolution display systems. "The pattern project helped Fujitsu to start developing the high-resolution display system in the early 1970s, which is now probably one of the most important products in the computer system," explained a Fujitsu manager.[139] Moreover, the results are being used in the 5th-generation computer project.[140]

Indeed, by the mid-1980s, the resulting technologies were increasingly in use. "After the project ended, people said some 70 percent of the subsidies were wasted, but now everyone finds the results very valuable," explained Professor Aiso of Keio University in late 1987.[141]

In the long term, the jump the makers got in the processing of Chinese characters and other non-roman symbols could give them a critical edge in offering computer processing in other languages with non-roman symbols, such as Chinese, Korean, Thai, Arabic, Hindi, and Urdu. But the effort need not have been started over 18 years ago.

> It was too premature for pattern recognition actually to be used as a system, so it seemed the project was a failure. There were, however, several key technologies for components that are used now and that will be used in future computer systems. [142]

Some of the PIPS Project results are now being used some years after the project ended; yet, when the project was undertaken, it was not the best use of the government's money or the firms' researchers. By ignoring the computer makers' opinions when setting the research agenda and not requiring them to fund part of the project, MITI ended up spending 10 years and some $66.67 million on a project that did not have a significant impact on the competitiveness of the computer firms. While such long-term projects would prove to be useful in the 1980s, the firms had more fundamental deficiencies in the 1970s that would have been better addressed.

While hardware development, like that done in the Pattern Information Processing, New Series, and DIPS-11 Projects, was undoubtedly given top priority by MITI and the computer makers, the floundering Japan Software Co., which would go bankrupt in late 1972, was a thorn in their sides, reminding them of their inability to create sophisticated software. Another problem disturbed the nation's planners in the early 1970s: Japanese computer users' demand for custom-made applications software was draining the nation's relatively small pool of software engineers. The only way to encourage people to use standardized programs was by offering them easy-to-use programs at low prices. A bottleneck in the supply of high-quality, low-priced software programs could ultimately choke the hardware industry. And, with only expensive custom-made software available, small companies and individuals—a large part of the economy—would be unable to cash in on potential productivity gains through computerization.

Nor could the problem be solved through imports. It was particularly important that Japanese language programs be developed, because most Japanese were not comfortable using computer software based on English writing systems and grammar. If computers were to be used widely, Japanese makers would have to offer reasonably priced software in the Japanese language—something IBM was not yet offering. With the Japan Software Co. on the brink of bankruptcy, MITI in 1970 was busily preparing for the creation of a different type of software institution, one that would not develop software itself but rather would help existing software houses get the funds they needed to develop standardized software packages.

The difficulty small software firms had obtaining loans posed a primary obstacle to the development of a vibrant software industry. With little collateral, and no ties to the powerful banks of the *keiretsu*, fledgling software houses were shunned by banks; with an underdeveloped stock market and virtually no venture capital, they had nowhere to turn unless they wanted to become subcontractors of major hardware vendors. Now they had the Information Processing Promotion Association (IPA), which was established by MITI in 1970 to promote the efforts of small independent software houses to develop standardized general-purpose software programs. IPA financed the development of specific types of programs, guaranteed loans to help software firms develop programs, operated a registration system for software programs to help reduce redundant development and promote smooth distribution, and rented out software programs for low fees. By renting out software packages at low monthly rental fees, just as JECC did for hardware, IPA hoped to stimulate both the supply and demand for standardized packages.

The government's financial commitment to IPA was relatively small. From 1970 to 1980, IPA received a total of 17.2 billion yen ($57.33 million) in initial capital subsidies; it arranged for loans of 106.3 billion yen ($354.3 million), and guaranteed loans averaging 4.15 billion yen ($13.8 million) a year (Table 19). The 17.2 billion yen in subsidies pales in comparison to the 70 billion yen funneled into the 5-year New Series Project. The loans and loan guarantees were relatively large in absolute amounts, but, in contrast to other projects in which funds were concentrated on a handful of companies, those through IPA were scattered over hundreds of small soft-

Table 19 Government Financial Assistance to IPA, 1970–1980 (unit: billion yen)

	1970	1971	1972	1973	1974	1975	1976	1977	1978	1979	1980	Total
Balance of loans Guaranteed by IPA	2.200	3.900	3.000	4.200	6.200	7.900	7.900	3.300	2.600	2.900	2.500	4.200[1]
Ceiling on loans IPA was authorized to make	4.200	12.400	20.800	20.800	20.800	20.800	20.800	20.800	20.800	20.800	20.800	—
Loans for promotion of information processing (From IBJ, LTCB, and JREB)	4.000	9.500	14.500	13.300	9.000	12.000	13.000	11.000	8.000	7.000	5.000	106.300
Government capitalization of IPA	0.200	0.400	0.450	—	—	—	—	—	—	—	—	1.050

Subsidies to IPA for consigning software development	0.300	0.400	0.370	0.790	1.000	1.320	1.730	2.048	2.280	2.580	2.780	15.600
Subsidies for IPA software programs survey register	0.002	0.003	0.003	0.004	0.004	0.004	0.003	0.002	0.002	0.002	0.002	0.031
Subsidies for information-processing technicians test	0.037	0.033	0.033	0.034	0.038	0.044	0.047	0.052	0.057	0.062	0.068	0.505
Subsidies for information-processing service companies register	—	—	0.001	0.001	0.001	0.001	0.001	0.001	0.001	0.001	0.001	0.009

Source: Annual *JECC Kompyūtā Nōto*; Annual *Denshi Kōgyō Nenkan*.
Note: 1. Annual Average Balance of Loan Guarantees

ware firms. Hardware development was consistently given priority over software. "There was a strong feeling in the government against giving money for software development," recalled Professor Aiso Hideo of Keio University, who has participated in several government projects.[143] Aiso remembered a time when he was asked by the Ministry of Finance (MOF), which inspects MITI's projects' accounts, to come and explain software to them. When Aiso said that it was hard to explain what software was in tangible terms, they said "It is just something in a black box. If you cannot explain it and it cannot be seen, we will not give any money for it!"[144]

Given this attitude, it is not surprising that MOF did not funnel huge funds into software in the 1970s. Nevertheless, IPA did guarantee 95 percent of MITI-approved bank loans for software firms and information-processing service companies, and it arranged low-interest loans for the companies from the LTCB, IBJ, and JREB.[145] IPA also paid firms to develop specific software programs that it felt were important but too risky and costly for the private sector to develop alone; this consignment of software work totaled 15.6 billion yen ($52 million) from 1970 through 1980 (Table 19). In cases where the government believed distribution of a program would be enhanced if IPA rather than a software house owned it, IPA tried to buy the program and promote its distribution by renting it out at low monthly fees.[146]

Despite the various methods IPA used to help nurture independent software houses, a vibrant sector of independent software houses has yet to emerge. The financial assistance did not have the effect MITI had intended. Loan guarantees, for example, did not necessarily induce banks to grant loans. Indeed, even with an IPA guarantee for 95 percent of the loan, many banks would not lend to small software businesses.[147] Banks investigated each firm; in cases where a company was deemed too risky, the bank did not make the loan because bad loans would reflect poorly on the bank's ability to evaluate credit-worthy customers.[148] As a result, IPA has guaranteed loans amounting only to about one-tenth to one-half of what it was authorized to guarantee (Table 19). By granting loan guarantees rather than loans, IPA left it to the market—the banks—to make the final decision about how to allocate their capital. One can only conclude that, in cases where the banks refused to lend, even with an IPA guarantee for 95 percent of a MITI-approved loan, MITI was approving losers and was fortunate that the market rejected them.

Upon first glance at the data, it seems that IPA was more successful in getting banks to lend to firms without an IPA guarantee than those with one. This is because there was an IPA system under which the IBJ, LTCB, and JREB granted loans to software-development and service companies without loan guarantees. There was no need for government guarantees because these loans were actually camouflaged government funds! Indeed, the government, using funds from the FILP budget,[149] bought the bonds of these banks on the condition that the bond money be used to provide low-interest loans to firms specified by MITI.[150] This type of arrangement allowed the Japanese government to give relatively "invisible" aid to the industry. From 1970 through 1975, these banks used government money from this invisible system to lend a total of 62.3 billion yen ($188.8 million) to small software companies (Table 19). Inaba Masahiro of the IBJ explained why the government used this camouflaged system to funnel funds to the software companies:

> The software houses were very small with small annual sales. From the banks' point of view, they were risky companies to whom we would usually lend through a *kyōchō yūshi* [cooperative financing] arrangement [whereby each bank lends a small amount]. But [pressuring banks to lend to very risky businesses] can create ill feelings, which we wanted to avoid. It was clear that, in the twenty-first century, software rather than hardware would be the core of the computer industry. We knew we had to promote the software industry, that it was necessary to supply it with a steady flow of very low-interest funds. Private banks like mine agreed to help. The question was how we would fund it. [In the end] we were able to use the government's money.[151]

By allowing the market to reject its loan guarantees, but forcing the IBJ, LTCB, and JREB to grant loans specified by MITI—without market veto—IPA was destined to promote the development of software programs that few firms ever used. Indeed, IPA manipulated the market so that software houses, desperate for cash, were more concerned with gaining IPA's approval than with making the type of software users demanded. Unlike JECC, which bought a computer from a maker only when a user applied to rent it, IPA did not require that a user demand a program before buying it or funding its development. Rather, IPA itself decided what the market wanted, paid for its development, and then tried to persuade users to rent or purchase it.

Not surprisingly, users have not been happy with the software IPA has offered. In 1975, IPA spent 1.3 billion yen ($3.94 million) to consign software development to private firms, yet sales and rentals of programs totaled a mere 60 million yen ($181,000).[152] From its beginning in 1970 through fiscal 1978, IPA spent some 10 billion yen ($33.33 million) to develop some 70 software programs, but very few of these programs were ever rented or sold.[153]

The fundamental flaw in IPA was that it funded software development without making sure that there would be any demand for the software to be developed. "The people that evaluated the proposals for software development were not the people who would use the software," explained Tsuji Junji, a former NEC engineer who now has his own software company.[154]

Another problem hindering the effectiveness of IPA was incompatibility of the software with Japanese makers' machines:

> The software depended heavily on the hardware. People could use IPA's software only if their computer happened to be compatible with the software. If it was not, they would have to change the software or hardware. It was a good idea, but in reality it was not used much.[155]

These problems in the IPA system were exacerbated by other characteristics of the Japanese software market that made promotion of independent software houses difficult at best. The reluctance of Japan's major computer companies to "unbundle" their software and hardware—to price them separately as IBM, under antitrust pressure, started to do in 1970—has made it very difficult for independents to survive, let alone thrive. Indeed, by keeping their hardware and software packaged in one system and by being willing to supply users with custom-made software, the computer makers did not give Japanese users a choice of purchasing cheaper software packages made by outsiders. This in turn reinforced Japanese computer users' "strong feeling that software is not a tangible product and that it should be free."[156] With all of these obstacles, it is not surprising that the government has had difficulty shifting market demand to standardized, general-purpose software packages.

Just a few years after IPA was established, MITI started yet another project to promote the floundering software industry: the Software Module Project, a 3-year effort started in 1973. With the bankruptcy of the Japan Software Co. in December 1972, MITI was anxious to assert its control and demonstrate its success in software. This was particularly crucial because, in the early 1970s, NTT proposed a joint-venture software company between itself and the computer companies to develop software for its data-communications systems.[157] The Ministry of Finance (MOF), by refusing to give NTT the money to establish the proposed company, prevented what would have been a battle between NTT and MITI. Even when NTT, after lobbying MOF, reapplied, MOF still did not yield.[158] The proposed company, composed of NTT, NEC, Hitachi, and Fujitsu, would have been almost a carbon copy of the defunct Japan Software Co.[159] After MOF's two rejections, NTT, realizing that it would be difficult to gain enough support, did not ask for the funds in its next budget proposal.[160]

MITI retained its hold on the software issue by establishing the Software Module Project, the first part of a 2-phase project. But this project, like IPA, was unsuccessful.[161] MITI provided 3 billion yen ($9.09 million) in subsidies[162] for the project, which concentrated 40 independent software companies[163] into five groups to develop various application programs.[164] This was peanuts compared to what it was funneling into hardware development. Unlike earlier software efforts and even many hardware projects, the subsidies covered a high percentage of the project's cost—75 percent.[165]

Each of the five groups, however, went its own way, with little management or coordination from a central body. There was not even agreement on the definition of a module. One group wrote its modules in FORTRAN, another used CPL; a group really did not know what the others were doing.[166] Like IPA, the project successfully developed the planned modules, but the software developed was not what users were interested in.[167] "Most users did not even know that the modules existed, and it is regrettable that, of those who did know, almost none actually thought of using them," explained one manager in the industry.[168]

In addition to administering various software projects and institutions, MITI also created several tax breaks in the early 1970s to help the fledgling independent software houses. In 1972, the government started allowing software firms to put 2 percent of their total software program sales in a non-taxable reserve called the software guarantee reserve fund;[169] these funds were to be used to modify programs already sold under their program warranty systems. In 1979, this was merged into a new software reserve fund, which allows firms to put in a special reserve 50 percent of income from the sales of general-purpose programs that have been registered with IPA.[170] This measure, however, has had little effect because very few packaged general-purpose programs have been sold.

Government efforts to promote software were limited in the early 1970s, and even those attempts were marked with repeated setbacks. It would not be until the 1980s that Japan Inc. would get serious about promoting software. When demand for technologically advanced software started to explode in the late 1970s and early 1980s, the demand for custom-made software (as opposed to standardized packages typical of U.S. software) would place a severe cap on the productivity of Japan's limited number of software engineers. Until a vibrant independent industry could be developed, users would be limited to those who could afford custom software or who were able to use English-language-based software efficiently. This in turn would continue to hinder the use and thus the sales of domestic computers.

Government intervention in the computer market reached its peak in the first half of the 1970s in a desperate attempt by the firms, backed by MITI and NTT, to survive against all odds. This was a time when, if left to the free market, Japanese makers would most likely have pulled out of computers. They would have been hesitant to pour their scarce resources into an industry where even RCA, with twice the world market share of Fujitsu, left the market. Private banks were also wary and thus often only matched government loans, required government loan guarantees, or lent money to firms only when the government bought the same amount of bank bonds in exchange. It was at critical times such as this—when the industry's survival was threatened by the IBM-370—that government support was critical. The state reduced the number of players in each market segment to allow each firm to achieve economies of scale; maintained high barriers against foreign products; pumped demand through JECC; and provided substantial financial support. Thus, though to a lesser degree than in the 1960s, government policy towards the industry in the early 1970s still involved substantially rigging the market in favor of domestic firms.

The detailed carving up of the market for the New Series Project fundamentally altered the nature of competition in the computer industry. While on the surface there were six computer firms, there were actually only two or three firms competing in any one market segment. A blend of competition and cooperation, along with the threat of IBM and the fear that the government would withdraw support if the firms did not advance, put tremendous pressure on the makers to invest heavily to cut costs and improve their technology. Together with a large dose of financial aid, these policies helped the makers catch up with IBM in hardware by the mid-1970s. "The Japanese manufacturers are extremely competent, especially NEC, Fujitsu, and Hitachi. We are not taking that competition lightly," stated IBM Chairman Frank Cary soon after the New Series Project machines started to hit the market.[171]

MITI had hoped to achieve much more. It had hoped the firms would be able to gain ground on IBM through the Pattern Information Processing Project. However, ignoring the firms' pleas that the plan was too future-oriented, the government proceeded with a project destined to have few short-term commercially viable results and thus little impact on the firms' competitiveness in the immediate future.

MITI had also been optimistic that a group of strong independent software houses would emerge through the promotion efforts of IPA and the Software Module Project. But, in establishing IPA to encourage the development of standardized general-purpose software programs, the government failed to build in market incentives to assure that it would develop software that met user demand. Similarly, the Software Module Project proceeded without sufficient attention to what type of software users desired.

The advances by the industry did not meet MITI's and the makers' highest expectations, and there was still a nagging fear about what would happen when the market was actually opened up to a free flow of foreign investment and imports. But catching up with IBM in hardware was nothing to be humble about. While RCA and GE had withdrawn from the computer business, the Japanese makers had not only survived, but had caught up with the world's computer giant in hardware. Profits from this achievement would help finance their efforts to leapfrog IBM in the period after 1975.

FIVE

Leapfrogging IBM? 1976 to the Present

In late 1975, when Japan began officially to open her computer market, the industry was feeling stronger. The response to the crises of the early 1970s—the introduction of the IBM-370, the sharp revaluations of the yen, the oil shock, and foreign pressure on Japan to open her market—had strengthened the Japanese economy in general and the computer industry in particular. The creation of a war mentality—a pulling together and tightening of belts to prevent the destruction of the small-island, resource-poor economy—has gotten Japan out of many a jam, most recently the economic upheaval caused by *endaka*—the sharp rise in the yen. By creating a sense of national emergency, both the government and the computer firms took the drastic steps needed to survive.

Indeed, much of the fear that a gust of free trade was going to be allowed to blow through the long-protected market was hype, exaggerated to force the computer makers to get their own houses in order. MITI really had no intention of opening the computer industry to the vagaries of a free market. As Americans would begin to understand only more than a decade later, a free market, to the Japanese, means a market without such formal constraints as tariffs, quotas, and prohibitions on foreign investment; it has nothing to do with whether competitive foreign products are actually purchased. There was never any question in MITI's mind but that informal restraints would continue. But MITI used the threat of market liberalization to pressure the industry into a so-called "re-

reorganization" *(saisaihensei)*. With the New Series and DIPS-11 projects drawing to a close, MITI, NTT, and the makers had already decided that the next research topic to explore was densely integrated chips called VLSI. They expected IBM to make full use of these chips in its Future Series of computers that would hit the market, the Japanese anticipated, in the late 1970s or early 1980s. NTT had already organized a project to make VLSI chips in its labs. Now MITI decided to make a larger industry-wide effort to push the technology. For the project, MITI wanted to reorganize the firms into two research groups, but the firms were reluctant. When Prime Minister Tanaka Kakuei gathered the presidents of the six computer firms together and hinted "Aren't three groups too many?" Fujitsu's Kobayashi Taiyū responded: "You say 're-reorganization,' but that is like a heart transplant—it is so dangerous that it could affect the very lives of the firms."[1]

After more jawboning and promises of subsidies, a process called *nemawashi*,[2] the firms agreed. They were rewarded. On the eve of liberalization, MITI Minister Komoto promised the computer makers they would not be abandoned:

> In view of the high expectations held for the independence and continued growth of Japan's computer industry, the Government is resolved to keep a careful watch on trends in the computer market with the aim of preventing any adverse effect on domestic firms which might lead to confusion in the computer market. . . . It is the opinion of MITI that the independence and future growth of Japan's computer industry following liberalization will hinge on the industry's ability to secure an appropriate share of the domestic market. While keeping a close watch on the trends in computer imports and installations, the Ministry will put into effect strong measures for the promotion of the domestic industry which will include, but not be limited to, encouraging the development of VLSIs for use in next generation computers and the securing of sufficient rental funds for domestic machines.[3]

Komoto's promise was backed by substantial government procurement. Such purchases accounted for some 19 percent of all computers sold in Japan in the late 1970s and early 1980s.[4] And MITI continued a reduced but still substantial package of financial aid. Subsidies and tax benefits in the period from 1976 to 1981 still totaled some 205.145 billion yen or $1.025 billion—equivalent to 25 percent of what the computer firms were investing in R&D and plant and equipment. Including low-interest loans, total government aid ($3.8 billion) was equivalent to 93.2 percent of the amount the computer firms invested ($4.084 billion) (Appendixes F and G). "Subsidies are still a source of nutrition," explained Maeda.[5]

Despite this support, MITI did have to adjust its policies in accordance with the official market opening. Clearly, it was no longer possible for the government to be as overt in its aid to industry without triggering complaints from abroad. Fortunately, with the increased competitiveness of the computer makers, they did not need government money as much as they used to. This shifted the power balance more towards the firms and away from MITI, causing its power to gradually wane. According to Maeda Norihiko, a former high lever MITI bureaucrat:

> Now [late 1980s] the firms are stronger financially and MITI weaker; if MITI tried to tell the firms to form three groups now [for joint product development and marketing, as in the New Series Project], it would not succeed.[6]

The firms' strength also made it more difficult for them to cooperate with one another.

The nature of government policies gradually changed to adapt to these new realities. While efforts in the 1960s had helped the makers build computers like those IBM had already put on the market, policies in the late 1970s assisted the firms in developing machines to compete with as yet unannounced IBM computers—to help them stake out a technological advantage. To get them started, MITI decided to focus their efforts on technology for manufacturing a new generation of chips.

Foreign observers are often critical of government intervention because they question the government's ability to choose new technologies in which to invest. But the decision to do research to develop technologies to produce VLSI was not a matter of picking a winner out of a hat. Dr. Leona Esaki, a top researcher at IBM and one of the few Japanese scientists to receive the Nobel Prize, said in a 1976 interview that the development of VLSI was definitely necessary for future advances in both software and hardware.[7] Dr. Yasuo Tarui, head of the VLSI project, said the Japanese based their predictions of what type of ICs would be coming out in the future on forecasts made by U.S. studies.[8]

It was clear to all in the industry that more highly integrated circuits was the path that computer advances would take. As the number of transistors on a chip increases, memory capacity and processing speed for a given size computer increase. Moreover, since the production cost per wafer is about the same no matter how many chips you can get per wafer, technology necessary to get more chips on each wafer and more transistors on each chip was critical to being competitive. The denser the chip, the smaller a computer's size, the greater its processing speed, and the lower its production cost.[9]

The problem was how to produce them: how to fit more chips on a wafer and transistors on a chip cheaply and without sacrificing reliability. To solve this problem it was necessary to develop a device that could draw as minutely as possible the pattern for a chip on a wafer. There was a consensus that existing optical-exposure techniques for drawing chip patterns on a wafer would not do and that a new technique—an electron-beam exposure system—would be needed to make the patterns small and accurate enough.[10]

Meanwhile, NTT, the phone company, had already been quietly pursuing its own VLSI project. Started in 1975, the 3-year project was part of NTT's heavy financial support of NEC, Hitachi, and Fujitsu through cooperative R&D projects and enormous procurement contracts. NTT's role was particularly important after liberalization because, as a government company, it was largely immune from pressures to open up its market. Indeed, all countries have national procurement policies. Likewise, since much of NTT's financial aid to the industry came in the form of high-priced equipment purchases, it did not officially constitute government subsidies. NTT spent a total of 310 billion yen ($1.55 billion) on R&D from 1976 through 1980,[11] of which 20 billion yen ($100 million) went to the 3-year VLSI project.[12]

NTT's project was aimed at developing the technology for producing a 64K-bit RAM for use in telecommunications. It was done cooperatively by NTT's laboratory, Fujitsu, Hitachi, and NEC.[13] Toshiba and Oki asked to participate, but NTT decided to limit the project to the three top computer and telecommunications firms.[14] When asked why NTT started a VLSI project, NTT President Yonezawa said: "The fact that we knew IBM was developing its FS [Future System] had a definite, though indirect, influence on the R&D theme we selected."[15] Yonezawa admitted that a visit to Bell Labs in the United States the previous year made him feel that Japan had to hurry up and research VLSIs.[16] "I didn't realize they had advanced so far," said Yonezawa after seeing Bell's experimental design of a machine that used electron beams to make VLSI masks.[17] At a lecture he gave soon after returning from the United States, he appealed to both NTT and the country as a whole to cooperate on basic technology for VLSIs, because he felt that Japan was behind the United States in VLSI research by three years.[18]

Starting in 1975, the project members experimented with using conventional photo-beam-exposure technology to produce a 64K-bit RAM; at the same time, they did research on the more advanced electron-beam-exposure device, which was considered necessary to make more highly integrated VLSIs. Using conventional light, it was possible at best to draw lines with a width of 2 microns, whereas, with an electron-beam device, they expected to be able to draw lines as narrow as 1 to 0.1 microns.[19]

The three firm–NTT lab group is credited with the development of several critical technologies up to the present; indeed, while the project was originally planned for only three years, it still exists today, over a decade later. In April 1977, NTT announced that they had successfully developed the photo-exposure technology for the production of the 64K-bit RAM.[20] NTT announced that this 64K was the first in the world, but people in the industry believed that IBM must have already developed it; sure enough, in late 1978, IBM announced a computer using 64K-bit RAMS.[21]

In April 1978, NTT announced that the project had created a prototype 128K-bit ROM (read only memory) by using an electron-beam-exposure system to draw the patterns directly.[22] This was the largest scale integration announced in the world.[23] Later that year, however, IBM announced that it had developed a VLSI with even higher integration—a 256 K-bit—by using technology to draw lines as narrow as 1 micron.[24] In early 1980 NTT announced that it had successfully made a prototype of a 256K RAM.[25] "NTT played a great role in the development of VLSI technology," according to Sakai Yoshio, senior researcher at Hitachi's Central Research Laboratory.[26]

MITI was not happy when NTT started its VLSI project because it felt that NTT was intruding into its territory.[27] So when MITI started a similar project a year later, it tried to persuade NTT to merge its project with the MITI effort. "We will cooperate with MITI on the part related to computers," was all MITI got out of NTT President Yonezawa.[28] Cooperation did not mean giving up its program and joining MITI's; rather it meant exchanging information.

If NTT would not join it, MITI wanted to beat it with a grander scale project including all of the five main computer makers. But the firms were not enthusiastic about following MITI's ambitious plan. This was partly because MITI wanted to set very high technological goals for the project—to develop the technology for producing memories with several million bits when the ICs being used in machines at the time were 2,000 to 4,000 bits. The firms were interested in doing research on the technology for manufacturing 64K RAMS—something attainable and commercially viable in the short run—as they were doing with NTT.[29] MITI was expecting the firms to put up money and scarce engineering resources. The firms were also reluctant to work as teams.

These two problems were ultimately resolved through another round of *nemawashi*—a process of negotiation and compromise. One of the problems was how to make two groups out of the three groups formed for the New Series Project. MITI solved this by dropping Oki from the project and adding Mitsubishi to the Fujitsu-Hitachi group. This pleased Fujitsu, which had long coveted the large Mitsubishi group market.[30] MITI felt Oki was technologically and financially inferior,[31] and that it would not be able to use VLSI technologies in sophisticated computers because it had not even commercialized the COSMO mainframe technology in the New Series Project.[32]

> The objective of the VLSI project was not to produce VLSI; it was to make the devices needed to make a top-level computer so that we would not be defeated by IBM. This would be a large-scale computer. The companies that would make large-scale computers raised their hands; Oki [had to] put its hand down.[33]

MITI also made it clear to Oki that it wanted Oki to specialize in terminals and peripherals.[34]

The second problem—what research to pursue in the project—was resolved by doing some R&D on more rapidly commercializable technology, which the firms desired, and some on the more long-term technologies that MITI wanted. The content of the research was also influenced by the developments made in the NTT VLSI project.

MITI's project lasted four years, from 1976 to 1979, and cost 72 billion yen ($360 million), 30 billion of which was funded by the government. The firms each contributed an equal amount to cover the remaining 42 billion yen.[35] The project aimed to make technology to produce VLSI having up to 1 million bits.[36] In comparison, the U.S. government spent a similar amount—$200 million (40 billion yen)—on its VHSIC (Very High-Speed Integrated Circuit) Project, which was undertaken between 1979 and 1984.[37] The U.S. effort, which targeted VLSI having up to 2 million bits/chips,[38] was focused on the development of VLSI for military use, requiring the ability to stand up to immense heat and shock; in contrast, the Japanese projects were concerned solely with commercial applications.

While the general topic of production technology for VLSI had been decided upon, it was still necessary to decide upon more detailed R&D themes and to divide up the labor. Tarui Yasuo, then of AIST's lab and currently a professor at Tokyo University of Agriculture and Technology, was the head of the committee given these tasks. He said that it was very difficult to get the firms to agree on specific research themes, and that they were particularly hesitant about doing cooperative R&D that would require that they divulge their own know-how.[39]

To avoid this obstacle and to encourage enthusiastic participation, they decided to select themes involving basic research that all firms would need for producing VLSI; this would decrease the need for firms to use their own know-how in the project and would get all firms interested because they would need the technology in the long run.[40] They chose 6 themes: micromanufacturing technology (especially technology for drawing narrower lines on wafers); silicon-crystal technology; and design, process, device, and testing and evaluation technology. The topics covered not only developing the technology for producing VLSI but also the technology and devices to test the reliability of the VLSI produced by the machines.

The first two themes were the most important. The first included devices such as the electronic beam and the X-ray beam, which were to draw more intricate patterns on VLSI. They decided to do two prototypes of the electron-beam drawing device, one in the first two years and the other, a refinement of the first, in the last two years. According to Dr. Tarui, they felt that, by doing it twice, they could get people from different firms with different backgrounds to brainstorm for the first prototype and then use the best ideas for the second and final prototype.[41] In an interview, Shimizu Sakae, Senior Managing Director of Toshiba, emphasized the importance of R&D on the electron beam:

> The timing of the project was critical; there was no electron beam and we needed a breakthrough to get ahead. The firms did not have any of the equipment for producing VLSIs, such as the electron beam or testing equipment.[42]

The second theme—silicon-crystal technology—was selected in order to find ways to decrease defects in VLSI. One problem was that, as transistors were made smaller in order to fit more on a wafer, tiny defects in the silicon crystals appeared.[43] It was also necessary to learn how to make good quality crystals in order to make larger wafers, which required attaining an even chemical composition over the entire wafer. With larger wafers, costs would be reduced dramatically, since more chips could be produced in a given production process. One problem explored under this theme was that of warps on wafers. Warping distorts the pattern drawn on the wafer, causing many defects.[44]

After deciding what specific topics to research, the cooperative research association had to determine how to divide up the labor among firms or groups of firms. Dr. Tarui said that, in the beginning, they asked each research member his first choice, but that everyone chose similar themes; thus they had to decide on the division and how much to mix researchers from different firms.[45] For the most important devices in the project, such as the electron-beam drawing device, they decided to have three parallel research labs work on the same thing independently, taking different approaches, in the hope that at least one would succeed.[46] Indeed, the project members tried a total of 7 different ways to get the electron beam to draw patterns on the wafer.[47] Each of the three groups was led by one firm; Dr. Tarui said that it would have been difficult to mix equal numbers of people from rival firms for research on the most important devices.[48] While research on the electron and X-ray-beam systems was done by several groups, each dominated by one firm, most of the technologies in the other 5 research areas were done by one group consisting of members of several different firms.[49]

There were four major labs. The Fujitsu, Hitachi, and Mitsubishi group made the Joint Computer Development Laboratories (CDL); Toshiba and NEC used their joint-venture NTIS lab, and there was a joint lab for all members including AIST's Electrotechnical Lab. NTT's lab exchanged information with the MITI project labs.

MITI's VLSI project had several positive results, some immediate, others more long-term, some purely technical, others resulting from the synergy of concentrating the top firms' efforts on one research topic. The project contributed greatly to the Japanese makers' ability to produce low-cost, high-quality VLSI in the late 1970s. "The VLSI project was so successful that it caused trade friction," according to Maeda Norihiko, a former top level MITI official.[50]

The project achieved most of its technical goals.[51] Within one year, it developed the variable-rectangle-beam system—the first in the world. This system made it possible to manufacture by electron beam chips having a line width of one micron.[52] It was more accurate and faster—¹⁄₁₀₀th the time—than a conventional electron beam.[53] By the end of the project, they were able to get line widths between 0.1-1 micron with the electron beam and with another device they developed—the X-ray-beam exposure system.[54] Both these systems can be used for making VLSI memory chips and logic chips.[55] Toshiba's Shimizu Sakae said that the VLSI project was very important in helping them produce 64K RAMS and more densely integrated 1-megabit chips; Toshiba and NEC jointly developed an electron-beam device under the project and are using it today in their VLSI efforts.[56]

In their research on crystals, project members found that impurities such as oxygen and carbon were primary causes of defects that occurred in the production of ICs when the temperature reached 600 to 900 degrees centigrade. They experimented to find the best temperature for minimizing wafer warping and other defects.[57] For the testing and evaluation technology, they developed a narrow laser-beam scanning device that could detect defects in the patterns drawn on a wafer.[58] Another important development was an evaluation technology for oxide and nitride layers using liquid crystals.[59]

The project resulted in some 1,000 patents.[60] Fifty-nine percent were held by individuals, 25 percent by groups dominated by people from one company, and 16 percent by groups consisting of several members of various firms.[61]

Perhaps the most important effect of the VLSI project was to induce the computer makers to take the risky step of committing themselves in VLSI.

> Japanese have the tendency that, if one does something, all will do it. That a project is assigned by the government is a clear sign that, if you are not on the bandwagon, you will miss something important.[62]

An important result of cooperative projects is that, by organizing the project, the government in effect takes the blame if it fails. Advanced VLSI research would have required a firm to go out on a limb; with the government project, the firms could take the risk collectively because a failure would not have been perceived as their fault.[63] As one maker put it:

> Because of the limited resources of a private firm, we domestic makers cannot allow a failure; we cannot deny that this [participation in MITI's VLSI project] was taking a big hedge against risk.[64]

Indeed, R&D in new areas is risky and inevitably involves some failures. By getting the firms to pool their financial and human resources, and by having three groups take different approaches to the same research problem, the probability of success was increased. Most important, all members of the research cooperative got access to the resulting patents at low cost.

The government's financing was also important.[65] All five firms would have had great difficulty carrying the financial burden of doing such comprehensive research. Indeed, the total cost of the MITI project was 72 billion yen from 1976 to 1979; Fujitsu's after-tax profits during this same period were only 35 billion yen,[66] and all the computer companies together invested only some 353.7 billion yen in R&D during that period.[67] Each firm had to spend only some 8.4 billion yen in MITI's VLSI project, yet it got access to the results of 72 billion yen of R&D, not to mention the benefits received from the NTT VLSI project. Nonetheless, Fukuta Masumi, the Deputy General Manager of Fujitsu's Compound Semiconductor Division, has argued that the government's value was in its coordinating efforts rather than its subsidies. "I believe there were results [in the VLSI project] not because of government financial support but because each company chose different fundamental themes."[68] The ultimate result was the same: By focusing on different themes and sharing results, the government project provided the firms with much more research per yen spent than they would have received if working alone.

The development of high-quality, densely integrated circuits has allowed the Japanese computer makers to increase their computer sales in both domestic and international markets. VLSI advances have been the key element in refinements of their "New Series" machines from the late 1970s up to Fujitsu's more recent announce-

Figure 2 Computer Imports and Exports, 1977–1983

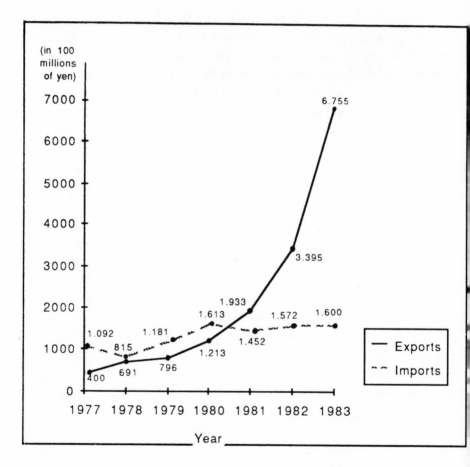

Source: Ministry of Finance "Customs Statistics"

ment of its M-780 mainframe, which exceeds IBM's top-of-the-line 3090 Sierra Series in price/performance.[69] Soon after the project ended there was a sharp increase in mainframe exports (Figure 2). By 1979, Fujitsu was neck-and-neck with IBM Japan in sales and, in 1980, was the first maker to top IBM in any country (Table 20). The project also helped the firms make deep inroads into the U.S. memory market, gave them the lead in the race to produce megabit RAMS,[70] and helped increase their telecommunications equipment sales. Since the firms participating in the project operated in several related markets, the firms and the government were able to receive a faster and greater return on their investment.

Table 20 Annual Sales Related to Information Processing, 1976–1982 (unit: Sales: billion yen; Share: percent (%))

	1976	1977	1978	1979	1980	1981	1982
Fujitsu	239.6	274.5	303.0	326.8	382.1	448.4	532.2
	(22.7)	(23.7)	(24.0)	(23.4)	(23.8)	(22.7)	(22.3)
IBM Japan	275.5	293.8	315.3	324.2	338.3	428.8	484.9
	(26.1)	(25.4)	(24.9)	(23.2)	(21.0)	(21.7)	(20.3)
NEC	114.0	137.6	166.9	200.8	240.4	332.5	424.7
	(10.8)	(11.9)	(13.2)	(14.4)	(14.9)	(16.9)	(17.8)
Hitachi	142.0	160.0	190.0	216.0	250.0	288.0	362.0
	(13.5)	(13.8)	(15.0)	(15.5)	(15.5)	(14.6)	(15.1)
Toshiba	59.2	59.1	43.0	50.4	80.3	95.0	140.5
	(5.6)	(5.1)	(3.4)	(3.6)	(5.0)	(4.8)	(5.9)
Oki	43.8	44.4	47.9	62.8	78.8	109.1	130.4
	(4.2)	(3.8)	(3.8)	(4.5)	(4.9)	(5.6)	(5.5)
Japan Univac	70.4	67.8	71.6	73.6	78.6	90.9	103.7
	(6.7)	(5.9)	(5.7)	(5.3)	(4.9)	(4.6)	(4.3)
Mitsubishi	32.0	38.0	45.0	53.0	62.0	73.0	94.0
	(3.0)	(3.3)	(3.6)	(3.8)	(3.9)	(3.7)	(3.9)
Burroughs	43.5	45.0	47.0	54.6	50.5	57.3	60.7
	(4.1)	(3.9)	(3.7)	(3.9)	(3.1)	(2.9)	(2.5)
Japan NCR	34.3	36.9	34.3	34.3	48.2	49.6	58.5
	(3.3)	(3.2)	(2.7)	(2.4)	(3.0)	(2.5)	(2.4)

Source: Shimoda Hirotsugu, *IBM to no 10 nen Sensō*, p. 178.

While the VLSI projects helped the firms keep up with IBM in hardware, MITI recognized that the makers still lagged far behind in software. Not until the 1980s would MITI funnel substantial financial aid into software, but MITI continued its efforts to help the small, fledgling software houses with the Software Production Technology Development Program.[71] The key problem was a dire shortage of programmers. To increase the productivity of Japanese software development, MITI patched together the 5-year (1976– 1981), 7.5-billion-yen ($37.5 million) program supervised by the Information Processing Promotion Agency (IPA); 17 software houses jointly established a new corporation—the Joint System Development Corporation (JSDC) to do the project work. IPA consigned the development of software tools to this organization, which in turn distributed the money to smaller software companies which did the actual development.[72] The JSDC was not a software company; rather it was a *madoguchi gaisha*—a window company—that functioned merely to coordinate the smaller member firms.[73] IPA would own the resulting software development tools and market them along with its other software products.

The project started with the goal of developing software that could automatically generate software applications programs. When it was acknowledged early on that the goals were virtually unattainable, the goals were scaled down from "automatic code generation" to the development of a library of working aids for software programmers;[74] along with this change, the budget was cut by a billion yen to 6.5 billion yen and the project extended by a year.[75] Despite the downscaling of the goals, the software tools it assigned to be developed failed to find a market amongst users.[76] In this project, as in earlier efforts, there was no attempt to get users involved in deciding what software tools to develop. Since the software companies were desperate for money, they were more intent on convincing the people overseeing government projects that they had a good product than in actually developing a bestseller. Maeda Norihiko, formerly of MITI and involved in MITI's later software efforts, stated that the primary goal of this project was to give financial aid to small and medium-sized companies; "It was not an economic rationale, it was a political one."[77] Others have maintained that the project failed because the alliance of small software companies with the large hardware vendors made it difficult for the various firms in the project to settle on common goals.[78]

Meanwhile, a more important project was developed—one that would improve the Japanese-language processing capability of Japanese computers.[79] The original plan for the 5-year (1979–1983) "Next Generation Computers Technology" project called for spending 47 billion yen ($235 million) to be borne half by the government, half by the participating firms;[80] in 1979 and 1980, the cost was borne equally by the public and private sectors, but, from 1981 on, the government, under pressure to pare its growing national budget deficit, cut its aid to 45 percent.[81] Professor Aiso has stated that this project helped the Japanese develop more sophisticated Japanese word processors.[82]

Just when things seemed to be going well, the Japanese industry was dealt a blow from which it has not yet fully recovered. In mid-1982, IBM, freed from a 13-year antitrust suit by the U.S. government, cooperated with the FBI in a sting to catch Hitachi and Mitsubishi stealing IBM technological secrets. "In all Hitachi's history, there was never a shock like that," admitted Hitachi's Vice-President Arami Masatomi.[83] Soon after IBM had settled its damages with these two companies, Fujitsu and IBM came out with a cooperative agreement covering Fujitsu's use of IBM-compatible software. Fujitsu Chairman Kobayashi Taiyū admitted that Fujitsu did not get caught in the sting because it did not have to steal IBM technology; it was getting it through Amdahl.[84] The firms have been forced to make licensing agreements with IBM involving huge sums. Hitachi, for instance, reportedly paid IBM 10 billion yen ($45.45 million) for the cost of the suit and for past use of software similar to IBM's, and is paying an estimated 8 to 12 billion yen ($36.36 million to $54.54 million) a year for current use; IBM also received the right to inspect new Hitachi machines to confirm that Hitachi is keeping the agreement.[85] IBM continues to put pressure on the Japanese makers. In 1985, it asked the American Arbitration Association to settle its complaint that Fujitsu was not honoring their original 1983 agreement covering IBM software;[86] this was resolved in September 1987 when the arbitrators decided that Fujitsu could have access to IBM's source codes—basic programs at the heart of IBM's mainframe computers—for a sum of $833.2 million.[87]

The risks in manufacturing computers that run on IBM-compatible software became increasingly clear. Indeed, firms that take an IBM-compatible strategy are under intense pressure to introduce a compatible machine as soon as possible after a new IBM machine is announced. "We have to make a complete break from the IBM standard in order to survive," said Yamamoto Kinko, the Managing Director of the Japan Information Processing Development Center (JIPDEC) and an active participant in Japan's computer industry since the late 1950s.[88] But such a move would prove to be easier said than done. Projects to date had all involved improving on the basic computer architecture and chip technology introduced by IBM in the early 1960s—all relatively clear steps. A move away from the IBM standard would require exploration of entirely new hardware and software frontiers.

Though the IBM *Supai Jiken* (spy incident) accelerated Japanese efforts to move away from the IBM standard, the Japanese had decided even before the embarrassing event that they would ultimately have to become independent of IBM in order to survive in the international computer market. Four projects would play a key role in this effort. The Supercomputer Project aimed to develop materials that would be the core of future computers. The 5th-Generation Computer Project attempts to create a radically new computer. The Sigma Project targets the development of a UNIX-based work station to be used for developing UNIX software. Japan hopes it can turn to UNIX if IBM suddenly increases the fees the Japanese IBM-compatible makers have to pay for information on IBM's operating systems. Finally, the TRON Project, a private sector project with indirect government backing, explores a totally new pure-Japanese standard, but one that is compatible with the current von Neumann computer architecture. By supporting these and other R&D projects, the government is substantially reducing the costs and risks for the firms to explore frontier technology and to break away from the IBM standard.

The "Supercomputer" Project,[89] a 9-year effort (1981–1989) under AIST's "Large-Scale R&D Program," is funded completely by the government at 23 billion yen ($104.54 million).[90] All six computer firms are involved. Advances in supercomputers are expected to be of critical importance in future computer systems. "This will be much more important than the Industrial Revolution," Michael L. Dertouzos, Director of the Laboratory for Computer Science at MIT, has asserted.[91] Dertouzos argues that supercomputers are the key to new knowledge and the linchpin to technological progress.[92]

The firms did not initially want to get involved in the Supercomputer Project because they thought there was not a large enough market for supercomputers; instead, they wanted a project to help them improve upon their IBM-compatible machines.[93] Why don't the firms refuse to join projects they are not interested in? "If we ever said, 'forget about Fujitsu [for a given project] and do it with someone else,' we would never be invited to join a government project again," explained Fujitsu's Tajiri.[94] For the Supercomputer Project, the government offered to fund the entirety, and the firms went along.

The primary goal of the project is the development of a prototype high-speed computer system that can process data 1,000 times faster than the supercomputers available when the project started. To reach this goal, two areas are being explored: densely integrated, high-speed logic and memory chips, and high-speed parallel processing techniques.[95] For the former, NEC, Toshiba, Hitachi, and Mitsubishi are studying gallium arsenide chips; Fujitsu, Hitachi, and NEC, Josephson junctions; and Fujitsu and Oki, HEMT (high electronic mobility transistor) devices.[96] The firms are researching these areas separately. In 1988, they decided that Fujitsu would be making the prototype using HEMT.[97]

High-speed chips will not only help the firms make supercomputers; they will also increase the speed of all computers and help the Japanese take the lead in developing new IC products. Moreover, low-cost, mass-manufactured gallium arsenide devices would revolutionize all electronics products and increase the competitiveness not only of Japan's computer and electronics industries but also its telecommunications, space, and numerically controlled machine-tools industries. By substantially reducing the costs and risks for the firms to explore these high-speed devices in this and other projects,[98] MITI is increasing the probability that the firms will be able rapidly to develop high-quality, low-cost devices.

Important advances in parallel processing, gallium arsenide, Josephson junction devices, and HEMT have already been made in the project,[99] and people from the companies participating in the project say that it is helping them significantly.[100] Indeed, the Japanese firms came out with a generation of supercomputers in 1983 and are now competing with the top U.S. supercomputer maker, Cray. Would the companies have gone into supercomputers even without the project? According to Oketani Kisaburō of Fujitsu:

> When the project was started, there were few supercomputers in use worldwide, so we thought there was not enough demand. I do not think that one company would have made such a big effort in supercomputers [as the project has].[101]

Yamamoto of JIPDEC emphasized the importance of the timing of the project; she believes the firms would have ultimately made the jump into supercomputers but that the project got them to commit themselves to it sooner and, through cooperation, to get the job done faster.[102]

MITI is not alone in helping the firms advance in high-speed chips. NTT also has its own supercomputer project, which involves Fujitsu, Hitachi, and NEC.[103] In early 1985, the NTT lab successfully developed a 1-K lead-based Josephson memory chip, which ranks as one of the fastest in the world,[104] and also a "pace-setting 4-K gallium arsenide memory."[105] These results are undoubtedly reducing the cost and accelerating the technological advances of Fujitsu, Hitachi, and NEC in the area of high-speed devices.

> I think that the Supercomputer Project will be the last [government project] in our attempt to catch up with America in hardware, because now

the firms are perfectly able to stand up on their own two feet. From now on, policies will be directed towards software.[106]

The importance of the supercomputer effort notwithstanding, MITI's primary effort to reduce the costs and risks for the firms to operate in the industry and do the research necessary to break away from the IBM standard is the 5th-Generation Computer Project.[107] This 10-year project, which started in 1982, is an ambitious attempt to make a major technological leap in artificial intelligence—to develop a "thinking" computer, one that can infer new knowledge from its data base and write its own software.

In contrast to the Supercomputer Project, which focuses on improving existing technologies, such as parallel processing, and developing clearly defined technologies, such as gallium-arsenide devices, the 5th-Generation Project has rather vague goals to be met by developing new concepts and technologies that the Japanese have yet to prove they can master.

The project members hope to produce a prototype machine by 1991, but the project director, Fuchi Kazuhiro, admits that he does not expect a 5th-generation machine to be commercialized until the late 1990s.[108] This long period of development is necessary because the 5th-generation computer involves completely new software and hardware concepts and technology.[109] The Japanese have had their greatest success in keeping up with advances in chips over the past three decades, starting with vacuum tubes for 1st-generation computers, transistors for the 2nd, ICs and LSIs for the 3rd and 3.5-generation machines, and VLSI for the 4th-generation machines in use today. These generations of computers have been based on the von Neumann design—they have a central processing unit that processes data sequentially. But the 5th-Generation Project aims to develop more sophisticated hardware that will process data much faster by doing it simultaneously. This hardware will require new, sophisticated software, an area in which Japan has always lagged behind. The 5th-generation machine will supposedly be able to infer knowledge based on data stored in its memory. Given the right information, for example, the Japanese expect that the computer would be able to write its own software for new applications and that it would be able to process and understand the meaning of a variety of symbols, including Chinese characters and photos. The Japanese expect that the 5th-generation machine would thus be able to "reason" at an elementary level, that it would be able to help doctors, managers, and others who analyze problems through complex sequences of inferences rather than depending solely on calculations.

Eight firms together with NTT are sending engineers to ICOT,[110] a central laboratory established in 1982 to conduct the research. They are: Fujitsu, Hitachi, NEC, Toshiba, Mitsubishi, Oki, Matsushita, and Sharp. NTT also has its own 5th-generation computer project, which it is conducting in cooperation with NEC, Hitachi, and Fujitsu.[111] At ICOT, researchers from different companies sit side by side working together,[112] something rather unusual compared to other projects. But ICOT also operates five other laboratories where the work is divided up. The chairman and directors of ICOT are designated by the Minister of MITI; there are some 200 members.[113]

According to the government's original plan, the 100 billion yen ($455 million) cost of the 10-year project was to be shared, but the firms refused. They believed the goals were far too vague, and they were particularly concerned that the project did not target an IBM-compatible machine.[114]

> Firms are, after all, firms, so of course they want to produce things they can make a profit on. The 5th-Generation [Project] idea was extremely new, so they naturally had doubts in the beginning.[115]

To encourage the firms to participate, the government agreed to fund the project completely for the first 3 years at a total cost of 8.3 billion yen ($34.5 million).[116] Later, government financial support for the project has been scaled down to 17.5 billion yen for the first 5 years, with 32.5 billion yen for the final 5 years; this decrease in financial support was coupled with a decision to focus ICOT efforts on the development of artificial-intelligence machines, leaving to the private sector alone the task of doing the R&D needed to apply the technology to commercial products.[117] Thus, though the firms still have not agreed to match government funds, MITI is planning to spend only its initially planned 50 billion yen.

The 5th-Generation Project has been hyped up in the press, raising expectations to unrealistic levels.

> When we read something about the 5th-Generation Project we think that a computer will be developed that will behave like a human being. But that is impossible. There are, however, many key technologies that are necessary for future machines, and we think that ICOT can develop those technologies.[118]

Although the project met its goals for the initial 3-year stage,[119] the final goal of the project—a prototype machine—will be more difficult to achieve. The project members may even find in the end that they have not taken the right path, one of the dangers of concentrating on a single approach. Even if their approach is right, they might not be able to complete a prototype system; indeed, the Japanese have had trouble in past projects that targeted vague goals, such as the PIPS Project and the work assigned to the Japan Software Co.

While the project is unlikely to result in a working prototype system, there will be important benefits to the industry. First, makers do expect some significant spin-offs from technology researched in the project;[120] some spin-offs have already been commercialized.[121] Second, the project has set an important guideline for the future path of research. Edward Feigenbaum, a specialist in artificial intelligence, has stated that the project "has focused attention on the right set of issues, properly structured."[122] Indeed, an increasingly important role of industrial policy towards the computer industry is to encourage firms to explore frontier technologies—such as artificial intelligence—that they will need in order to compete in the long-run. "Because of the 5th-Generation Project, there has recently been sudden excitement about artificial intelligence in Japan; the project has had a great impact."[123]

While the artificial-intelligence boom in Japan may not be long lived—the United States has had several booms in AI in the last few decades—the 5th-Generation Computer Project has, since the late 1970s when the project planning began, pressured Japanese computer makers to think about a new generation of non-IBM-compatible machines. Moreover, the project has substantially reduced the costs and risks involved in their exploring alternative strategies. Fujitsu has announced that it plans to decrease its dependency on IBM-compatible computers;[124] projects like the 5th-generation effort could help it come up with new options.

> We think government projects are significant because there are many things for us to challenge in the future, many that can be better done in a government project than a private one. . . . When profit decreases as it has in the last two years due to the recession, the increasingly higher yen, and trade friction, we, in our [corporate] research lab, are pressured to cut costs and to be more product-oriented. It is very difficult to propose a future-oriented technology because we will be asked "Is it necessary? How profitable will the results be?" So we believe that national projects are very very important when they are future-oriented—when they focus on very risky R&D that is very difficult for the private sector to challenge alone.[125]

Finally, the 5th-Generation Computer Project is training a few key young researchers of the major firms; these researchers will still be working in the industry in the 1990s when the battle to commercialize a 5th-generation machine will most likely occur. When a market for such computers does develop, the Japanese firms will, from the project effort, have a common approach and standard for their "thinking" machines; they will also have learned in the project not only what technologies will work, but also what will not work. Indeed, weeding out "failure" strategies in a government project reduces the risks and costs that each firm bears when it comes time to refine and commercialize the technology.

The Supercomputer and 5th-Generation Computer Projects are not the only efforts MITI has made to reduce the costs and risks for the firms in this transition to a different standard. In 1981, MITI started a 10-year project called the Basic Industrial Technology for the Next Generation Project, which includes efforts to develop new devices, such as 3-dimensional VLSI devices and super-lattice devices to speed up and improve computer processing, and to investigate the possibilities of biocomputers to mimic the human brain.[126]

MITI has also resorted to tactics to limit IBM's stranglehold on the industry. In early 1984, for example, MITI proposed a software-protection law that would protect copyrights on software for only 15 years instead of the 50-year protection provided by international copyright law. This proposed law would give MITI the authority to force a company to license its software to another firm in cases where MITI deemed it in the national interest or when a company had substantially altered the original software and wanted to sell it as a new product.[127] "We want to prevent firms from having to completely rewrite software that already exists," explained MITI's Kawano Hirobumi.[128] After long negotiations involving an un-usually strong U.S. lobby against the measure, the proposal was dropped. Had the law passed, Japanese makers, over the long run, could have saved a large part of the money they now have to pay for rights to use software similar to IBMs. That MITI would make such a politically explosive proposal at a time when trade frictions be-tween the two countries were very high suggests how desperate it felt about freeing the firms from IBM's software chains.

In addition, since the early 1980s when the fields of telecom-munications and computers increasingly overlapped, the govern-ment tried to hinder IBM's and other foreign firms' full-scale entry into the telecommunications–data-communications market. In late 1984, the Ministry of Post and Telecommunications (MPT) drafted a telecommunications law that, in the words of one U.S. govern-ment official, "takes us back to the feudal era, when foreigners were banned from Japan."[129] This attempt to increase barriers for foreign firms did not succeed due to heavy U.S. pressure.[130] But the battle between the United States and the MPT raged again in 1988 when the MPT changed its position on international value-added net-works to the detriment of foreign firms that have their own unique protocols. While a compromise on the issue was reached in Septem-ber 1988, the U.S. government is still dissatisfied and pushing for a completely free market.[131] Meanwhile, Japanese companies gained the breathing space to make advances in telecommunications.[132] Thus, despite the privatization of the NTT in 1985 and the govern-ment's repeated commitment to open up the telecommunications

market, inroads by foreign firms, though increasing, are still min-
uscule. As in computers, informal policies skew standards, delay
approvals, and make doing business in Japan's telecommunications
market difficult for foreign competitors. As Prime Minister Naka-
sone told a Diet committee in 1984, he supported free competition
for foreign companies in Japan's VAN market, but he warned that,
"if there is any effect on the people's welfare, we will have to put
up limits."[133] Foreign firms still face tremendous barriers.

While MITI's ultimate goal is to help the computer industry
create a new standard in order to reduce dependence on IBM, it has
also, as an interim measure, encouraged the industry to diversify its
risk by starting a large software project in 1985—the Sigma Project—that uses AT&T's UNIX as the operating standard.[134] "We've
got to find another standard," remarked Tomioka Susumu, manager
of Fujitsu's software division that is developing UNIX for Fujitsu.
"We're moving away from the IBM system, and UNIX is . . . a
strong candidate."[135] "It is really necessary to develop a software
standard and UNIX is excellent for software development and R&D,"
agreed Yasui Masaya, Assistant Director of MITI's Data-Processing
Promotion Division, about the choice of UNIX for the Sigma Project.[136]

The project is aimed at increasing software productivity—reducing redundant software development and increasing the efficiency
of software engineers and programmers—in order to alleviate what
is expected to be a shortage of some 600,000 software engineers by
1990.[137] The idea of developing a software system to generate software automatically was taken from the earlier, unsuccessful Software Production Technology Development Project from 1976 to
1981, the results of which the Sigma Project is using.[138]

Begun in April 1985, the project is scheduled to be completed
in 1990. There are 164 firms participating in it, including all of
Japan's leading computer and software firms and the recently privatized NTT, and also the subsidiaries of foreign firms like IBM,
AT&T, Hewlett Packard, DEC, Unisys, Data General, and Oli-
vetti. The total cost is estimated at 25 billion yen ($147 million),
of which the government will supply approximately one half.[139]

With Sigma, Japan hopes to create the infrastructure—the necessary environment—for programmers to develop applications software more efficiently.[140] This infrastructure will consist of a national-policy company—the Sigma Center, user sites, and an elaborate network connecting the two. The Sigma Center will house a database containing the basic software tools that are to be developed in the project.[141] Software programmers using Sigma work stations will have on-line access to the Sigma database via networks. With this standard, small software makers will no longer be dependent on the large hardware vendors, who up to now have forced the small makers to use their various operating systems and tools.[142] Several of Japan's computer makers are already marketing machines based on the UNIX standard. The project hopes to satisfy and stimulate further this increase in demand for UNIX programs.

The project is progressing on schedule and meeting its intermediate goals; but, even if wholly successful, it will at best be an interim move to buy time. It in no way helps the makers become independent; in fact, it simply throws them into the arms of another huge foreign competitor—AT&T. There are also technological limits to UNIX. "It is very good for researchers, but it is not good when used in networking and is very bad in respect to security," Hitachi's Kuwahara has stated. "There are many other architectures; the expectations for the Sigma Project are too high."[143]

AT&T in many ways holds all the cards. MITI bureaucrats are already worried about Sigma's dependence on UNIX, because they fear that AT&T may demand rights to any resulting software, since it is based on the UNIX system.[144] "The copyright problem, in various ways, is becoming more severe; AT&T has recently begun to assert its copyright on UNIX," JIPDEC's Yamamoto complained in late 1987.[145]

But will the Sigma work station be the best for software development? Despite growing interest in Sigma machines, industry surveys predict that low-end, desk-top versions of mainframes, such as IBM's 9370 and DEC's VAX station 2000, will be leading the way in software development. A lot will depend on price. Sigma officials have proposed a price of about 3 million yen ($20,000), but recent prototypes are going for as low as half that.[146] Forecasts for the potential market for the Sigma work station vary from MITI's low of 10,000 by 1990, the project's prediction of 50,000 to 60,000, and the computer manufacturers' optimistic hopes for some 100,000 units by 1990.[147] With the project still incomplete, it is difficult to tell whether the Japanese firms will be able to make a top-of-the-line machine that they can sell at competitive prices without losing money over the long run. But IBM's announcement in April 1988 that it would increase royalty fees on its 32,000 patents from about 1 percent to as much as 5 percent of sales revenue[148] may give Sigma the push it needs.

It is largely due to the corner the Japanese have been backed into that a recent effort to establish a new all-Japanese standard for computers and other electronics products has been met with great fanfare. The TRON[149] Project, started in 1984 and headed by Sakamura Ken, a lecturer at the University of Tokyo, is, unlike projects discussed thus far, officially a private-sector initiative. Collaboration between firms without direct government intervention, increasingly common in Japan, has been facilitated by the close relationships formed by the companies in numerous government projects over the last few decades. For example, Hitachi and Fujitsu, which have cooperated with one another in several MITI projects, are collaborating on the development of a 32-bit TRON microprocessor.[150] But, as we shall see, projects that are officially private can have substantial government backing.

TRON, like the Sigma Project, is another interim step to try to break away from IBM. To quote Toda, who heads the NTT's research lab:

> IBM could double or triple its price and we could not complain. Japanese firms are very troubled by this prospect, and that is why everyone is saying let's go along with the TRON chip (microprocessor).[151]

Yamamoto of JIPDEC agreed:

> There is a feeling that in the future Japan may no longer be able to use America's operating systems (OS) freely. We must create and promote the diffusion of a Japanese operating system standard.[152]

TRON is lauded in Japan as a pure Japanese answer to their problem; it is not only independent of Western standards; it is also being designed so that it can process the Japanese language. It is viewed as a potential saviour of the Japanese culture, countering the opinion of many computer specialists that the Japanese language must be put into roman letters in order to be used efficiently by computers. "It is a *Hi no Maru* [Rising Sun] operating system," JIPDEC's Yamamoto has proudly boasted.[153]

The project is incredibly—many would say unrealistically—ambitious. It plans to build a completely new standard—something Japan has never done. Moreover, the goal is for this to become *the* international operating system and interface standard that all companies would adopt for products ranging from simple personal computers to complex computer networks.[154] This would make all other standards obsolete.

Despite these ambitious goals, all Japan's major computer companies, electronics firms, and NTT have joined the TRON association, as have subsidiaries of foreign companies such as IBM and AT&T. By the end of May 1987, the members totaled 60 firms.[155] The government gave the project a big boost in November 1987, when the Ministry of Education announced that TRON would be the operating system standard for the computers that will be used by Japan's 27 million schoolchildren.[156] Not only will this provide a strong immediate demand-pull for the project; it also means that, upon graduation, Japanese students will be comfortable working with TRON and will probably, given the opportunity, purchase TRON machines for their companies and homes. NTT has also agreed to use TRON in its computer networks.[157]

But all this hoopla is more the result of an over-confident industry desperate to divorce itself from IBM and to prove to the world that Japanese are indeed creative than a technologically sound answer to the industry's problems. While it is too early to make definitive conclusions, it is clear that, at best, TRON will be one of many standards Japanese makers will use as a temporary hedge against IBM; at worst, by encouraging a desperate industry to race headlong down the wrong path, TRON could be a disaster. According to one Hitachi manager:

It is a good thing that a new architecture—TRON—was proposed by Japan, because most new computer technology comes from abroad. But there are many problems that need to be solved to make TRON a reality. . . . TRON is a very good architecture that Japan can boast of; it can be one of the standards, but I do not think the whole world will use TRON.[158]

Toda of NTT has expressed a similar view: "Companies need to have insurance for their businesses, so firms that take the TRON path, will also take other paths."[159] But a more damning judgment has been put forth by one of Japan's most highly revered telecommunications and computer experts, Inose Hiroshi, former Dean of Tokyo University's Engineering Department: "I am not optimistic about TRON; the only benefit is that it is not a DEC or IBM standard; there is no evidence that TRON is a better architecture."[160]

Japan's computer industry is clearly at the crossroads. In the late 1970s, the government and the makers could continue to follow the path IBM had blazed, but, by the early 1980s, it became apparent that continuing to follow IBM would be tantamount to self-destruction. With IBM squeezing down hard on Japanese firms using its proprietary software technology and with software becoming an ever-increasing proportion of a total system's cost, the writing is on the wall. But where to go and how to get there is far from clear.

What is certain is that Japan's huge vertically integrated and diversified electronics firms will not give up easily. To quote Ota Hideo of Mitsubishi:

We are not thinking of loss or profit just for computers, but for the whole company. And we use computers in all our businesses. When we cannot follow computer technology, we will be in trouble all over."[161]

It is also clear that the government will continue to play an important role in supporting the industry. "It's like a parent," explained Amaya Naohiro, formerly a high-level MITI man; "if the children grow, the parents' role declines, but still children need advice."[162] With heavy protectionism and subsidization no longer politically possible, MITI is increasingly targeting R&D. According to Maeda, formerly of MITI:

Our companies still need this [R&D] help. Without government help, they would not conduct R&D like that in the 5th-Generation Project. MITI's role is to pressure them to look into the distant future. IBM may be an exception, it may not need this aid. But Fujitsu, Hitachi, and NEC are not big enough.[163]

"We are entering the age of consortia," according to Hitachi's Kuwahara.[164] MITI's role is to manage the ever-increasing elaborate coordination among Japanese firms, government labs, and the recently privatized NTT. "The peak of MITI's power and importance was with the New Series Project in the early 1970s; if we say it was 100 then, it is still 40 or 50 now," explained Tajiri of Fujitsu.[165] "National projects are still very very important," to quote Kuwahara of Hitachi.[166]

The next decade will be very costly and risky, as the firms move to a new standard and try to convince current users to continue using their computers, despite the fact that their new machines will not be compatible with their old ones. MITI's industrial policy will continue to play a critical role in reducing the costs and risks Fujitsu and the other makers must bear in this transition stage. But the ball is really in the makers' court now; the government can help, but it is the firms that must come up with radically new technology.

"The IBM era is over," conjectured Aiso Hideo, the head of the 5th-Generation and Supercomputer Projects, in late 1987.[167] Whether Aiso's estimate is correct or not remains to be seen.

SIX

Cooperation and Competition

for Competitive Advantage

The Japanese government has intervened extensively in the computer market over the past three decades in an attempt to build a competitive computer industry. Were these efforts for naught or did they really contribute to the industry's development? Some may argue that the government's efforts have been a failure. Not everything went the way the government would have liked. The six Japanese computer firms, for example, refused to be merged into a few larger computer companies. Dependence on the IBM standard has made the industry very vulnerable. Japanese computer users have yet to be persuaded to use standardized software packages, and the resulting drain on the productivity of the nation's small pool of software engineers threatens to hit crisis proportions by the 1990s. Japan has also missed out on the boom in minicomputers and personal computers; and computer exports have not shown the impressive gains of exports in Japan's steel, auto, semiconductor, and consumer-electronics industries. The industry, with less than a 10-percent share of the world computer market, is far from undermining the dominant position of IBM.

Yet, MITI did succeed in its broader goal of encouraging the development of an internationally competitive computer mainframe industry. Despite IBM's dominance, the Japanese invested heavily. I have shown that their decision to do so was financially viable because the government agreed to bear part of the high costs and risks of investment in R&D and plant and equipment. Without this government support, the Japanese computer companies would have foundered on several occasions. Instead, they consistently increased their share of the domestic market so that today Japan is the only industrialized country in the free world where IBM is not the market leader. Japan now supplies hardware to IBM competitors around the globe, including ICL of Britain, Siemens and BASF of Germany, and Amdahl and National Advanced Systems of the United States. Honeywell, which for almost two decades supplied NEC with technology, has recently turned to NEC for technology and next-generation computers. While exports of computer-related equipment totaled only $6.9 billion in 1985, the annual growth rate of exports in the 1980s has been on the order of some 60 percent a year.[1] In 1972, Japan imported almost 8 times what she exported in computer-related equipment; today exports exceed imports 4-fold.[2]

More important than these numbers is the technological foundation that a vibrant computer industry has provided, preparing the makers to advance quickly in the upcoming years. While the Japanese have not done well in export markets so far, they are keeping up with all the key technologies, and most would agree that Japan is ahead in areas such as new ceramic materials and gallium arsenide. NEC, a huge producer of personal computers for the Japanese market, has its own standard, which has thus far hindered its exports; but other PC makers like Toshiba and Epson are doing well, and NEC may yet emerge a winner. There is also potential in Asia for Japanese computers. Demand from Korea, Taiwan, China, and Thailand for sophisticated computer equipment will undoubtedly increase sharply in the future as their economies continue to expand rapidly. Japan, with advanced technologies for processing non-roman characters, is the best positioned to benefit from this demand. The Japanese future is far from the bleak picture the numbers suggest.

The domestic computer industry has also helped Japanese firms take dominant world positions in such key industries as semiconductors and numerically controlled machine tools; Fanuc Ltd., an offshoot of Fujitsu, for example, is the world's largest maker of numerically controlled machine tools. The computer industry has also provided the technological foundation for Japanese firms to enter new industries that use computer technology such as optoelectronics and factory automation. MITI's success in nurturing a domestic computer industry would be grounds enough for saying that government policies have succeeded. The ripple effect on other industries, though difficult to measure precisely, adds weight to that conclusion.

The overall effort has been successful because the government has generally structured its policies in ways that did not squelch the individual initiative of each company. Tailoring these policies continuously to meet the changing needs of the industry as it evolved over time, the government kept an appropriate balance between helping the firms and pressuring them to advance (Table 21). Success was also contingent on a private sector that was willing to invest its own resources and work hard to improve quality and technology, and cut costs.

The Japanese government promoted the computer industry by altering the market environment in two primary ways: reducing costs and risks to encourage firms to enter and invest heavily in the industry; and reducing the number of players in each market segment to promote economies of scale in R&D and production.

In the late 1950s and early 1960s, Japanese electronics and telecommunications firms faced insurmountable odds in going into the computer business. IBM had a 70-percent share of the world computer mainframe market, and the rest was dominated by large U.S. companies such as Sperry Rand (UNIVAC), RCA, and GE. Fujitsu was just a tiny telecommunications maker with annual sales of $6.4 million.[3] To encourage firms to invest in computers, it was necessary to reduce the costs and risks of entering and staying in the industry—MITI needed to give domestic firms advantages and to handicap foreign firms. It did this by establishing JECC to finance

Table 21 Changes in Policies, Technologies, and Market Share in the Computer Industry, 1958–1982 (unit: %) (Share of Annual Deliveries [Rental/Purchase] of General Purpose Computers)

	1957	1958	1959	1960	1961	1962	1963	1964	1965	1966	1967	1968	1969
Related Events								(1) Japan joins the OECD and changes status in GATT. (2) Matsushita withdraws from the computer industry				U.S. pressure on Japan to open computer and other markets increases	
General Policy Decisions	Computer designated strategic by law.		(1) Decision that IBM patents are necessary. (2) IBM allowed to establish wholly owned subsidiary to produce in Japan.										
Year	1957	1958	1959	1960	1961	1962	1963	1964	1965	1966	1967	1968	1969
Japanese Market Share (%)		6.9	21.5	27.3	18.2	33.2	29.7	42.8	52.2	53.6	47.2	56.5	57.4
Foreign Market Share (%)		93.1	78.5	72.7	81.8	66.8	70.3	57.2	47.8	46.4	52.8	43.5	42.6
Technological Changes	IBM introduces 2nd-generation computers, e.g. the IBM 1401.						IBM starts producing 2nd-generation computers in Japan.	IBM announces its 360 series, the world's first 3rd-generation computer.	(1) IBM starts to produce the 360 series in Japan (2) Results of Fontac Project begin to be used in domestic machines.			Japanese bring out more advanced computers, though still much less advanced than the IBM 360.	

Protectionism	(1) MITI flooded with applications to import the IBM 1401. (2) Tariff on computers increased to 25% from 15%.	Government procures about 25% of all domestic computers in the 1960s. Government control over foreign exchange and imports.	Tariffs decreased to 15% for GATT members.		Import Quotas in effect throughout the 1960s
Financial Assistance	Relatively minor assistance	From 1961–1969, a total of $132 million in subsidies and tax benefits, $410 million in loans. Total aid equivalent to 188% of what firms invest in R&D and plant and equipment during that same period.			
Cooperative R&D Projects	Government and university labs tinker with elementary computers	First project—"Fontac Proj-ect"—margin-ally suc-cessful		MITI's "1966 Project" to counter 360	NTT starts its first computer project, the DIPS-1
JECC	Negotia-tions over how to establish JECC	JECC es-tablished JECC.	Between 1961 and 1969 an average of 65% of all domestic computers rented out through JECC.		

Table 21 Changes in Policies, Technologies, and Market Share in the Computer Industry, 1958–1982 (unit: %) (Share of Annual Deliveries [Rental/Purchase] of General Purpose Computers) (cont.)

	1970	1971	1972	1973	1974	1975	1976	1977	1978	1979	1980	1981	1982
Related Events		"Nixon Shocks"— sharp revaluation of the yen.		Oil Shock									
General Policy Decision			Decision made to liberalize computer market at end of 1975										
Year	1970	1971	1972	1973	1974	1975	1976	1977	1978	1979	1980	1981	1982
Japanese Market Share	59.7	58.8	53.2	51.4	48.4	55.8	56.7	66.4	67.2	69.6	72.5	72.2	74
Foreign Market Share	40.3	41.2	46.8	48.6	51.6	44.2	43.3	33.6	32.8	30.4	27.5	27.8	26
Technological Changes	IBM announces the 370, a very advanced machine that threatens the survival of many computer companies around the world; RCA & GE withdraw from the industry.					Results of "New Se- ries" and DIPS-11 projects start to hit the market	Japanese makers con- sidered competi- tive with IBM in hardware	IBM's new 303X se- ries of machines hits the market.	Results of VLSI proj- ect start to be used in Japanese computers		Japanese makers cap- ture some 70% of world 64k RAM mar- ket.		
Protectionism	(1) Slow dismantling of quotas and tariffs. Formal quotas end in 1972, but still strong pressure on the private sector to "Buy Japanese." (2) Government Procurement—25% of all Japanese computers.										(1) Market officially liberalized (2) Government Procurement: 25–30% of all Japanese computers		

	1970–1975				1976–1981		
Fin. Asst.	From 1970–1975: $632 million in subsidies and tax benefits, $1.24 billion in government loans. Total aid equivalent to 168% of what the firms invest in R&D and plant and equipment during that same period.				1976–1981: $1.02 billion in subsidies and tax benefits; $2.78 billion in government loans. Total aid equivalent to 93% of what firms invest in R&D and plant and equipment during that same period.		
Coop. R&D projects	Pattern-Recognition Computer Project begins.	MITI's "New Series" Project to counter IBM 370 begins.	NTT's DIPS-11 Project to counter IBM 370 begins.	Japanese government and companies start to give more attention to software.	VLSI Project begins.	Super-Computer Project begins.	5th-Generation Computer project begins.
JECC	1970–1975: 40% of domestic computers rented out through JECC.				1976–1981: 19% of domestic computers rented out through JECC.		11% rented out through JECC.

computer rentals, negotiating with foreign firms to get U.S. technology at low prices, protecting the firms from foreign imports, and subsidizing the firms.

Without JECC it is highly unlikely that the firms could have financed the renting out of their computers. Japanese firms had to rent their computers in order to compete with IBM's extensive rental system. But they did not have the money to finance rentals, nor could they borrow enough. Fujitsu would have had to borrow about 35.1 billion yen extra from 1961–1969 in order to finance the machines it sold to JECC for rental during those years;[4] this would have meant more than doubling its investment in R&D and plant and equipment.[5] Given the high risk in the industry and the conservatism of Japanese banks, it is unlikely that Fujitsu could have gotten the loans necessary to make such an investment; Fujitsu's debt-equity ratio was already high,[6] and it was not yet recognized as a top company.

The establishment of JECC made it much easier for its member firms to price competitively. By offering computers at monthly rental fees set some 40 percent below IBM's,[7] JECC boosted the market share of domestic computer companies. After JECC was established, the Japanese makers' market share jumped from 18.2 percent in 1961 to 33.2 percent in 1962 and to 52.2 percent by 1965.[8] By producing greater quantities of computers, they were able to gain scale economies and increase their market share. JECC's management of a price cartel also assured the companies that their profits could be reinvested rather than whittled away in price wars.

JECC provided critical financing, but the companies also needed technology. MITI helped Japanese companies purchase technology from foreign companies at low cost by acting as a mediator; this prevented a foreign firm from playing the Japanese firms off against one another in order to raise the price. In some cases, the government used its control over foreign investments to force foreign firms to cooperate. MITI, for example, refused to allow IBM to produce in Japan until it agreed to offer all its basic computer patents to Japanese firms at low prices.

A protected environment was necessary to allow the industry to take root. Unless IBM and other foreign makers were controlled, most users would have chosen foreign machines over inferior domestic ones. By handicapping IBM in a web of bureaucratic regulations over foreign-exchange conversion, imported parts, exports, and the type and volume of machines they could produce, MITI made it virtually impossible for Japanese firms to buy foreign computers when there was even a vaguely comparable domestic product available. When Japan did finally begin to open its computer market, MITI continued to offer security to domestic firms by promising that it would supervise the market and prevent any dramatic drop in their market share.[9]

Once the firms entered the market, government subsidies and low-interest loans helped reduce the costs and risks and raise the profit expectations of doing business in computers. Financial aid was particularly critical in periods when IBM came out with a new-generation computer that threatened to wipe out its competitors. The government plowed large sums of money into the computer industry. A conservative estimate shows that some $542 million in subsidies, tax benefits, and loans were granted to the industry from 1961 to 1969, equivalent to some 188 percent of what the firms themselves invested in the industry during that period.[10] This does not include the huge benefits from procurement by NTT and other government institutions. "It was because they received a stable flow of profits from NTT that firms like Fujitsu, Hitachi, and NEC could invest so much in computers," explained Takeuchi of the LTCB.[11]

Indeed, government financial aid was far more important than suggested in other studies of Japan's industrial policy. The Hudson Report, for example, states that government loans to the Machinery and Information Industries

> have not only been relatively small in recent years, but were no more than 2.5 percent of total investment even at the height of infant industry encouragement in the early sixties. . . . With regard to outright subsidies, the amounts with few exceptions, tend to be small.[12]

The Hudson Report statistics include machinery along with computers, which may help to account for the discrepancy between their study and this one; nonetheless, the report uses its statistics to argue that Japanese government aid has been very small. This study shows that, at least in the computer industry, financial assistance has been very large in comparison to private-sector investment in the industry.

The timing of government financial aid was also critical. In the early 1960s, IBM brought out the 360 series when the Japanese makers had not even finished the FONTAC Project, which aimed to make a much less sophisticated machine. Without government financial assistance, together with protection and the JECC system, the firms would not have been able to rent their computers, which were far inferior to the newly introduced 360 series. Without the subsidies and cooperative efforts of the Super High-Performance Computer Project, it would have been very difficult for the firms to develop a prototype machine to counter the 360; the project provided 12 billion yen in R&D subsidies;[13] from 1961 to 1965, the firms had invested only 11.2 billion yen in R&D on computers.[14]

The government's role was critical in propping up the domestic computer industry in the early 1970s when the IBM-370 was introduced. At that time, the Japanese economy was reeling from the effects of a drastic revision of the yen-dollar exchange rate, a sharp increase in oil prices, and pressure to open up their computer market. GE and RCA, and technological partners of Toshiba and Hitachi, withdrew from the computer business, viewing it as too tough a market to compete in. And the Japanese government, under heavy U.S. pressure, reluctantly promised to liberalize the computer market at the end of 1975. The Japanese computer firms would have been hard put to remain in the computer business without government aid. From 1970 to 1975, estimated government subsidies and tax benefits to the industry were equivalent to 56.73 percent of the estimated total investment by the private sector in R&D and plant and equipment;[15] if low-interest loans are included, total government assistance ($1.877 billion) was 168 percent of the amount the private sector invested in R&D and plant and equipment.[16] Even after the computer market was officially opened to foreign firms and imports (1976–1981), direct government aid was still equivalent to some 25 percent of what the firms were investing in R&D and plant and equipment, and, including loans, 93 percent.[17]

The government tried to award its subsidies, loans, and tax benefits in ways that promoted technological advancement and discouraged inefficiency. In several R&D projects, the firms were required to match government subsidies. This pressured them to make a commitment to the project and increased the probability that they would commercialize the project results to get a return on their investment. In general, financial aid favored the most competitive firms; the more consumers asked to rent a firm's computers, the larger the advance it received through JECC, and the greater the tax benefit it received through the computer buyback loss reserve. In cases where the government did not tie government funds to performance, such as in the Japan Software Co. and IPA cases, inefficiency ensued.

Protectionism, JECC, and financial aid, by reducing costs and risks for a few select firms, helped determine which firms operated in the computer market as a whole—who played in the computer business game. R&D projects, on the other hand, were concerned with determining which firms did what type of R&D and production—who was on what team and what was their winning strategy. The goal of MITI's manipulation of the market structure was to help strengthen the industry as a whole by having each player specialize.

The government's strategy for structuring markets was flexible, changing in response to IBM's moves, the firms' own strategies, NTT's needs, and external economic shocks. In the late 1960s when the United States started to pressure Japan to open up her computer market, MITI felt there were too many computer firms and sought to reduce the number to two or three through mergers. Failing in this effort, MITI instead encouraged concentration by promoting cooperation amongst the companies on R&D and specialization by each company in their strongest market segments. In each case, the government sought to preserve incentives to produce high-quality products. The ultimate criterion of a firm's success was always its ability to commercialize the results of the projects.

The government encouraged the most competitive firms in a given market segment to increase their investment by assigning them R&D related to that market segment. By excluding weaker firms from government-sponsored R&D in those fields, the government discouraged them from entering those markets; this allowed the "winners" a larger share of the market. There are risks in this strategy, particularly in a fast-growing and changing industry like computers. It is true that many great inventions in the United States have been made by small start-ups, but, in mainframes and chips, size was critical and the strategy was thus important. Fujitsu, Hitachi, and NEC, which had proven to be the most advanced in making computer mainframes, were generally assigned the mainframe research in the projects set up by both MITI and NTT. Those three companies continue to be Japan's top three mainframe makers today. Toshiba, Oki, and Mitsubishi, which tended to lag somewhat behind in the technologies needed for large-scale computers, were assigned peripherals and small computers. Mitsubishi and Toshiba continue to concentrate on smaller computers, while Oki's strength is still in peripherals. This was not a case of MITI picking winners in different market segments. MITI picked firms that had already proven themselves competitive in their respective areas. MITI policy acted as leverage to reinforce their positions as market leaders. Since the firms tended to train researchers and invest money in the areas MITI assigned them in an R&D project, they continued to build up expertise in those areas.

By using R&D projects to encourage specialization, MITI helped the companies gain economies of scale in production. The small number of computers Japanese companies manufactured and sold compared to IBM made it very difficult for Japanese companies to match IBM's production and research costs per computer. In the late 1960s, for example, Japan's top three computer firms each manufactured about 2 computers of any given model for every 100 computers IBM manufactured of that model-type.[18]

The Japanese government helped narrow this gap, not only by encouraging Japanese companies to specialize in different market sectors, but also by encouraging them to pool their resources for

R&D. By giving all members of a research association access to the resulting technology at low cost, each firm was able to get more R&D results per yen spent. In the case of the Super High-Performance Computer Project, the government completely funded the project; the firms had only to contribute researchers. Even in cases where the firms paid part of the cost, the amount of R&D results a firm received per yen spent was enormous compared to if it had done the work alone. For example, the government spent 30 billion yen on the VLSI Project, the five firms a total of 42 billion yen. Thus, though each firm spent only 8.4 billion yen, it got access to the results of 72 billion yen worth of research. From 1976–1979, the entire private sector invested only 353.7 billion yen in R&D in the computer industry,[19] an average of 70.74 billion yen for each of the five computer firms. Each firm, by itself, would have found it difficult to finance the amount of research that came out of the joint VLSI Project. By giving subsidies and reducing redundancy through cooperation, the government substantially reduced the cost of R&D to the firms. Without MITI's VLSI Project, explained Matsukara Yasuo, General Manager of NEC's VLSI development division, each company would have spent 5 times as much on R&D to develop electron-beam technology.[20] According to Fujitsu Chairman Kobayashi Taiyū:

> There is no denying the fact that our company is benefiting immeasurably from cooperation with other organizations. Direct outlays made by our company are by no means the only R&D funds we can take advantage of.[21]

Cooperative R&D projects also helped accelerate the technological progress of the industry by coordinating the research programs of different firms and getting each firm or team of firms to take different approaches to a given problem. "Its a question of competing against time," explained former MITI official Maeda Norihiko.[22] In the VLSI Project, for example, the most important R&D themes—the electron-beam and X-ray-exposure systems—were researched in three parallel groups, each dominated by one company; these three groups explored a total of 7 approaches to drawing minute lines on wafers. In the New Series Project, three groups worked on different computer series to counter the IBM-370; and, in the Supercomputer Project, Fujitsu and Oki are focusing on HEMT; NEC, Toshiba, Hitachi, and Mitsubishi on gallium arsenide; and Fujitsu, Hitachi, and NEC on Josephson junction devices.[23] There are always failures in R&D; if one firm has to go through 3 approaches to find a successful one, time will be lost. By having a few firms approach the problem differently, and agreeing to give all participants access to the research results, the probability that one will succeed is greatly increased, and the time it takes to develop a successful technology can be cut substantially.

> One of the reasons for NTT's R&D efforts is that there is always a high probability of failure in R&D. Each company worries about failing and is relatively conservative. In these cases, we at NTT, like the rest of the government, do not exactly tell the firms "It is okay to fail," but we let them make a riskier decision than they would if it was their company alone, so that they can try to develop various technologies in different ways.[24]

Fujitsu Chairman Kobayashi agreed that Japanese companies benefit greatly from cooperative R&D:

> The Japanese industry and R&D institutes are very cooperative and often go on "division-of-labor" arrangements. This gives us a considerable edge over IBM, which has to do everything on its own.[25]

In the early research projects, in which specific commercial products were targeted, there were sometimes problems between partners. As the firms became stronger, these became worse; for example, Fujitsu and Hitachi did not cooperate on technological development in the New Series Project. In later years, the government dealt with this problem by concentrating on basic or production technology that was one step removed from product development. "If R&D content is too close to commercialization, cooperation will not go far," explained Shimizu Sakae, Senior Managing Director of Toshiba.[26]

> It is useless to have too much competition—it can double or triple the development costs. Sharing in government projects is very important, particularly when the industry is immature and has too many things it needs to explore.[27]

The government made every effort to assure that the companies had to compete to survive. Subsidies were given to those companies that proved themselves in the marketplace. Companies that did not come out with competitive products were excluded from the projects; for example, when Oki failed to come out with a computer series following its participation in the New Series Project, MITI decided that it had fallen behind and excluded Oki from the next major project.

MITI tried to ensure that market incentives operated even in the cooperative projects. There were usually at least two firms involved in researching any given theme; a government grant could thus not be used to strengthen a company's monopoly position. Exceptions exist, such as the Japan Software Co., which researched the software for the Super High-Performance Computer Project alone and ultimately became so inefficient that it went bankrupt. But, while the firms cooperated on research and development, it was up to each to beat the competition in getting its research to the marketplace. Since several firms had access to project results, the situation where one company develops a key technology but then decides not to use it, such as RCA and its VCR technology, was less likely to occur.

Just as the division of labor in R&D projects promoted both cooperation and competition, so did the pooling of resources in a centralized computer-rental firm. On the one hand, JECC promoted cooperation by serving as a centralized sales arm for the computer firms and by functioning as the manager of the industry's price cartel. On the other hand, JECC pressured the firms to compete in order to survive. By requiring that JECC approve all the computers to be rented through it, MITI pressured the firms to increase the local content of their computers in the 1960s. With several firms competing for JECC money, a firm had to continuously bring out more advanced computers to attract customers. This pressure was particularly strong because users could trade in a computer after 15 months. The fact that price discounts were not allowed on machines rented through JECC pressured the firms to compete on quality, cost, service, and technology rather than price.

Classical economic theory would suggest that elaborate price and

R&D cartels, heavy subsidies, and policies promoting "winners" would lead to firms with highly inflated costs, excess staff, slow advances in technology, and high prices. But the industry has steadily narrowed its gap with IBM and increased its market share at home and abroad. This study suggests that state policies can accelerate an industry's development if structured in ways that maintain forces of market competition.

Even if one accepts the notion that targeting was critical to Japan's evolving comparative advantage in computers, it does not mean that policies have always been effective. This case and others show that there have been both successes and failures. While a systematic comparison of industrial policy in several countries and industries is necessary to determine what conditions are most critical to success, this study suggests several important to nurturing infant industries.

The most important is to structure policies in ways that keep competitive forces intact. One way of helping ensure this is by promoting domestic competition among several firms to provide incentives to cut costs, advance technologically, and provide quality goods at reasonable prices. The Japan Software Co. and the IPA failed because they did not have strong incentives to compete; JECC succeeded, in large part, because it promoted competition. A lack of competition—a "national-champion" strategy—may help explain France's failure to develop a viable computer industry.

It is also very important for the business community to have substantial input into the process by which policies are selected and implemented. The process of government-business cooperation, negotiation, and compromise is critical for two reasons: Managers know more about the market than bureaucrats; and cooperation in the selection and implementation processes increases the private sector's commitment to the policies.

Business input also functions as a check on government proposals. When the government oversteps itself and makes a proposal that goes sharply against market forces, opposition from the private sector can prevent it from enacting policies that would have led to serious failures. Merging the six computer firms into two or three firms, for example, would have caused far more harm than good. While there have been exceptions, such as the Japan Software Co., major blunders have been surprisingly few. It is precisely because neither the state nor the private sector is able to dominate the policymaking process that policies tend to be market-conforming.

Japan's efforts in computers did require a large share of the nation's resources, much of which could have been put to good use on parks, sewers, or housing. Supporting computers required a general societal consensus that what was good for industry was good for Japan. In Japan, most sectors of society allow the bureaucracy, in concert with industry, to decide what is in the national interest.[28] Citizens thus did not question the government's decision to funnel low-interest loans and subsidies into the computer industry; when there was opposition, it usually came from the Ministry of Finance. Targeting industries in countries where citizens have more influence on government policy would most likely require a broader societal commitment to the targeted industry, such as that of many Americans for its defense industry.

A stable institution—one that does not change directions every time an administration changes—is also important in implementing industrial policy. Government support must be continuous over a long period of time or firms will not risk contributing key engineers to R&D projects or investing in technologies that may not have immediate prospects for commercialization. It is highly doubtful that the computer firms would have continued to invest in computers in the 1960s and early 1970s without MITI assurance that they would be protected from IBM, would receive subsidies and various tax benefits, and would continue to be able to rent their computers through JECC over the long term. Continuous government support must be, and in the computer case was, contingent on the firms' becoming more competitive.

The impartiality of MITI was also critical. The computer makers trusted the government to be fair and consistent in deciding which companies would be involved in a given R&D project, which would do what R&D, and which would be responsible for developing the final prototype. It is a process of *gibu ando teiku* (give and take) in which the firms trust that, if they are not assigned their first choice in the divvying up of the labor in one project, they will be given an important part in another project.[29]

A relatively large domestic market also seems to be important for an effective industrial policy. While the world market is the most important in the long run, demand in the domestic market, which can be isolated with protectionist measures, is critical in the infant-industry and growth stages. The Japanese computer makers, for example, would not have been able to gain the economies of scale necessary to become competitive without heavy domestic demand. Indeed, a major role of the government, through JECC, procurement and protectionist policies, was to stimulate the demand for computers in Japan and to assure that the bulk of demand was met by supplies from domestic makers.

It is also important to have access to foreign markets and to be able to control foreign access to the domestic market. Japan had both. In the 1950s and 1960s, the United States encouraged the development of industry in Japan; U.S. firms readily sold their technology cheaply to Japanese firms, and Japan was given easy access to the U.S. market. Sales of Japanese VLSI, peripherals, and mainframes in the United States have clearly contributed to the ability of Japanese companies to get returns on their investment. Japan was not only able to export a substantial amount to the United States; it was also able to keep foreign firms out of its own large domestic market. The Japanese government was able to keep IBM on a leash, obstruct other foreign firms with high walls, and pour huge subsidies into specific industries with little complaint from Western nations. In the 1980s, the international environment has changed dramatically. It is unclear whether other countries can implement comprehensive industrial targeting policies like those of Japan towards its computer industry. Korea is facing barriers to its flow of exports to the United States and is being sharply criticized for protecting its domestic market from foreign imports.

As for successful cooperative R&D projects, four factors seem to be critical. Having the private sector contribute funds to a project seems to help assure its success. While 100-percent government-funded projects were not all failures, the two most effective projects—the New Series and VLSI Projects—were only partially funded by the government. Moreover, the PIPS and 5th-Generation Computer Projects, the two that the private sector would never have participated in if the government had not promised to fully fund the work, have not and most likely will not have a substantial impact on the competitiveness of the computer firms.

Having clear and specific goals also seems to influence the success of a cooperative venture. The New Series, VLSI, DIPS, and Supercomputer Projects all had relatively clear goals and have contributed substantially to the industry's competitiveness. In contrast, the Japan Software Co. work and IPA had vague goals and were largely failures. Even the PIPS Project, while resulting in some important spin-offs, was not as successful as hoped, in large part because it involved exploring unknown territory which could not be easily defined. The objectives of the 5th-Generation Project are also rather obscure; it is thus not surprising that the private sector does not expect it to result in a 5th-generation machine prototype. Shimizu Sakae, Senior Managing Director of Toshiba, drew an analogy between the PIPS and 5th-generation efforts, saying that he expects the 5th-Generation Project, like PIPS, to result in commercial spin-offs of parts of the technology rather than in a full system.[30] This is not to say that future-oriented research should not be promoted; rather it suggests that it is more difficult to target frontier areas, and that there are likely to be fewer benefits per unit cost than when targeting specific goals. Industrial policy will tend to be more successful when used to catch up with others—when a clear target can be defined—than when used to explore unknown technologies.

Third, the more basic the R&D topics, the easier it is for rival firms to cooperate. While there have been some cases of R&D done jointly by members of several firms, such as the research on silicon crystals in the VLSI Project, most so-called "cooperative" R&D has consisted of "cooperation' to divide up the research and share the results.

Finally, a healthy dose of trust is important to a project's success. Trust is by no means the result of some superior ethical standard in

Japan; rather there are institutional factors that discourage firms from breaking agreements.[31] The computer makers also compete in other areas such as consumer electronics, telecommunications, and semiconductors; abrogating responsibility in one area raises the possibility of retaliation or ostracization in another. Strong university ties also increase trust among researchers in different firms.[32] An understanding that there will be a continuity of projects targeting computers also compels the firms to toe the line; they know that, if they misbehave, the government can easily leave them out of the next project. Indeed, the importance of the government as a mediator cannot be overstated in this regard. The lack of an impartial umpire and coordinator in the United States appears to be a factor contributing to problems at Sematech, the U.S. semiconductor industry's recent response to the Japanese challenge.

This study also suggests two other important, broader conditions. One is that countries where macroeconomic policies encourage investment and savings rather than consumption are likely to be more conducive to targeting than countries that encourage the opposite. The development of the Japanese computer industry was clearly facilitated by macroeconomic policies that encouraged firms to invest their profits and citizens to save rather than consume. These savings, funneled through various institutions, were used to finance targeting policies. The other is that industrial policy is most likely to be successful when aimed at "linkage" industries that affect other industries. For example, Japan's semiconductor industry has helped the consumer-electronics, computer, and other industries by providing them with cheap parts; in turn, these industries provided the semiconductor makers with a huge market for their products. Promotion of the steel industry helped the auto industry by providing it with cheap, high-quality steel; promotion of computers has helped the Japanese numerically controlled machine-tools industry take a large chunk of the world market; it has also helped increase the competitiveness of many industries that use computer-automated factories, and has provided the technological foundation for Japan to enter other industries, such as the biotechnology, optoelectronics, and space industries.

These conditions, it must be noted, would only apply to the effectiveness of policies targeting infant industries. Efforts to encourage the retrenchment of declining industries would inevitably require different conditions. Rarely would there be a national consensus on the need for retrenchment; linkages, macro policies, and access to foreign markets would be irrelevant in most cases. Clearly, the problem of entrenched managements, heavy sunk costs, and political problems such as unemployment make the successful targeting of sunset industries different from boosting rising stars. In particular, protectionist policies aimed at helping declining industries in the short run are in danger of becoming permanent features of the environment. The United States finds it difficult now to dismantle policies protecting its steel and auto industries. Japan has had similar problems as exemplified by continued support of its silk industry.

The principle of comparative advantage suggests that it is most efficient for countries to specialize in those products in which they have a natural comparative advantage. Countries with huge populations but little capital or technology would be better off developing labor-intensive industries like textiles, nations rich in natural resources, by making products that make use of their advantage in raw materials. Yet Japan, despite a clear disadvantage in capital and technology-intensive industries after World War II, decided to develop its own steel and computer industries. Japan used industrial policies to help firms gain a competitive advantage in the marketplace. In the computer case, we have seen that Japan was able to purchase many of the givens, such as patents, components, and machinery, and to develop those it could not buy, such as a labor force skilled in information processing. In most cases, Japan first bought the "given" and gradually developed competitiveness in making it. This study suggests that nations can create comparative advantages by changing their factor endowments and that, in the computer case, industrial policy has played a key role in encouraging and facilitating this change.

The way in which the Japanese government helps create comparative advantages in specific industries may seem unconventional, if not grossly inefficient, from a Western point of view. The kind of targeting policies used by the Japanese clearly create market inefficiencies. Encouraging cooperative R&D projects, concentration of firms in specific market segments, and price cartels all run contrary to the classical economic principle that perfect competition brings about an optimal allocation of resources. But this study shows that Japan, on balance, avoided such inefficiencies, at least in the long run, because policies were structured in ways that encouraged—in fact required—that the companies make better products at lower costs to survive.

The development of Japan's computer industry suggests that Japan's innovative mixture of cooperation and competition may have benefits that we in the West are only beginning to understand. Most U.S. scholars would agree that competition is critical to industrial development. Many would also concede that, at least in some cases, firms of a reasonably large size and market share are more able to invest heavily in R&D and bring the fruits of those efforts to the market rapidly. But we in the United States do not believe it is possible to gain the benefits of market power without incurring its potential negative side effects—high prices and inefficiency. The Japanese, in the computer case, have an innovative solution: By having several firms, they get the benefits of competition; but, by having temporary cooperative alliances, they also receive the benefits—economies of scale in production and R&D—of relatively large, dominant firms. While one case does not a theory make, the potential of using a mix of cooperation and competition for competitive advantage needs to be acknowledged and further explored.

The notion that the state can help create comparative advantages has serious implications for the United States. It means that in no area, including computers, is the United States assured of having a leadership role. The conditions that have enabled it to become a leader in high technology sectors may, over a long period of time, be countered by other factors emerging in foreign nations. The United States may still remain a leader in basic technology, but, if other countries have a better infrastructure for introducing, managing, and commercializing that technology into products cheaply and quickly, they may reap the most benefits from that research. Does this mean that the United States needs a Japanese-style industrial policy?

Clearly it would be politically difficult for the United States to use the tools Japan has used to target its computer industry. But the close interaction between the U.S. government and businesses in the defense sector, the long-term commitment of substantial public resources to defense, and the societal consensus on the necessity of a strong military show that it is possible for the United States to develop a strategic industrial policy towards a specific sector. While it is unlikely that the United States would intervene as extensively in non-defense sectors as Japan has done in computers, there is still much America and other advanced nations could learn from Japan's effort to create competitive industries. Whether the United States chooses to learn is a question of priorities, institutions, and political will.

Learning from Japan does not necessarily require mimicking Japanese ways; various means can be used to achieve a given end. MITI's role in Japan's relatively smooth transition from labor-intensive to more capital- and knowledge-intensive industries suggests that it is important to have some non-partisan group or institution to watch and evaluate how the international economic environment and its division of labor is changing and map out, using different sets of assumptions, possible long-term scenarios of where the United States might fit into the global economy. Even if this institution or group does not actively intervene in the economy à la MITI, it could at least provide information and a forum for debate so that U.S. citizens, businesses, and the government could better understand the possible long-term ramifications of their strategies. Topics for study and debate might include the long-term effects of the huge U.S. federal and trade deficits or of the withdrawal of U.S. firms from industries that have linkages to other key sectors.

The computer case also emphasizes that there can be substantial benefits from inter-firm collaboration. It also suggests that cooperation is more effective when the firms have to contribute a substantial amount of the required funds and when aid is tied to performance. Domestic competition can be crucial, especially in cases where a decision is made to buffer domestic firms temporarily from foreign competition, and the threat of unleashing foreign competition can be effective in pressuring firms to cut costs and improve their products.

For the foreseeable future, the United States will be under increasing pressures to protect and subsidize industries facing international competition. Rather than confronting the damage with piecemeal policies, the government might consider trying to improve the situation by using policies that pressure the firms to improve their competitive position in exchange for government aid. If the Japanese case says anything, it is that it is not protection and promotion policies per se that spur industrial development or economic inefficiencies; it is the way they are structured. Whether or not we believe intervention is good, it often happens anyway. We would be better off using policies that encourage, not discourage, competitive firms.

Notes

Notes

1. MARKET-CONFORMING POLICIES

1. *The Wall Street Journal,* 24 June 1982, p. 22.
2. Takahashi Kenkichi, Nishida Shōhei, and Ōhashi Takashi, *Kompyūtā Gyōkai,* p. 220. The share data are for general-purpose computers, which include mainframes and personal computers.
3. *Hi no Maru,* literally the round shape of the sun, refers to the round sun on the Japanese flag. When used with "computers," it is analogous to Americans' calling IBM computers "the Stars-and-Stripes Computers."
4. Peter Katzenstein, ed., *Between Power and Plenty,* pp. 324–325.
5. Chalmers Johnson, *MITI and the Japanese Miracle,* pp. 18–19.
6. Thomas K. McCraw, "Regulation in America: A Review Article"; David Vogel, "Why Businessmen Distrust Their State."
7. Robert Ballon, "Management Style," p. 119.
8. Eleanor M. Hadley, *Antitrust in Japan,* pp. 390–391, 448.
9. Western economists also acknowledge the problem of excessive competition. F.M. Scherer notes: "While we generally assume that price competition is good among oligopolists because it reduces monopoly profits, it is sometimes argued that competition among oligopolists burdened with high fixed costs has a tendency to become "cutthroat" or "ruinous," and that it should be restrained through price-fixing agreements or mergers." (F.M. Scherer, *Industrial Market Structure and Economic Performance,* p. 212.)
10. MITI, *Sangyō Kōzō no Chōki Bijion,* p. 2.
11. Joseph A. Schumpeter, *Capitalism, Socialism, and Democracy,* p. 84.
12. Scherer, p. 407.
13. G.B. Richardson, *Information and Investment, A Study in the Working of the Competitive Economy,* pp. 49, 68–70.
14. Almarin Phillips, *Market Structure, Organization, and Performance,* p. 230.
15. Schumpeter; John Kenneth Galbraith, *American Capitalism: The Concept of*

Countervailing Power, Henry Villard "Competition, Oligopoly, and Research."

16. Scherer, p. 417.
17. Ibid., p. 438.
18. Paul Krugman, ed., *Strategic Trade Policy and the New International Economics.*
19. Bruce R. Scott and George C. Lodge, eds., *U.S. Competitiveness in the World Economy;* Laura Tyson and John Zysman, eds., *American Industry in International Competition.*
20. Johnson, *MITI and the Japanese Miracle;* T.J. Pempel, "Japanese Foreign Economic Policy: The Domestic Bases for International Behavior."
21. James Abegglen, "The Economic Growth of Japan," p. 35.
22. Johnson, *MITI and the Japanese Miracle,* p. 316.
23. Ibid., p. 315.
24. Richard J. Samuels, *The Business of the Japanese State, Energy Markets in Comparative and Historical Perspective.*
25. Hugh Patrick and Henry Rosovsky, eds., *Asia's New Giant,* p. 47.
26. Ibid., pp. 15–20.
27. Ibid., pp. 44–45.
28. James C. Abegglen and George Stalk, Jr., *Kaisha, The Japanese Corporation,* p. 5.
29. Hugh Patrick, "Japanese Industrial Policy and Its Relevance for United States Industrial Policy," pp. 18–19.
30. Ezra Vogel, *Comeback;* William Ouchi, *The M-Form Society.*
31. Leonard Lynn, *How Japan Innovates: A Comparison with the U.S. in the Case of Oxygen Steelmaking.*
32. Merton Peck and Shuji Tamura, "Technology," p. 557.
33. Fumio Kodama, "A Framework of Retrospective Analysis of Industrial Policy."
34. Imai Kenichi, "Gijutsu Kakushin kara mita Saikin no Sangyō Seisaku," pp. 194–198.
35. Philip H. Trezise and Yukio Suzuki, "Politics, Government, and Economic Growth in Japan," pp. 798–799.
36. Richard Caves and Masu Uekusa, "Industrial Organization," p. 489.
37. Imai Kenichi, "Tekkō"; Yamawaki Hideki, "Tekkō Gyō."
38. Peck and Tamura, p. 572.
39. Mitsubishi Electric engineers were also caught in the same IBM-FBI sting.

2. *Changing Competition to Favor Domestic Firms, 1957–1969*

1. The consensus was formed in the Computer Technology Committee of the Japan Electronics Industry Development Association (JEIDA), established in 1958 based on a 1957 law that designated the electronics industry, including computers, as strategic to the nation's long-term development. A Tokyo

University professor headed the committee, which included other academics, MITI and Japan Telegraph and Telephone (NTT) officials, and representatives of each of the Japanese computer makers. ("JECC Monogatari" [The JECC story] in *Kokusan Denshikeisanki Nyūzu*, Tōkyō: JECC, 1 May 1980, segment 8, no. 124.) Also interviews with Yoshioka Tadashi, Director and advisor of JEIDA, formerly of MITI, 27 November 1987; Miyano Motoyuki, Managing Director of the Leisure Development Center, formerly of MITI, 24 November 1987; Yamamoto Kinko, Managing Director of JIPDEC, 3 December 1987; and Toda Iwao, head of NTT's Communications and Information Processing Laboratory in Yokosuka, 5 December 1987.

2. Interview with Yoshioka Tadashi.

3. Interview with Miyano Motoyuki.

4. Interview with Toda Iwao.

5. Interviews with Okazaki Kōtarō, a Director and section chief of the Operations Department, the Industrial Bank of Japan (IBJ), 4 December 1987; and with Takeuchi Hiroshi, Managing Director of the Long-Term Credit Bank of Japan, 8 December 1987.

6. Interview with Okazaki Kōtarō.

7. Discussion with Kajiwara Yasushi, Director and General Manager, Corporate Banking Department no. 5, IBJ, 4 December 1987.

8. Interview with Okazaki Kōtarō.

9. Interviews with Toda Iwao of NTT and Okazaki Kōtarō of IBJ.

10. Interview with Takeuchi Hiroshi.

11. Cited in Franklin M. Fisher, John J. McGowan, and Joen E. Greenwood, *Folded, Spindled, and Mutilated: Economic Analysis and U.S. vs. IBM*, p. 176.

12. For the text and general discussion of the 1957 law, see *Denshi Kōgyō Nenkan*, 1962, pp. 136–48.

13. Ibid., p. 161.

14. Interview with Yoshioka Tadashi.

15. *Kompyūtopia*, December 1973, p. 23.

16. In 1937, it was incorporated as the Japan Watson Tōkei Kikai Kabushiki-gaisha (Japan Watson Business Machines Inc.).

17. As Nihon (Japan) IBM.

18. *Denshi Kōgyō Nenkan*, 1976, p. 683. The Foreign Capital Law is sometimes translated as the Foreign Investment Law.

19. The Foreign Exchange Control Law of 1933, the Foreign Exchange and Foreign Trade Law of 1949, and the Foreign Capital Law of 1950. These laws were drafted as the Japanese government started to construct its industrial-policy machinery to regulate the flow of foreign exchange, investment, and goods into and out of Japan. While essential in the years following World War II to cope with balance-of-payments problems, they were used by the government into the 1970s to stifle foreign efforts to penetrate the Japanese market.

20. The Foreign Exchange Control Law of 1933 and the Foreign Exchange and Foreign Trade Law of 1949 gave the government control over foreign currency transactions. (JECC, *Kokusan Denshikeisanki Nyūzu* "JECC Monogatari," segment 3, no. 119, 1 December 1979.)

21. Matsuo Hiroshi, *IBM Ōkoku o Obiyakasu Fujitsu,* p. 152. In this case, MITI used the 1950 Foreign Capital Law.

22. JECC, *Kokusan Denshikeisanki Nyūzu* "JECC Monogatari," segment 2, no. 118, 1 November 1979.

23. "JECC Monogatari," segment 3, no. 119, 1 December 1979.

24. Ibid.

25. Ibid., segment 4, no. 120, 1 January 1980, p. 6.

26. *Kompyūtopia,* December 1973, p. 24.

27. JECC, *Kokusan Denshikeisanki Nyūzu,* "JECC Monogatari," segment 5, no. 121, 1 February 1980, p.3.

28. Ibid. IBM opened its patents to the firms but did not make its know-how available; know-how was made available only to IBM Japan. (*Denshi Kōgyō Nenkan,* 1966, p. 283.)

29. Uozumi Tōru, *Kompyūta Sensō,* p. 57.

30. *The Japan Economic Journal,* 3 November 1964, p. 2.

31. With the exception of Matsushita, these firms have roots from the Meiji period in either heavy electrical machinery, including power plants and other industrial machinery, or telecommunications; each is closely tied to one of the 6 largest postwar *keiretsu* industrial groups, groups of firms bound together by interlocking shares, directorates, and close long-term supplier-buyer relationships. Matsushita was established in 1918 and produced simple electric consumer products like lights for bicycles.

32. Interview with Yoshioka Tadashi.

33. Japan also accepted GATT's Article 14 (no government subsidies of exports). (Johnson, *MITI and the Japanese Miracle,* p. 263.)

34. One such example was MITI's aborted attempt in 1963 to wrestle substantial new, discretionary powers in a proposed Special Measures Law for the Promotion of Designated Industries (*Tokutei Sangyō Shinkō Rinji Sochi Hōan*). The rejection of this law, due to private-sector concerns that MITI was trying to institutionalize excessive control over their business affairs, was an outgrowth of the system of negotiation and compromise among government and businesses in the policymaking process. While MITI did not get the extra powers the law would have granted it, many of the ideas expressed in the proposed law, such as cartels and subsidies, were incorporated in MITI's subsequent industrial policies. See Johnson, *MITI and the Japanese Miracle,* pp. 255–267, for details about the law and the reasons why it did not pass.

35. Ekonomisuto Editorial Board, ed., *Sengo Sangyō Shi e no Shōgen,* I, 142–143.

36. Interview with Shiina Takeo by Michael Berger, late 1984.

37. *Kompyūtopia*, October 1974, pp. 29–30.

38. Ibid.

39. Interview with Ishii Yoshiaki, General Manager of JECC's Research Division, 19 July 1984.

40. Data on IBM exports and production are not available and thus must be estimated. According to Nikkō Shōken Kabushiki Gaisha Chōsabu, *Tōshi Geppō*, February 1969, p. 50: as of 1967, 98% of Japan's computer-related exports were IBM Japan's exports; thus, we can use Japan's exports of computers as an indicator of IBM Japan's exports. Since IBM accounted for most of the foreign machines used in Japan, we can use the data for purchases of foreign computers in Japan as an indicator of the sum of imports and IBM Japan production used in Japan. By adding the data on exports to the data on foreign computer purchases in Japan and then subtracting imports, we can estimate IBM Japan's production. Data on imports are from *JECC Kompyūtā Nōto*, 1970, p. 22; data on exports and on purchases of foreign computers are from *JECC Kompyūtā Nōto*, 1979, pp. 10–11, 27.

41. JECC, *Kokusan Denshikeisanki Nyūzu*, "JECC Monogatari," segment 4.

42. Uozumi, p. 86.

43. Ibid.

44. *Nihon Keizai Shimbun* (Japan's economic news), 2 June 1965.

45. Ibid., 19 March 1965.

46. Ibid., 2 June 1965.

47. Ibid.

48. Uozumi, pp. 87–88.

49. Takeuchi Hiroshi, *Gendai no Sangyō: Denki Kikai Kōgyō*, pp. 299–300.

50. Ibid.

51. Uozumi, p. 79.

52. Today's Mitsui Bussan.

53. Today's Nihon UNIVAC.

54. Uozumi, pp. 78–79.

55. MITI used a similar strategy to restrain America's Digital Equipment Corporation (DEC) from dominating Japan's minicomputer market. MITI allowed Hewlett Packard into Japan only on the condition that it make a joint venture with Yokogawa Electric, with the Japanese partner holding 51% of the shares, and arranged for Sharp and Takeda Riken to form a joint venture to import Data General technology to produce and sell Data General machines in Japan. Again, the aim was to use Hewlett Packard and Data General to counter the market power of DEC. (Uozumi, pp. 78–79.)

56. Nihon Denshi Kikai Kōgyōkai, *Denshi Kōgyō 30 Nenshi*, p. 102.

57. Ibid., pp. 101–103.

58. Ibid., p. 81.

59. *Denshi Kōgyō Nenkan*, 1970–1971, p. 634.

60. MITI's 1966–1971 project to develop a Super High-Performance Computer.
61. _Denshi Kōgyō 30 Nenshi,_ pp. 102–103.
62. Ibid., p. 102.
63. Usui Kenji, Terasawa Yasuo, and Numakura Hōzo, _Nihon no Denshi Kōgyō—Shisutemuka no Ayumi,_ p. 286.
64. Richard Caves and Masu Uekusa, _Industrial Organization in Japan,_ pp. 90–91.
65. The government was forced to reduce the rate to 15% for GATT members in 1964 when Japan changed to Article 11 status in GATT and entered the OECD. It had set the tariff on peripherals at 15% with a rate of 10% for GATT members, but raised it to 25% (15% for GATT members) in the late 1960s when the Japanese makers decided to invest heavily in producing peripherals. (MITI Chōsa Kai, _Genkō Yunyū Seido Ichiran._)
66. The quota on computers ended in 1972, that on peripherals in 1971. (Ibid.)
67. "JECC Monogatari," segment 18, no. 134, 1 March 1981, p. 8.
68. Ibid.
69. "JECC Monogatari," segment 19, no. 135, 1 April 1981, p. 8.
70. "JECC Monogatari," segment 20, no. 136, 1 May 1981, p. 8.
71. "IBM wa Ya ni Hanatareta Tora da," (IBM is a tiger let loose in a field), _Bungeishunjū,_ September 1982, p. 103.
72. Interview with Takeuchi Hiroshi.
73. _Asahi Shimbun_ (Asahi News), 6 June 1961.
74. _Yomiuri Shimbun_ (Yomiuri News), 14 September 1961.
75. Interview with Inose Hiroshi, 7 December 1987.
76. "JECC Monogatari," segment 18, p. 8.
77. _Asahi Shimbun,_ 6 June 1961.
78. "JECC Monogatari," segment 19, p. 8.
79. Ibid.
80. Uozumi, pp. 202–203.
81. "JECC Monogatari," segment 19.
82. Shūgiin, Teishin Iinkaigiroku, Kokkai 65 (The Lower House, communications committee proceedings, Diet no. 65), 25 March 1971, p. 10.
83. Shūgiin, Shōkō Iinkaigiroku, Kokkai 63 (The Lower House, commerce committee proceedings, Diet no. 63), 23 April 1970, p. 20.
84. All shares are of computers in monetary value. (_Kompyūtopia,_ January 1983, pp. 92, 95.)
85. Ibid., p. 93.
86. Government procurement data are not available; they are estimated from data on computers in use at government-related institutions. In the 1960s, on average about 25% of domestic computers were used in government offices; thus we assume that on average the government bought or rented about 25% of domestic makers' computers each year. Data from JECC, _Kompyūtā Jitsudo Jōkyō Chōsa._

87. Interview with Takeuchi Hiroshi.
88. *Nihon Keizai Shimbun,* 7 October 1961; Uozumi, p. 120.
89. Dokusen Bunseki Kenkyūkai, "Nihon IBM" p. 275.
90. *Denshi Kōgyō Nenkan,* 1971–1972, p. 172.
91. *JECC Kompyūtā Nōto,* 1979, p. 10.
92. *Denshi Kōgyō Nenkan,* 1971–1972, p. 234.
93. Ueno Hiroya, *Nihon no Keizai Seido,* pp. 30–38.
94. Interview with Takeuchi Hiroshi.
95. Originally named the Japan Export Bank.
96. For example, in its 1963–1964 annual statement, the LTCB stated: "Responding to the brisk demand for industrial capital funds, our Bank, specializing in long-term financing, endeavored to supply smoothly long-term industrial funds in co-operation *(sic)* with the government." (Edward J. Lincoln, *Japan's Industrial Policies,* p. 23.)
97. Interview with Takeuchi Hiroshi.
98. Lincoln, p. 24.
99. Interview with Inaba Masahiro, Assistant Manager, Business Coordination Department, IBJ, 4 December 1987.
100. Lincoln, p. 24.
101. These banks not only helped funnel resources to the steel industry, but also to computers. In 1967, just as the government was stepping up its efforts to nurture the industry, the IBJ increased its shares in Fujitsu to 1.9% of the shares, to become one of Fujitsu's top 10 shareholders and lenders. As of March 1982, the IBJ's share of Fujitsu stock was up to 2.8%, making it Fujitsu's 4th largest shareholder and one of its top lenders. In September 1966, the IBJ became the 8th largest shareholder of Hitachi with a 1.4% share; by March 1982, it was Hitachi's 4th largest shareholder (2.6% of the shares) and the largest lender. The IBJ has been particularly important for these firms because neither is a member of the two largest *kinyū keiretsu*— Sumitomo and Mitsubishi. The NEC, a member of the enormous Sumitomo group, has been the recipient of few loans from the IBJ.
102. T.J. Pempel, "Japanese Foreign Economic Policy," p. 152.
103. Kozo Yamamura and Jan Vandenberg, "Japan's Rapid-Growth Policy on Trial: The Television Case," p. 240.
104. Usually BOJ guidance is referred to as "window guidance" *(madoguchi shidō).*
105. Yamamura and Vandenberg, p. 240.
106. Chalmers Johnson, *MITI and the Japanese Miracle,* p. 210.
107. *The Wall Street Journal,* 22 September 1988, p. 35.
108. Interview with Yoshihara Junji of MITI's AIST's Technology Research and Information Division, 28 March 1984.
109. I have not found, either through interviews or documents, any evidence that these have been repaid.
110. Tsuruta Toshimasa, *Sengo Nihon no Sangyō Seisaku,* p. 47.

111. Joseph Pechman and Keimei Kaizuka, "Taxation," p. 356.

112. Interview with Maeda Norihiko, Senior Managing Director of the Association of Information Service Industries, formerly of MITI, 28 February 1986.

113. Dokusen Bunseki Kenkyūkai, ed. "Nihon Denshin Denwa Kōsha (NTT)," pp. 134–135; discussions with Professor Uekusa Masu of Tōkyō University and Professor Nanbu Tsuruhiko of Gakushuin University.

114. Interview with Tajiri Yasushi, Deputy Section Chief, Marketing Department, Computer Systems, International Operations, 1 December 1987.

115. Shūgiin, Teishin Iinkaigiroku 25, Kokkai 71 (The Lower House, proceedings no. 25 of the communications committee, Diet no. 71), 27 June 1973, p. 19.

116. Shūgiin, Teishin Iinkaigiroku 14, Kokkai 65, 13 April 1971, pp. 9–10.

117. Ibid. p. 10.

118. *Nihon Kaihatsu Ginkō Tōkei Yōran.*

119. Nihon Densen Kikaku Kobushikigaisha, *Hojokin Benran.*

120. Interview with Toda Iwao.

121. Interview with Toda Iwao.

122. *Kompyūtopia,* April 1969, p. 30.

123. Interview with Tajiri Yasushi.

124. Nihon Denshin Denwa Kōsha 25 Nenshi Iinkai, ed., *Nihon Denshin Denwa Kōsha 25 Nenshi,* III, 249.

125. Nihon Chōki Shinyō Ginkō Sangyō Kenkyūkai, *Shin Jidai ni Chōsen suru Nihon no Sangyō,* p. 233.

126. Ibid., p. 230.

127. Interview with Aiso Hideo, Professor at Keio University and currently the head of Japan's 5th-Generation and Supercomputer Projects, 20 November 1987.

128. Nihon Chōki Shinyō Ginkō Sangyō Kenkyūkai, *Shin Jidai ni Chōsen suru Nihon no Sangyō,* p. 10.

129. Interview with Inose Hiroshi, 3 November 1987.

130. Nihon Denshi Kikai Kōgyōkai, *Denshi Kōgyō 30 Nenshi,* pp. 81–82. To receive the subsidies, Fujitsu, NEC, and Oki formed a research cooperative association as required by the Mining Industry Technology Research Association Law of 1961. Fujitsu developed the main processor and the card punch; NEC, a sub-computer, paper-tape reader, and magnetic disk device; and Oki, a different sub-computer, a card reader, line printer, paper-tape punch, and typewriter (*Kompyūtopia,* December 1974, pp. 39–40); the software was consigned to a U.S. firm—Computer Usage Corporation—for $170,000 (61.2 million yen). (*Denshi Kōgyō Nenkan,* 1966, p. 278.)

131. Interview with Yoshioka Tadashi.

132. Interview with Tajiri Yasushi.

133. *Kompyūtopia,* December 1974, p. 94.

134. *Denshi Kōgyō Nenkan,* 1966, pp. 279–281. NEC used Honeywell technology for its NEAC-2200 series; Hitachi based its HITAC-8000 on a machine of its partner, RCA.

135. Discussions with Hirose Kōichi, Deputy General Manager of JECC's Research Division, 1984.

136. Matsuo, *IBM Ōkoku o Obiyakasu Fujitsu,* p. 144.

137. *Denshi Kōgyō Nenkan,* 1967, p. 241.

138. MITI, *Agency of Industrial Science and Technology* (AIST), pp. 10–12.

139. *Denshi Kōgyō 30 Nenshi,* p. 108.

140. *Denshi Kōgyō Nenkan,* 1966, p. 260.

141. Shūgiin, Kessan Iinkaigiroku no. 21, Kokkai 71 (The Lower House, settlement-of-accounts committee proceedings no. 21, Diet no. 71), 12 July 1973.

142. *Denshi Kōgyō 30 Nenshi,* p. 82.

143. Nomura Securities Research Institute, *Zaikai Kansoku,* May 1969, p. 77.

144. Interview with Inose Hiroshi, 7 December 1987.

145. MITI's Kōgyō Gijutsuin, *Ōgata Purojekuto ni yoru Chōkō Seinō Denshikeisanki,* p. 9.

146. Ibid., pp. 8–10; *Kompyūtopia,* June 1973, p. 17.

147. The specific hardware goals were: addition speed of 50 nanoseconds with average speed of 200–300 nanoseconds and main memory capacity of 1MB. For the magnetic-disk device, the goal was to have an average access time of 72.5 ms, memory of 1,000 MB, and data transfer speed of .72 MB per second. *Ōgata Purojekuto ni yoru . . . ,* p. 10.) The final prototype had a minimum addition time of 50 nanoseconds, and its average speed was 250 nanoseconds. The goals for the main memory and magnetic-disk device were also met. (*Kompyūtopia,* June 1973, p. 15; *Electronics,* 24 May 1971, pp. 42–49.)

148. Interview with Inose Hiroshi, 7 December 1987.

149. First, the project tried to increase the basic processor's speed by use of pipeline processing, which enables the basic processor to divide each instruction into several parts and execute different parts of several instructions simultaneously. In the final evaluation, AIST admitted that the pipeline control mechanism did not work well for calculations in which storing, loading, and branching are repeatedly done; they were not able to achieve a full performing pipeline-control method. Second, the project also originally hoped to develop a letter-recognition device that could read 26 capital letters, 26 lower-case letters, 46 Japanese katakana characters, 10 numerals, and up to 20 miscellaneous symbols; but the goal was reduced, and the final prototype could read only 26 capital letters, 10 numerals, and 8 other symbols. Third, while they had hoped to develop a core memory with a cycle time of 100 nanoseconds, they were able to get it down only to 150ns.

(*Kompyūtopia,* June 1973, p. 17; *Electronics,* 24 April 1971, pp. 42–43, 24 May 1971, p. 47.)

150. Usui Kenji, Terasawa Yasuo, and Numakura Hōzo, p. 289.

151. The new main memory includes a high-speed temporary storage area that holds data temporarily both before it enters the CPU and after it comes out from the CPU; it is critically important because input-output devices were very slow, leaving the CPU idle during input-output operations. By having this temporary storage area separating the CPU and input-output devices, which operate at different speeds, the faster device (CPU) could continue operation while the slower devices (input-output devices) performed their functions.

152. The project members, in cooperation with NTT, established a standard "input-output interface 69," which was used in this project and in NTT's DIPS-1 Project (to be analyzed later in this chapter). (*Denshi Kōgyō Nenkan,* 1973, pp. 312–315; *Ōgata Purojekuto ni yoru . . . ,* p. 17.)

153. Interview with Yoshioka Tadashi.

154. Interview with Kuwahara Yutaka, head of the R&D Administration Office, Hitachi's Central Research Laboratory, 9 December 1987.

155. Interview with Aiso Hideo.

156. *Denshi Kōgyō Nenkan,* 1967, p. 246.

157. *Ōgata Purojekuto ni yoru . . . ,* p. 202.

158. Ibid., p. 17; *Kompyūtopia,* June 1973, p. 15.

159. MITI had been pushing the idea of a specialized software consulting firm as a joint venture among the 6 computer makers since the end of 1964, but the firms were not willing to commit resources to a joint venture until MITI promised NEC, Fujitsu, and Hitachi that the software work for the Super High-Performance Computer Project prototype would be consigned to the newly established software firm and arranged for the IBJ to carry part of the venture's financial burden. The firm was initially capitalized at 35 million yen, with the firms each bearing 30% of the burden and the IBJ the remaining 10%. Later they added 70 million yen in capital in the same proportions. (*Denshi Kōgyō Nenkan,* 1967, pp. 244–245; *Kompyūtopia,* June 1973, p. 13.)

160. *Kompyūtopia,* May 1975, p. 107.

161. *Nihon Keizai Shimbun,* 5 July 1966.

162. Uozumi, p. 172.

163. Ibid.

164. Interview with Inose Hiroshi, 3 November 1987 in Cambridge, MA, and 7 December 1987 in Tokyo.

165. *Kompyūtopia,* February 1973, pp. 28–29.

166. Programs written in conventional source languages such as Fortran, Cobol, or PL/1 would be compiled into the intermediate or "common" language

from which they would then be recompiled into machine language for a specific computer model. (*Electronics*, 24 May 1971, p. 42.)

167. Shūgiin, Kessan Iinkaigiroku no. 21, Kokkai 71 (The Lower House, settlement-of-accounts committee no. 21, Diet no. 71), 12 July 1973, p. 27. This 3 billion yen was from a total of 4.7 billion yen allotted to software development for the project.

168. *Kompyūtopia*, June 1973, p. 17.

169. Uozumi, p. 172.

170. *Kompyūtopia*, February 1973, p. 27.

171. Interview with Yamamoto Kinko, 28 February 1986.

172. *Kompyūtopia*, February 1973, pp. 27–30; interview with Yamamoto Kinko, 28 February 1986.

173. Interview with Yamamoto Kinko, 28 February 1986.

174. Interview with Aiso Hideo.

175. *Denshi Kōgyō Nenkan*, 1970–1971, p. 118.

176. *Kompyūtopia*, February 1973, pp. 27–30.

177. Uozumi, p. 172.

178. *Nihon Keizai Shimbun*, 3 July 1972.

179. *Kompyūtopia*, February 1973, pp. 27–30. A major cause of the losses, however, was the high rental fee Japan Software paid for use of Fujitsu's FACOM 230-60 in their work. The rental fee alone of 20 million yen a month took a large chunk of the money consigned to the Japan Software Co. (*Daiyamondo*, 12 August 1972, p. 80.)

180. Shūgiin, Kessan Iinkaigiroku 21, Kokkai 71 (The Lower House, settlement-of-accounts committee no. 21, Diet no. 71), 5 July 1973, p. 29. According to the Japan Software union, Fujitsu gave money to Japan Software engineers to entice them to retire and join a new software company of Fujitsu's called SSL. (Sōhyō Zenkoku Kinzoku Rōdō Kumiai Tōkyō Chihon, Nihon Sofutowea Shibu, *Ikarimote, Kompyūtopia no Tobira o Tatake*, pp. 77–78.) According to other government documents, in May 1972 Fujitsu's Naitō—President of Japan Software—wrote a memo to other Fujitsu executives describing his strategy of bankrupting Japan Software: In order to weaken Japan Software financially, Fujitsu would no longer order anything from it and would establish a new software company and try to attract Japan Software technologists to the new firm. (Shūgiin, Yosan Iinkai no. 4, Bunka Kaigiroku no. 3, Kokkai no. 72 [The Lower House, proceedings no. 3 of the fourth section of the budget committee, Diet no. 72], 7 March 1974, p. 44.)

181. Shūgiin, Kessan Iinkaigiroku no. 21, Kokkai no. 71 (The Lower House, settlement-of-accounts committee no. 21, Diet no. 71), 5 July 1973, p. 29.

182. Interview with Yoshioka Tadashi.

183. Sangiin, Shōkō Iinkaigiroku 17, Kokkai 63 (The Upper House, proceedings no. 17 of the commerce committee, Diet no. 63), 6 May 1970, p. 7.
184. In 1954, a Tokyo University professor and his student developed a new circuit they called a parametron, which they felt was more advanced than the vacuum tube.
185. Interview with Toda Iwao.
186. *Kompyūtopia*, October 1973, p. 43.
187. Shūgiin, Teishin Iinkaigiroku 12, Kokkai 65 (The Lower House telecommunications committee no. 12, Diet no. 65), 24 March 1971, p. 6.
188. Shūgiin, Shōkō Iinkaigiroku 30, Kokkai 61 (The Lower House, commerce committee proceedings, no. 30, Diet no. 61), 6 June 1969, pp. 21–22; Interview with NTT's Toda Iwao.
189. Interviews with Aiso Hideo and Toda Iwao.
190. *Kompyūtopia*, September 1971, p. 129.
191. Interview with Toda Iwao.
192. While the 1966 project targeted an average time to execute commands of 0.245 microseconds and a magnetic-disk memory of 1,000 MB, the DIPS-1 Project targeted a slower average execution time of 0.63 microseconds and a smaller disk memory of 233 MB. The final DIPS-1 machine met these goals. (*Kompyūtopia*, March 1971, p. 144; *Denshi Kōgyō Nenkan*, 1973, p. 478.) The machine-language software was standardized, although they did not have enough time to fully develop the applications software for the DIPS-1 system, making it somewhat behind the middle level of IBM's 370 series. (Shūgiin, Teishin Iinkaigiroku 25, Kokkai 71 [The Lower House telecommunications committee no. 25, Diet no. 71], 27 June 1973, p. 19.) The targeted standardization of the logic circuits of the electronic switching machine (which connects to the computer) was abandoned mid-project; this would have taken more time than originally estimated, and the firms wanted to finish the system as quickly as possible. (*Nihon Denshin Denwa Kōsha 25 Nenshi*, II, 683.) The project also made the memory device more economical: Made smaller and lighter, it required less electricity. (*Kompyūtopia*, October 1973, pp. 73–76.)
193. DEMOS-E (Dendenkōsha Multi-Access On-line System—Extended) is a scientific and technical calculation service provided by an on-line link between users' terminals and the DEMOS-E Center Computer. The service actually started in March 1971 as DEMOS, and was extended—DEMOS-E—in late 1972 when the larger and more sophisticated DIPS-1 machines came out and made it possible to offer better service. The service can be used for the various calculations done in the structural design of buildings, circuit analysis, financial accounting, and other work such as linear programming and simulation. This service is on-line, thus available to many users simultaneously. As of 1981, there were 65 centers around Japan ser-

vicing about 1,800 users. The DRESS service (NTT Real-Time Sales Management System) which started in September 1970, also upgraded its services when the DIPS-1 machines became available. It is used for inventory control and sales management. Like DEMOS-E, it links users to a computer in the DRESS center. As of March 1981, it had centers in 64 cities nationwide, with some 1,500 users. (Japan Information-Processing Development Center, *Computer White Paper,* 1981, pp. 55–56.)

194. *Nihon Denshin Denwa Kōsha 25 Nenshi,* II, 683.
195. Interview with Hitachi's Kuwahara Yutaka.
196. Interview with Aiso Hideo.

3. INCREASING SUPPLY AND DEMAND: THE JAPAN ELECTRONIC COMPUTER COMPANY (JECC)

1. *JECC 10 Nenshi,* pp. 50–51; *JECC Kompyūtā Nōto,* annual.
2. Interview with Ishiguro Ryūji, Director of the Japan Development Bank's Center for Research on Investment in Plant and Equipment, 12 November 1984.
3. JECC, *Kokusan Denshikeisanki Nyūzu,* "JECC Monogatari," segment 7, no. 123, 1 April 1980, p. 3; segment 5, no. 121, 1 February 1980, p. 3; and segment 11, no. 127, 1 August 1980, p. 8.
4. Interview with Yoshioka Tadashi.
5. "JECC Monogatari," segment 12, no. 128, 1 September 1980.
6. Ibid., segment 7.
7. Ibid., segment 23, nos. 139 and 140, 16 August 1981, p. 8.
8. The process of negotiation and compromise in which the idea of JECC as a national computer company was transformed into one where it was owned by the private sector but largely financed by the state is similar to the notion of "reciprocal consent" that Richard Samuels develops in his book *The Business of the Japanese State, Energy Markets in Comparative and Historical Perspective.*
9. "JECC Monogatari," segment 5, p. 3.
10. Ibid., segment 9, no. 125, 1 June 1980, p. 2.
11. *Denshi Kōgyō Nenkan,* 1962, pp. 154–158.
12. "JECC Monogatari," segment 21, 1 February 1982, p. 8.
13. Various discussions with Hirose Kōichi, Deputy Manager of JECC's Research Division, 1984; Interview with Ishii Yoshiaki, General Manager of JECC's Research Division, 19 July 1984.
14. *Kompyūtopia,* December 1973, pp. 26–27.
15. Foreign machines were on average being used for 4 years.
16. Government institutions purchased most of the remainder.
17. *JECC Kompyūtā Nōto,* 1970, p. 52.
18. Interview with Tajiri Yasushi.

19. See Appendix B.
20. Interview with Tajiri Yasushi.
21. Ibid.
22. Interviews with Takeuchi Hiroshi of the LTCB and Inaba Masahiro and Tamaki Makoto of the IBJ.
23. *JECC 10 Nenshi,* pp. 50–51, 59.
24. Interview with Ishiguro Ryūji of the JDB.
25. See Appendix B.
26. Fujitsu annual financial reports; Dokusen Bunseki Kenkyūkai, *Nihon no Dokusen Kigyō,* I, 292; *Denshi Kōgyō Nenkan,* 1979, p. 447; *JECC Kompyūtā Nōto,* 1979, p. 377.
27. Nikkō Shōken Kabushiki Gaisha Chōsabu, *Tōshi Geppō,* February 1969, p. 46.
28. "JECC Monogatari," segment 23.
29. *Dempa Shimbun* (Electric wave news), 4 April 1967, p. 2.
30. Ibid., 22 April 1967, p. 2; *Nihon Keizai Shimbun,* 30 December 1968.
31. *Nihon Keizai Shimbun,* 28 April 1968, p. 4.
32. Nihon Denshi Kōgyō Shinkō Kyōkano, Denshikeisanki Sangyō Chōsa Iinkai, ed., *Waga Kuni no Denshikeisanki Sangyō Mondai Ten to Sono Taisaku,* (Tokyo, 1970), section 4, p. 29.
33. *Nihon Keizai Shimbun,* 4 July 1967; *Denshi Kōgyō Nenkan,* 1971–1972, p. 83.
34. Of the 281 machines traded in between 1962 to early 1967, only 59 had been re-rented; the remaining were left in inventory. (*Nihon Keizai Shimbun,* 23 February 1967.)
35. *Denshi Shijō Yōran* 1972–1973, pp. 235–236; *Nihon Keizai Shimbun,* 22 September 1966.
36. *Nihon Keizai Shimbun,* 18 October 1966.
37. Nihon Jōhō Shori Kaihatsu Kyōkai, eds., *Kompyūtā Hakusho,* 1969, p. 44; Jimmy Wheeler, Merit E. Janow, and Thomas Pepper, *Japanese Industrial Development Policies in the 1980s,* pp. 96, 142.
38. MOF, *Zeisei Chōsa Kai,* p. 31.
39. *JECC 10 Nenshi,* p. 26.
40. Interview with Ishii Yoshiaki of JECC.
41. *JECC 10 Nenshi,* p. 51.
42. *Dempa Shimbun,* 27 December 1969, p. 2.
43. *Tōyōkeizai* (Oriental Economist), 24 January 1970, p. 42.
44. *Ekonomisuto* (The economist), 12 May 1970, p. 22.
45. *Nihon Keizai Shimbun,* 4 July 1967; Dokusen Bunseki Kenkyūkai *Nihon no Dokusen Kigyō,* 1971, V, 277.
46. *JECC 10 Nenshi,* pp. 60–62.
47. *Nihon Kaihatsu Ginkō Tōkei Yōran,* 1971, p. 400.
48. Calculated using data from: *JECC Kompyūtā Nōto,* 1979, pp. 10–11, 377;

Nihon no Dokusen Kigyō, I, 292; *Denshi Kōgyō Nenkan*, 1979, p. 447; and *Kompyūtā Warudo* (Computer world), 31 May 1982, p. 21.

49. *Tōyōkeizai*, 24 January 1970, p. 42.
50. *Kokusan Denshikeisanki Nyūzu*, 12 December 1970, p. 1.
51. Nihon Jōhō Shori Kaihatsu Kyōkai, eds., *Kompyūtā Hakusho*, 1972, pp. 117–120, 1975, pp. 57–58.
52. *Computer White Paper*, 1973, p. 24.
53. MOF, *Zeisei Chōsa Kai, Zen Shiryō Shū;* MOF, *Zeisei Chōsa Kai Kankei Shiryō Shū.*
54. See Appendixes D and F.
55. Calculated using data from: *JECC Kompyūtā Nōto*, 1979, pp. 10–11, 377; *Nihon no Dokusen Kigyō*, I, 292; *Denshi Kōgyō Nenkan*, 1979, p. 447; *Kompyūtā Warudo*, 31 May 1982, p. 21.
56. *Kompyūtopia*, July 1975, p. 77.
57. Ibid.
58. Iwahori Y., *Hitachi no Keiei*, p. 201.
59. Uozumi, p. 190.
60. Fujitsu's March and September 1973 financial reports.
61. Interview with Tajiri Yasushi of Fujitsu.
62. JECC annual financial reports; Nakae Gōki, *Kompyūtā Sangyō no Shijō Senryaku*, p. 292. The loans for 1976–1978 are estimated because the data are not available. They are estimated using the data for JDB loans to JECC and assuming that JDB loans accounted for 48% of the total loans during these 3 years; 48% is estimated by calculating the percent of JDB loans in total loans immediately before and after the 1976–1978 period.
63. See Appendixes E and G.
64. Fujitsu annual reports; *JECC Kompyūtā Nōto*, 1979, p. 377; *Denshi Kōgyō Nenkan*, 1979, p. 447; *Kompyūtā Warudo*, 31 May 1982, p. 21.
65. Calculated using data from: *JECC Kompyūtā Nōto*, 1979, pp. 10–11; Shimoda Hirotsugu, *IBM to no 10 nen Sensō*, p. 178; *Kompyūtā Warudo*, 31 May 1982, p. 21.
66. Interview with Oketani Kisaburō, section chief, Market Planning Department, Fujitsu, 1 December 1987.

4. STRENGTH THROUGH CONCENTRATION, 1970–1975

1. Johnson, *MITI and the Japanese Miracle*, p. 284.
2. Interview with Yoshioka Tadashi.
3. Johnson, *MITI and the Japanese Miracle*, p. 285.
4. *Nihon Keizai Shimbun*, 8 July 1971, p. 1.
5. *Ekonomisuto*, 17 July 1973, p. 86.
6. Nihon Denshi Kikai Kōgyōkai, *Denshi* 12.10:19 (1972).

7. Shūgiin, Shōkō Iinkaigiroku 7 (The Lower House commerce committee proceedings no. 7, Diet no. 65), Kokkai 65, 5 March 1971, p. 10.
8. Ibid., no. 65, Diet no. 63, 23 April 1970, p. 17.
9. An article summarizing MITI's Industrial Structure Deliberation Council's Information Industries Division's 1974 interim report, in MITI, *Tsūsan Jānaru* 7.8:63 (November 1974).
10. *Kompyūtopia,* October 1971, p. 154.
11. Uozumi, pp. 90–92.
12. *Dempa Shimbun,* 27 March 1971, p. 2.
13. *Kokusan Denshikeisanki Nyūzu,* 20 December 1971, p. 2.
14. *Dempa Shimbun,* 26 March 1971, p. 2.
15. *Nihon Keizai Shimbun,* 2 November 1985, p. 5.
16. Interview with Tamamura Tomio, former high-level manager at IBM Japan, 27 October 1984.
17. The 370-155, 370-135, and System 3 machines (*Kompyūtopia,* October 1971, p. 154).
18. In the early 1970s, MITI rejected IBM's request to produce its 370-145 model in Japan. IBM tried to get around MITI by reducing the performance of the 370-155 to about the level of the 370-145, but continuing to call it a 370-155, adding only "submodel 2." But MITI seems to have caught on to IBM's strategy by 1972, when it demanded that IBM stop producing its 155 model if it wanted permission to manufacture its larger, more advanced 370-158 model in Japan. (Uozumi, pp. 99–100.) Thus, by 1974, IBM Japan was allowed to manufacture the 370-115, 370-125, 370-135, and 370-158. (*Kompyūtopia,* July 1974, p. 31.) MITI also rejected IBM's request to produce its larger 370-168 in Japan, delaying it until the late 1970s.
19. Ezra Vogel, p. 142.
20. *JECC Kompyūtā Nōto,* 1979, p. 160.
21. MITI Chōsa Kai, *Genkō Yunyū Seido Ichiran,* annual.
22. Uozumi, p. 194.
23. *Denshi* 12.10:21 (1972).
24. Government procurement data are not available; they are estimated from data on computers in use at government-related institutions. From 1970 through 1975, on average about one-fifth of domestic computers were used in government offices; we can thus assume that, on average, the government bought or rented approximately 20% of domestic computer makers' computers each year. Data from JECC *Kompyūtā Jitsudo Jōkyō Chōsa,* annual.
25. *Denshi* 12.1:14 (1972); 70.5 billion yen were to be funneled into computer development, 60 billion yen in loans to shore up JECC, 7 billion yen for ICs, and 10 billion yen for software development. (*Ekonomisuto,* 17 July 1973, p. 85.) Calculated at 330 yen to the dollar.
26. *Kompyūtopia,* October 1971, p. 153.
27. *Kompyūtā Hakusho,* 1972, p. 390.

28. *Denshi* 12.3:6 (1972).
29. Includes about 65 billion yen in subsidies for mainframe and peripheral equipment development, 33.1 billion yen in loans from JDB to JECC, 5.2 billion yen in subsidies for R&D on integrated circuits, and approximately 5.7 billion yen in subsidies and 10 billion yen in loans for software. Calculated at 330 yen to the dollar.
30. Shūgiin, Ōkura Iinkaigiroku 5, Kokkai 76 (The Lower House finance committee proceedings no. 5, Diet no. 76), 3 December 1975, p. 10.
31. Using subsidies from the general budget as an indicator.
32. Ogura Masatatsu and Yoshino Naoyuki, "Zeisei to Zaisei Tōyūshi," p. 106.
33. Shūgiin, Shōkō Iinkaigiroku 6, Kokkai 65 (The Lower House commerce committee proceedings no. 6, Diet no. 65), 3 March 1971.
34. Interview with Takeuchi Hiroshi.
35. Calculated at 330 yen to the dollar.
36. Firms' annual financial reports. Calculated at 300 yen to the dollar.
37. This is the sum of the following calculations (at 300 yen to the dollar): *Subsidies:* New Series Project: 13.38 billion yen by 22.5 percent = 3.01 billion yen ($10.03 million) (the Fujitsu-Hitachi group got 45% of the subsidy, thus we assume Fujitsu got 22.5%); Pattern Recognition Project: 3.37 billion yen/5 firms = 0.674 billion yen ($2.25 million); NTT's VLSI Project: 6.67 billion yen/ 4 firms = 1.67 billion yen ($5.56 million); JECC advance: 1.34 billion yen by 45% = 0.603 billion yen ($2.01 million) (in 1975, 45% of the computers JECC purchased were from Fujitsu; thus we assume Fujitsu got 45% of the benefits received through JECC) (*Kompyūtā Warudo*, 31 May 1982, p. 21); Interest savings from JDB loans to JECC: 3.75 billion yen by 45% = 1.69 billion yen ($5.63 million). *Tax Benefits:* Experimental R&D credit: 2.1 billion yen/ 6 firms = 0.35 billion yen ($1.17 million); Computer buyback reserve benefit: 5 billion yen by 45% = 2.25 billion yen ($7.5 million); Special depreciation: 1.2 billion yen/ 6 firms = 0.2 billion yen ($0.67 million). The subsidies and tax benefits total $34.83 million (10.45 billion yen). Data from Appendix D.
38. Fujitsu is assumed to have accounted for one-third (26.87 billion yen or $89.56 million) of the industry's total investment (80.6 billion yen). Aid to Fujitsu of $34.83 million is 39% of Fujitsu investment ($89.56 million). Appendixes D and E.
39. *Loans:* Fujitsu received the benefit of 45% of the JDB loans to JECC (46 billion yen), equal to 20.7 billion yen ($69 million). It also received 45% of the benefit of up-front cash through JECC (13.8 billion yen), equal to 6.21 billion yen ($20.7 million); direct loans to Fujitsu from the government's JDB and the Import-Export Bank: 1.875 billion yen ($6.25 million). This totals $95.95 million (28.79 billion yen). Data from Appendix D and from Fujitsu's 1975 financial statement.
40. *Total benefits:* $34.83 million plus $95.95 million equals $130.78 million.

Fujitsu invested an estimated $89.56 million and had pre-tax profits of $33.06 million (9.92 billion yen) in 1975. Data from Appendixes D and E, and Fujitsu's 1975 financial statement.

41. Interview with Amaya Naohiro, 7 December 1987.
42. Interview with Miyano Motoyuki.
43. These attempts to consolidate key industries led not only to an increase in mergers but also an increase in the number of cartels exempt from the antitrust law. These exemptions covered a wide range of products: By the 1970s, large parts of steel, textiles, electric machinery, and precision instruments were produced under cartel conditions. (Imai Kenichi, "Japan's Industrial Organization," pp. 111–112.)
44. Shūgiin, Shōkō Iinkaigiroku 21, Kokkai 63 (The Lower House commerce committee proceedings no. 21, Diet no. 63), 17 April 1970, p. 25.
45. *Tōyōkeizai,* 24 January 1970, p. 42.
46. Matsuo Hiroshi, *Daitanna Chōsen, Fujitsu no Monogatari,* p. 207.
47. *Kompyūtā Hakusho,* 1972, p. 99.
48. Interview with Yoshioka Tadashi.
49. Annual reports of the firms.
50. Interview with Tajiri Yasushi.
51. Interview with Yoshioka Tadashi.
52. Letter in *Fujitsu Nyūzu,* Fujitsu's internal magazine, November 1971, reprinted in *Fujitsu Shashi,* II, 134–136.
53. When TRW left data processing in the early 1970s, Mitsubishi made a technological agreement with Xerox.
54. See Appendixes D and F.
55. Uozumi, p. 14.
56. *Kompyūtopia,* July 1974, p. 30.
57. Interview with Tajiri Yasushi of Fujitsu.
58. Shimoda, *IBM to no 10 Nen Sensō,* p. 158.
59. Uozumi, p. 140.
60. *Tōyōkeizai,* 20 April 1974, p. 87.
61. Jōhō Sangyō Shimbunsha, *Nihon Jōhō Sangyō Shimbun* 263:1 (15 July 1974).
62. *Kompyūtopia,* February 1975, pp. 16–26.
63. The resulting Fujitsu M-190 machine was very similar to the Amdahl-470/V6 computer. (*Kompyūtopia,* February 1975, pp. 16–26.)
64. Matsuo, *Daitanna Chōsen, Fujitsu no Monogatari,* p. 212.
65. Kobayashi Taiyū, *Tomokaku Yatte Miro,* p. 119.
66. Ibid.; Kashiwabara Hisashi, *IBM o Furueagaraseta Otoku, Ikeda Toshio to Fujitsu Yarōtachi,* p. 179.
67. Kashiwabara, p. 176. Calculated at 330 yen to the dollar.
68. Ibid., p. 180.
69. Ibid., p. 184.

70. *Electronics,* 27 March 1980, p. 128.

71. Kashiwabara, p. 184.

72. Ibid., pp. 199–200; *Tōyōkeizai,* 1972, new spring special large issue (no specific date given), pp. 149–150.

73. A total of 70.3 billion yen in subsidies was given for the New Series Project. The Fujitsu-Hitachi group received about 45% of this—or 31.6 billion yen (Uozumi, p. 14.); Fujitsu got half of this: 15.8 billion yen. Dollars calculated at 330 yen to the dollar.

74. Calculated at 330 yen to the dollar.

75. Fujitsu's sales to JECC were 30.1% of JECC's purchases in 1972, 37.7% in 1973, 46% in 1974, 45% in 1975, and 48.8% in 1976. Calculated by taking the total benefit of JECC subsidies and loans to the industry in these years and calculating the benefit to Fujitsu by using these percentages. (*Denshi Kōgyō Nenkan,* 1979, p. 447 and *JECC Kompyūtā Nōto,* 1979, p. 377.) Calculated at 330 yen to the dollar.

76. Fujitsu annual financial report. Calculated at 330 yen to the dollar.

77. Kashiwabara, p. 199.

78. *Bungeishunjū,* September 1982, p. 101.

79. Ibid., p. 102.

80. Ibid., pp. 102–103.

81. *Zaikai Kansoku,* January 1976, p. 41.

82. The very first machine was bought by NASA. (Kashiwabara, p. 216.)

83. Matsuo, *IBM Ōkoku o Obiyakasu Fujitsu,* p. 77.

84. Indeed, before Fujitsu had even come out with its M-160 computer (1976), Hitachi unexpectedly brought out an M-160 (1975), forcing Fujitsu to call its machine the M-160II; and, when Hitachi put out the M-180 in 1976, Fujitsu put out an M-180II in 1977. A study by Julian Gresser argues that the 160 and 160II, and 180 and 180II have the same price/performance, but technical specifications of the computers show that the 160II is clearly positioned between Hitachi's 170 and 160 and the 180II between the Hitachi 180 and 170 (Table 17). (Julian Gresser, *High Technology and Japanese Industrial Policy: A Strategy for U.S. Policymakers,* p. 13.)

85. From 1977 on, Fujitsu and Hitachi continued to fill out the M-series, with Fujitsu bringing out the 130, 140, 160S, and 200, and Hitachi bringing out the 150 and 200H.

86. Interviews with Tajiri Yasushi of Fujitsu, Maeda Norihiko and Amaya Naohiro, both formerly of MITI.

87. Interview with with Hitachi's Kuwahara Yutaka.

88. Interview with Yamamoto Kinko, 28 February 1986.

89. Interview with Kuwahara Yutaka.

90. Interview with Tajiri Yasushi.

91. *Nihon Keizai Shimbun,* 22 September 1971.

92. Uozumi, p. 135.
93. *Nihon Keizai Shimbun*, 8 March 1973.
94. NEC was responsible for the ACOS-200, 300, 400, and 500 and Toshiba the middle level 600 and 700; the larger-scale 800 and 900 were to be developed separately by both Toshiba and NEC and were given last priority in the plan. (Uozumi, pp. 135–136.)
95. For example, the ACOS-200 model was sold by NEC as the ACOS-77 series NEAC system 200 and by Toshiba as the ACOS-77 series TOSBAC system 200. (*Kokusan Denshikeisanki Nyūzu*, 1 June 1974, p. 1.)
96. Uozumi, p. 135.
97. *Kompyūtopia*, June 1975, p. 110.
98. Uozumi, pp. 135–136.
99. *Tōyōkeizai*, 26 July 1975, p. 91, and 29 April 1974, p. 87.
100. *Kompyūtopia*, July 1974, pp. 30–37.
101. Ibid., p. 40.
102. The NEC-Toshiba group received a subsidy of some 28 billion yen, which was to cover half of their R&D costs for the project. (*JECC Kompyūtā Nōto*, 1972, p. 90.)
103. The ACOS-800 and 900.
104. *Tōyōkeizai*, 26 July 1975, p. 90.
105. For NEC, by June 1979, 529 ACOS-200 systems were installed, 150 ACOS-300, 58 ACOS-400, and 91 ACOS-500 machines. For Toshiba, there were 61 ACOS-600 systems and 49 ACOS-700 systems installed. For the ACOS-800 I and II, and ACOS-900 I and II, which came out in 1978, there were 16 of the 800 and 4 of the 900 installed by June 1979. (*Kompyūtopia*, January 1980, p. 17.)
106. *Electronics*, 27 March 1980, p. 121.
107. Ibid., 11 March 1985, p. 17.
108. *Tōyōkeizai*, 6 June 1970, p. 55.
109. *Ekonomisuto*, 17 October 1972, p. 48.
110. *Nihon Keizai Shimbun*, 23 October 1971.
111. Oki was in charge of the peripheral and terminal equipment, and Mitsubishi developed the CPU and magnetic-disk devices for the new series. (*Ekonomisuto*, 17 October 1972, p. 48.) Mitsubishi Sogo Research Institute was responsible for developing the software. Xerox technology was used for the software (*Kokusan Denshikeisanki Nyūzu*, 1 June 1974, p. 1.)
112. *Kompyūtā Hakusho*, 1972, p. 391.
113. Giving Mitsubishi 8%, Oki 47%, and Sperry Rand 45% of the shares. (*Denshi Kōgyō Nenkan*, 1973, p. 254.) Their alliance for the New Series Project further complicated their already complex relationships with Oki UNIVAC and Japan UNIVAC. They agreed that their COSMO series would not compete with the machines then being produced by Sperry Rand and Oki UNIVAC; and Oki UNIVAC, in exchange, promised not to sell ma-

chines like those of Mitsubishi and Oki. (*Nihon Keizai Shimbun,* 25 November 1971.) Mitsubishi also agreed to make magnetic-disk devices for Oki UNIVAC. (*Denshi Kōgyō Nenkan,* 1973, p. 254.)

114. *Kokusan Denshikeisanki Nyūzu,* 1 June 1974, p. 1.

115. The machines competed in the middle and lower end of the computer market. While they were called "general-purpose," they were most sophisticated for use in industrial control. Indeed, Mitsubishi was the leader in the field of industrial control systems in the mid-1970s. (*Electronics,* 25 November 1976.)

116. The subsidies granted for the New Series Project were granted on the condition that the recipients produce a computer series using the R&D. A related reason was that MITI felt that Oki was lagging behind the others technologically. (Uozumi, pp. 169–170.)

117. *Kompyūtopia,* January 1980, p. 17.

118. Interview in "IBM wa Ya ni Hanatareta Tora da," *Bungeishunjū,* September 1982, p. 101.

119. Interview with Maeda Norihiko, 30 November 1987.

120. Ota is deputy manager of Mitsubishi Electric's electronic products and systems group. (*Electronics,* 27 March 1980, p. 126.)

121. *Electronics,* 27 March 1980, p. 126.

122. *Kokusan Denshikeisanki Nyūzu,* 25 August 1973, no. 44, p. 1.

123. Interview with NTT's Toda Iwao.

124. Hitachi made the smallest of the 3 models, which was aimed at countering the IBM-370-158; NEC worked on the middle model to compete with the 370-168, and Fujitsu the largest model having twice the performance of the 370-168. (*Denshi Kōgyō Nenkan,* 1975, p. 373.)

125. *Nihon Keizai Shimbun,* 5 July 1973.

126. Shūgiin, Teishin Iinkaigiroku, Kokkai 71 (Lower House telecommunications committee, Diet no. 71), 11 July 1973, p. 4.

127. Their new machines were compatible with the earlier DIPS-1 software and peripherals. (Interview with Toda Iwao; JECC, *Japan Computer News,* January 1977, p. 7.) The most advanced DIPS-11 machine had twice the performance of the DIPS-1 and cost half as much; its weight, floor space, and use of electricity was one-fourth to one-half that of the DIPS-1. Overall, the DIPS-11 machines were a 40% improvement in price/performance over the DIPS-1. (*Kompyūtopia,* March 1976, p. 112.)

128. Interview with Maeda Norihiko, 28 February 1986. The Hitachi-10 model was positioned between its M-series 170 and 180 models, the NEC-20 model between its ACOS-700 and 800, and Fujitsu's 30 model was very similar to its M-190. (Based on the information and sources in Table 17 of this chapter and on information from *Denshi Kōgyō Nenkan,* 1977, pp. 318–319, 328.) Completed in late 1975 and early 1976, the machines underwent testing at NTT labs and were put into use in NTT's data-

communications services from 1977. (*Kompyūtopia*, January 1977, p. 116.)

129. *Electronics*, 8 January 1976, p. 103.

130. PIPS was the second computer project under AIST's Large-Scale Program.

131. *Denshi* 11.10:13 (October 1971).

132. *Denshi* 21.7:46 (July 1981).

133. *Japan Computer News*, September 1977, pp. 4–5. The project was to improve upon the makers' next generation mainframes. Oki did not participate in the project because it did not make large-scale computers; it depended on UNIVAC for them. (Interview with Yoshioka Tadashi.)

134. MITI Kōgyō Gijutsuin (AIST), ed., *Ōgata Purojekuto, Patān Jōhōshori Shisutemu Kenkyū Kaihatsu Seika Happyōkai Ronbunshū*, pp. 1–8; *Japan Computer News*, August 1981, pp. 4–5 and September 1977, pp. 4–5; various articles by participants in the project in *Kōgyō Gijutsu*, the monthly magazine of AIST, July 1981, pp. 24–28; interview with Shimizu Sakae, Toshiba's Senior Managing Director, 3 February 1986.

135. Interview with Yoshihara Junji of AIST's Technology Research and Information Division, 28 March 1984.

136. Interview with Yoshihara Junji of AIST.

137. Interview with Kuwahara Yutaka of Hitachi.

138. Interviews with Shimizu Sakae and Aiso Hideo.

139. Interview with Fujitsu's Tajiri Yasushi.

140. Interview with Yamamoto Kinko, 28 February 1986.

141. Interview with Aiso Hideo.

142. Interview with Kuwahara Yutaka of Hitachi.

143. Interview with Aiso Hideo.

144. Ibid.

145. *Denshi Kōgyō Nenkan*, 1973, p. 230.

146. *Computer White Paper*, 1973, p. 25.

147. *Kompyūtopia*, March 1976, p. 48; interview with Isahai Kenji, General Manager of JECC's Research Division, 14 January 1986.

148. Interview with Isahai Kenji.

149. *Denshi Kōgyō Nenkan*, 1973, p. 231.

150. Shūgiin, Shōkō Iinkaigiroku 18, Kokkai 63 (Lower House, commerce committee no. 18, Diet no. 63), 8 April 1970, p. 8.

151. Interview with Inaba Masahiro of IBJ, 4 December 1987.

152. Minamisawa Noburō, *Nihon Kompyūtā Hatten Shi*, pp. 173–174. Calculated at 330 yen to the dollar.

153. *Kompyūtopia*, March 1978, p. 72. Since the software programs promoted by IPA were not those demanded by users, it is not surprising that the software-program survey register, a system to provide both users and software makers with information on what programs already exist, has largely been a failure. This system, an attempt to reduce redundant investment and to

encourage users to rent or buy registered programs, might have been more effective had the programs registered been those users demanded. (*Kompyū-topia*, March 1976, p. 40.) Calculated at 300 yen to the dollar.

154. Interview with Tsuji Junji, President of Tsuji Shisutemu Keikaku Jimusho Company, 7 December 1987.

155. Interview with Fujitsu's Tajiri Yasushi.

156. Interview with Aiso Hideo.

157. *Kompyūtopia*, May 1971, pp. 25–30.

158. There were also legal obstacles to a public-policy company like the NTT starting up a new company. (*Kompyūtopia*, May 1971, p. 28.)

159. Ibid., p. 29.

160. Ibid., p. 30.

161. Minamisawa, p. 188.

162. *Computer White Paper*, 1976, p. 32.

163. *Datamation*, September 1976, p. 97.

164. These applications were in 5 major categories: operations research, automatic control, business data processing, business management, and design calculations. (Minamisawa, pp. 187–188.)

165. Ibid., p. 188.

166. *Datamation*, September 1976, p. 97.

167. Interview with Yoshioka Tadashi.

168. Cited in Minamisawa, p. 188.

169. *Computer White Paper*, 1976, p. 33.

170. *JECC Kompyūtā Nōto*, 1981, pp. 219–222.

171. *Electronics*, 9 June 1977, p. 105.

5. LEAPFROGGING IBM? 1976 TO THE PRESENT

1. *Ekonomisuto*, 17 July 1973, p. 87.

2. *Nemawashi* literally means digging around the roots, which is done before transplanting a tree. It is very commonly used in Japan to refer to the negotiations and compromises that occur among different parties to lay the groundwork for action, in this case, the establishment of 2 groups for an R&D project.

3. *Computer White Paper*, 1976, p. 7.

4. Hitachi, NEC, and Fujitsu are the primary beneficiaries of this government largess: As of June 1980, 30.5% of the government's computers were Fujitsu machines, 30.1% were from NEC, and 24.5% from Hitachi; only 4.6% of the government's machines were from IBM. (*Kompyūtopia*, January 1983, p. 95.) This huge government market is important to IBM, but has proved elusive; and the issue of opening the market to foreigners is a sensitive one.

So much so that, in the late 1970s, when an IBM executive implied dissatisfaction with the government's procurement policy, there was such an uproar that IBM Japan President Shiina Takeo went to MITI to apologize. (Uozumi, pp. 10–31.) Foreigners cannot complain about tariffs. The Japanese have gradually decreased their tariffs on computers and related equipment in accordance with GATT negotiations. In April 1983, they were reduced from a 1978 level of 10.5% on computers and 17.5% on peripherals to 4.9% and 6% respectively. (*JECC Kompyūtā Nōto*, 1985, p. 167.)

5. Interview with Maeda Norihiko, 30 November 1987.
6. Ibid.
7. Uozumi, pp. 160–162.
8. Tarui Yasuo, *IC no Hanashi, Toranjisuta kara Chō LSI made*, pp. 136, 139, 152.
9. Ibid., p. 142.
10. Ibid., p. 158, and *Electronics*, 23 December 1976, p. 6E.
11. *JECC Kompyūtā Nōto*, 1981, p. 280.
12. *Tōyōkeizai*, 5 July 1975, p. 72.
13. Ibid., pp. 72–74.
14. *Kompyūtopia*, August 1975, p. 92.
15. Ibid., p. 93.
16. Ibid.
17. Ibid. Masks are like a negative through which light is passed to impose designs on a wafer.
18. Ibid.
19. JECC, *EDP in Japan*, 1977, pp. 51–53.
20. *JECC Kompyūtā Nōto*, 1979, p. 232.
21. *Denshi* 19.1:9 (January 1979).
22. *Denshi* 18.5:37 (May 1978).
23. *Japan Computer News*, June 1978, p. 6.
24. *Denshi* 19.1:9 (January 1979).
25. *JECC Kompyūtā Nōto*, 1981, p. 283.
26. Interview with Sakai Yoshio, 9 December 1987.
27. *Kompyūtopia*, August 1975, pp. 91–92.
28. Ibid., p. 93.
29. Uozumi, pp. 154–155.
30. Ibid., pp. 128–129.
31. Interview with Koezuka Masahiro, Deputy Director of MITI's Electronics Policy Division, 26 May 1984.
32. Uozumi, pp. 169–170. Oki ultimately got access to the VLSI Project technology through NTT, to whom it has had close ties historically on telecommunications equipment.
33. Interview with Yoshioka Tadashi.

34. *Kompyūtopia,* July 1975, p. 73.
35. *Denshi* 16.7:9, 14 (July 1976).
36. Shimura Yukio, *IC Sangyō Daisensō,* p. 3.
37. Ibid.
38. Ibid., p. 11.
39. Tarui, p. 143.
40. Ibid., p. 144.
41. Ibid., p. 146.
42. Discussion with Shimizu Sakae, Senior Managing Director of Toshiba, 3 February 1986.
43. Tarui, pp. 144–145.
44. Ibid.
45. Ibid., p. 147.
46. Ibid., pp. 144–145.
47. Ibid., p. 156.
48. Ibid., p. 147.
49. Ibid., p. 50.
50. Interview with Maeda Norihiko, 28 February 1986.
51. Tarui, p. 170.
52. *Japan Computer News,* September 1977, p. 7.
53. *EDP in Japan,* 1977, pp. 53–54.
54. *JECC Kompyūtā Nōto,* 1981, p. 183.
55. Ibid.
56. Discussion with Shimizu Sakae, Senior Managing Director of Toshiba.
57. Tarui, p. 168.
58. Ibid., p. 169.
59. Barry Hilton, "Government Subsidized Computer, Software, and Integrated Circuit Research and Development by Japanese Private Companies," p. 16.
60. Ibid.
61. Tarui, p. 149.
62. Interview with Nishimura Taizo, General Manager of Toshiba's International Operations, Electronics Components Division, 3 February 1986.
63. Discussion with Charles Cohen, long-time Tokyo Bureau Chief of *Electronics* magazine, 14 January 1986.
64. Uozumi, p. 156.
65. Fujitsu's Tajiri Yasushi mentioned money as a key benefit of the project to Fujitsu.
66. Fujitsu annual reports.
67. See Appendix G.
68. Interview with Fukuta Masumi, 7 February 1986.
69. *Electronics,* 25 November 1985, pp. 20–21.
70. Discussion with Todoriki Itaru; *Electronics,* 30 September 1985, pp. 30–32.

71. *Sofutowea Seisan Gijutsu Kaihatsu Keikaku.* This project was a consolidation of the failed Software Module Project, in progress 1973–1975.
72. The firm was capitalized at $1.85 million. (*Datamation,* September 1976, p. 97.)
73. Interview with Yamamoto Kinko, 3 December 1987.
74. Ibid.
75. Hilton, p. 13.
76. Interview with Yoshioka Tadashi; interview with Tsuji Junji, 7 December 1987.
77. Interview with Maeda Norihiko, 30 November 1987.
78. Interview with Tsuji Junji; interview with Ogino Yuji, Managing Director of IDC Japan Ltd., 20 November 1987.
79. The Promotion of the Development of Technology for Next Generation Computers Project (*Jisedai Denshikeisanki Kihon Gijutsu no Kaihatsu Sokushin*). This project is often referred to as Phase II of the VLSI Project. Aiso Hideo, "Overview of Japanese National Projects for Information Technology," p. 8.
80. The 6 major computer makers participated along with Matsushita and Sharp.
81. Hilton, pp. 14–15. The exchange rate used is 200 yen to the dollar.
82. Aiso, p. 8.
83. *Tōyōkeizai,* 1 February 1986, p. 34.
84. Interview with Fujitsu Chairman, Kobayashi Taiyū, in *Bungeishunjū,* September 1982, pp. 98–99.
85. Shimoda, *IBM to no 10 Nen Sensō,* pp. 60–61.
86. Talk by George H. Conrades, Group Executive, Asia-Pacific Group IBM, at Tokyo Foreign Correspondent's Press Club, 12 February 1986.
87. *The Wall Street Journal,* 16 September 1987, p. 2; 30 November 1988, p. A3.
88. Interview with Yamamoto Kinko, 28 February 1986.
89. *Kagaku Gijutsu yō Kōsoku Keisan Shisutemu.*
90. *JECC Kompyūtā Nōto,* 1985, p. 109.
91. *Business Week,* 26 August 1985, p. 60.
92. Ibid.
93. Interview with Fuchi Kazuhiro, 2 August 1985.
94. Interview with Tajiri Yasushi.
95. Interview with Yamamoto Kinko, 28 February 1986. The Supercomputer Project is in many ways a sub-project of the 5th-Generation Computer Project because both the Supercomputer-Project results related to high-speed chips and parallel processing will be incorporated into the 5th-Generation Project in its final stage.
96. *Electronics,* 13 January 1982, p. 71.
97. Interview with Aiso Hideo.
98. Gallium arsenide is also being studied in the Optoelectronics Project (large-

scale project at AIST), 1979–1987, fully funded by the government at 18 billion yen, and in a 10-year government-financed project on future electron devices starting in 1981. (*Electronics*, 8 September 1983, pp. 94–95.) By 1984, the project members had already developed prototypes for products; Fujitsu, for example, had developed a gallium arsenide chip. (*Electronics Week*, 29 October 1984, p. 22.)

99. *Denshi Kōgyō Nenkan*, 1986, p. 186.

100. Interview with Kitagawa Noriyoshi, of NEC's Second LSI Division, 3 February 1986, and discussion with Hiyaguri Toshio, Director and General Manager of Fujitsu's Computer Group after he gave a talk on Fujitsu's Supercomputer efforts at the Tokyo Foreign Correspondent's Press Club, 4 December 1985. Interview with Yamamoto Kinko of JIPDEC, 3 December 1987.

101. Interview with Oketani Kisaburō of Fujitsu.

102. Interview with Yamamoto Kinko, 3 December 1987.

103. Interview with Yamamoto Kinko, 28 February 1986; *Electronics*, 25 February 1985, p. 31.

104. *Electronics*, 25 February 1985, p. 31.

105. Ibid., 2 September 1985, p. 11.

106. Interview with Yamamoto Kinko, 3 December 1987. In 1985, the 1978 law that promoted machinery and information industries expired and was not extended (as it had been since its origin as a law to promote the electronics industry in 1957). Instead, the government revised the 1970 Information Processing Promotion Association (IPA) law into the "Law Pertaining to the Promotion of Information Processing" (*Jōhō Shori no Sokushin ni Kansuru Hōritsu*); Yamamoto argued that these actions indicated the government's strong intention to focus on software rather than hardware in the future. (See *JECC Kompyūtā Nōto*, 1987, pp. 61–62 about the laws.)

107. *Denshikeisanki Kiso Gijutsu no Kenkyū Kaihatsu Dai Go Sedai Kompyūtā*

108. Interview with Fuchi Kazuhiro.

109. The project involves software and hardware for 3 sub-systems: the data base, the inference and problem-solving system, and the man-machine interface.

110. The Institute for New Generation Computer Technology.

111. Interview with Yamamoto Kinko, 28 February 1986.

112. Interview with Hitachi's Kuwahara Yutaka.

113. Unpublished overview of the project given to me by one of the project's leaders, Professor Aiso Hideo of Keio University.

114. Interview with Fuchi Kazuhiro.

115. Interview with Yamamoto Kinko, 3 December 1987.

116. *JECC Kompyūtā Nōto*, 1985, p. 106.

117. Report by IDC Japan (International Data Corporation).

118. Interview with Kuwahara Yutaka of Hitachi.

119. *Electronics,* 23 July 1984, pp. 33–34; 12 January 1984, p. 75; and 3 December 1984, pp. 57–63. These include prototypes of a sequential-inference machine, a parallel-inference machine, a relational data-base machine, and a basic software system.

120. Discussion with Shimizu Sakae, Toshiba Senior Managing Director.

121. Interview with Okamura Yūji of the Electronics Policy Division of MITI's Machinery and Information Industries Bureau, 3 December 1987. Mitsubishi, for example, has used ICOT's sequential-inference system in its Melcom Psi computers.

122. Edward A. Feigenbaum and Pamela McCorduck, *The Fifth Generation, Artificial Intelligence and Japan's Computer Challenge to the World,* p. 135.

123. Interview with JIPDEC's Yamamoto Kinko, 3 December 1987.

124. *Nihon Keizai Shimbun,* 15 November 1986, p. 9.

125. Interview with Hitachi's Kuwahara Yutaka.

126. Aiso, pp. 8–9; Hilton, pp. 10–11.

127. *Business Week,* 13 February 1984, p. 110A.

128. Ibid.

129. *Electronics,* 19 November 1984, pp. 29–30.

130. Ibid., 24 April 1985, pp. 24–25.

131. Stephen Kreider Yoder, "Japan Proposal May Boost Participation by U.S. Firms in Telecommunications," *The Wall Street Journal,* 13 September 1988, p. 22.

132. The United States and Japan reached an understanding in 1987 (in the Market Oriented Sector Specific [MOSS] talks) that both countries would have free access for firms entering the international VAN services market—that firms would be able to use their own protocols—the rules that determine how computers interconnect within the network. Subsequently, the MPT stated that companies offering such services would have to replace their proprietary protocols with standard ones recommended by the Consultative Committee of International Telephone and Telegraph, an international standard-setting body. In a letter in May 1988, William Verity, U.S. Secretary of Commerce, complained to Nakayama Masaaki, the Minister of Post and Telecommunications, that "this position ignores the extensive scientific and financial resources invested by telecommunications firms in developing proprietary protocols, and it would present a significant barrier to the ability of U.S. firms to offer competitive services to the Japanese market." In mid-September 1988, bowing to trade pressure, the MPT made a concession: It will grant licenses to a company that uses a unique protocol if the company's business is willing to provide the technology to connect with other, incompatible networks and if the company promises to divulge certain technical details. (*The Wall Street Journal,* 13 September 1988, p. 22.)

133. Cited in Leslie Helm, "A New Path Onto NTT's Turf for U.S. Giants," *Business Week,* 5 March 1984, p. 45.

134. *Electronics,* 10 June 1985, pp. 30–31. Sigma stands for Software Industrialized Generator and Maintenance Aids *(Sofutowea Seisan Kōgyōka Shisutemu no Kōchiku, Unei).*

135. *Electronics Week,* 10 June 1985, p. 30.

136. Ibid., p. 31.

137. Aiso, p. 11.

138. Interview with Yoshioka Tadashi.

139. *JECC Kompyūtā Nōto,* 1985, p. 89; IDC Report on Sigma Project. Calculated at 170 yen to the dollar.

140. Interview with Tsuji Junji, 7 December 1987, and information from his book, *Jōhōshori Sangyōkai,* pp. 129–130.

141. These tools include multi-task software for word processing and networking. There will also be tools designed for specific applications such as processing office work, doing scientific calculations, and for systems control. (IDC Japan Report, 1988.)

142. Ibid.

143. Interview with Kuwahara Yutaka.

144. Shimoda Hirotsugu, *Kasumigaseki no Haiteku Kokka Senryaku,* p. 175. (Kasumigaseki is the part of Tōkyō where all of the ministries' offices are located.)

145. Interview with Yamamoto Kinko, 3 December 1987.

146. IDC Japan Report, 1988.

147. Ibid.

148. *The Wall Street Journal,* 11 April 1988, p. 2.

149. TRON stands for Real Time Operating-System Nucleus.

150. *The Japan Economic Journal,* 8 November 1986.

151. Interview with Toda Iwao, who heads the NTT's research lab.

152. Interview with Yamamoto Kinko, 3 December 1987.

153. Ibid. This is analagous to an American calling an Apple or IBM standard a "Stars-and-Stripes" standard.

154. The standard would be available in 5 types: I-TRON, for use in industry, allows the operator to switch among many different tasks operating at high speeds; B-TRON establishes a common interface among personal computers, word processors, and work stations; C-TRON establishes an interface that the NTT has already agreed to use in its integrated-service digital-network computer, which is expected to hit the market in the 1990s; M(acro)-TRON, aimed at coordinating and controlling data processing networks; and the TRON chip, a 32-bit microprocessing unit. (IDC Japan Report, 1988.)

155. Ibid.

156. *The Japan Times,* 18 November 1987, p. 20.

157. IDC Japan Report, 1988.
158. Interview with Kuwahara Yutaka, a Hitachi manager.
159. Interview with Toda Iwao.
160. Interview with Inose Hiroshi, 7 December 1987.
161. *Electronics,* 27 March 1980, p. 122.
162. Interview of Amaya Naohiro, 7 December 1987.
163. Interview with Maeda Norihiko, 30 November 1987.
164. Interview with Kuwahara Yutaka.
165. Interview with Tajiri Yasushi.
166. Interview with Kuwahara Yutaka.
167. Interview with Aiso Hideo.

6. COOPERATION AND COMPETITION FOR COMPETITIVE ADVANTAGE

1. *JECC Kompyūtā Nōto,* 1987, p. 30. An exchange rate of 200 yen to the dollar was used.
2. *JECC Kompyūtā Nōto,* 1987, pp. 30–31. Exchange rate of 330 yen to the dollar used for 1972 data, 200 yen for 1980 data.
3. Fujitsu's March 1961 financial statement.
4. Fujitsu accounts for 25% of the machines that were rented through JECC during this period. Thus, we assume that they would have had to borrow about 25% as much as JECC did. Fujitsu's share is calculated using data from: Dokusen Bunseki Kenkyūkai, *Nihon no Dokusen Kigyō,* I, 292; *Denshi Kōgyō Nenkan,* 1979, p. 447; and *JECC Kompyūtā Nōto,* 1979, p. 377. 35.1 billion yen is 25% of 140.42 billion yen, the amount JECC borrowed from 1961 to 1969. (See Table 7.)
5. The computer companies invested a total of 103.9 billion yen of their own funds during this period. Since Fujitsu accounted for 25% of the machines that went through JECC, we assume that it accounted for approximately 25% of the investment in the industry, or about 26 billion yen. If Fujitsu had had to invest 35.1 billion yen in its own computer-rental system, it would have had to more than double its estimated investment in the industry of 26 billion yen.
6. Fujitsu's debt-equity ratio in 1969 was 4.11. (Fujitsu's financial statement.)
7. *Denshi Kōgyō Nenkan,* 1962, pp. 154–158.
8. See Table 1.
9. *Computer White Paper,* 1976, p. 7.
10. See Appendix A.
11. Interview with Takeuchi Hiroshi of the LTCB.
12. Wheeler, Janow, and Pepper, p. 157.
13. *Denshi Kōgyō 30 Nenshi,* p. 108.
14. Ibid., p. 82.

15. See Appendixes D and E.
16. Ibid.
17. Appendixes F and G.
18. More specifically, in small computers, while IBM produced and sold 11,150 of its 360-30 machines, Fujitsu sold only 946 of its FACOM-230-25, NEC sold 351 of its NEAC-2200/200, and Hitachi sold 178 of its HITAC-8210. For middle-sized computers, the numbers are even more dramatic. IBM produced 5,200 of its 360-40; Fujitsu produced 157 of its FACOM-230-35; NEC produced 101 of its NEAC-2200/500, and Hitachi 174 of its HITAC-8400. Thus, in small machines, Hitachi's production scale was 1.4% that of IBM's, NEC's 3.1%, and Fujitsu's 8.5%. In medium-sized computers, Hitachi's was 3.34%, NEC's 1.94 % and Fujitsu's 3.02%. (*Denshi Kōgyō Nenkan,* 1974, p. 419.)
19. See Appendix G.
20. *The Economist,* 5 April 1980, p. 75.
21. *The Oriental Economist,* January 1980, p. 29.
22. Interview with Maeda Norihiko, 30 November 1987.
23. *Electronics,* 13 January 1982, p. 71.
24. Interview with Toda Iwao.
25. *The Oriental Economist,* January 1980, p. 29.
26. Interview with Shimizu Sakae.
27. Interview with Kuwahara Yutaka.
28. For discussions of the limited participation of Japanese citizens in government policymaking and their willingness to let the bureaucracy make decisions in the national interest, see: Chalmers Johnson, *MITI and the Japanese Miracle,* pp. 315–317; Chalmers Johnson, "Who Governs? An Essay on Official Bureaucracy"; T.J. Pempel, "Japanese Foreign Economic Policy," pp. 146–149; and T.J. Pempel, *Policy and Politics in Japan, Creative Conservatism,* pp. 1–45.
29. Interview with Tajiri Yasushi of Fujitsu.
30. Interview with Shimizu Sakae.
31. Interview with Tajiri Yasushi and Oketani Kisaburō of Fujitsu, and Kuwahara Yutaka and Sakai Yoshio of Hitachi.
32. Interview with Kuwahara Yutaka.

Appendixes

Appendix A Government Financial Assistance, 1961–1969 (unit: billion yen, million dollars; ¥360 = $1)

	1961	1962	1963	1964	1965	1966	1967	1968	1969	Total Yen	Total Dollar
SUBSIDIES											
1. Mining Subsidies[1]	.042	.096	.142	.184	.119	.120	.087	.243	.193	1.23	3.42
2. 1966 Project	—	—	—	—	—	.370	1.19	2.030	2.780	6.37	17.70
3. DIPS-1 Project	—	—	—	—	—	—	—	7.500	7.500	15.00	41.67
4. Interest Savings[2]	.012	.036	.081	.153	.308	.133	.312	.402	.592	2.03	5.64
5. Subsidy due to JECC Advance[3]	.070	.180	.270	.510	.850	.810	.950	2.240	2.210	8.10	22.50
TAX BENEFITS[4]											
1. Computer Buyback Reserve	—	—	—	—	—	—	—	1.40	2.30	3.70	10.28
2. Special Depreciation for Equipment Used in Experimental R&D	2.50 (.25)	2.50 (.25)	2.50 (.25)	6.30 (.63)	4.50 (.45)	1.30 (.13)	8.70 (.87)	11.00 (1.10)	12.20 (1.20)	51.50 (5.13)	143.06 (14.30)[5]
3. Special Depreciation for Equipment Important to Rationalization	8.00 (.80)	7.00 (.70)	7.50 (.75)	6.20 (.62)	5.20 (.52)	3.60 (.36)	4.90 (.49)	6.80 (.68)	9.10 (.91)	58.30 (5.83)	162.00 (16.20)[5]
TOTAL SUBSIDIES AND TAX BENEFITS:										¥47.39	$131.71

Appendix A (cont.)

	1961	1962	1963	1964	1965	1966	1967	1968	1969	Total Yen	Total Dollar
LOANS											
1. To JECC from JDB[3]	0.40	0.80	1.50	2.50	5.50	8.00	6.00	8.00	18.00	50.70	$140.83
2. Upfront Cash Loan through JECC[3]	0.80	2.02	3.12	5.82	9.78	9.63	11.61	27.28	26.95	97.01	269.47
TOTAL LOANS:										147.71	410.3
TOTAL LOANS, SUBSIDIES AND TAX BENEFITS:										¥195.10	$542.01

Sources: Denshi Kōgyō Nenkan; JECC Kompyūtā Nōto; Kompyūtā Hakusho; Tax data from Zeisei Cbōsa Kai, 1970, p. 31.

Notes: [1] Includes FONTAC Project.

[2] Interest Savings from low-interest JDB loans to JECC; see Appendix C for calculations.

[3] See Chapter 3 for calculations.

[4] Reduction in government revenue due to tax measures.

[5] Assumed conservatively that 10% went to the computer industry.

There are slight discrepancies due to rounding.

Appendix B Private-Sector Investment in Computer-Related R&D and Plant and Equipment, 1961–1969
(Unit: billion yen, million dollars) (¥360 = $1)

	1961	1962	1963	1964	1965	1966	1967	1968	1969	Total Yen	Total Dollars
1. Computer Industry Investment in Plant and Equipment	1.98	1.70	2.40	3.00	3.50	3.80	5.90	8.60	10.90	41.78	116.06
2. Computer Industry Investment in R&D	—	—	11.20[1]	—	—	6.30	8.40	12.20	24.00[2]	62.10	172.50
TOTAL INVESTMENT BY THE PRIVATE SECTOR:	103.9 billion yen									103.9	288.60

SUBSIDIES AND TAX BENEFITS AS PERCENT OF INVESTMENT: 45.61%

LOANS, SUBSIDIES, AND TAX BENEFITS AS PERCENT OF INVESTMENT: 187.78%

Sources: MITI, Shuyō Sangyō no Setsubi Tōshi Keikaku; 1961–1965 data from Denshi Kōgyō 30 Nenshi, p. 82. 1966–1968 data from Nihon Denshi Kōgyō Shinkō Kyōkai, Waga Kuni Denshikeisanki Sangyō no Mondai Ten to Sōno Taisaku p. 72.

Notes:

1. 11.2 billion yen for 1961–1965.

2. Data not available; I estimate at 24 billion.

There are slight discrepancies due to rounding.

Appendix C Estimated Interest Expense on Alternative Private
Financing of Computer Rentals, 1961–1981
(unit: billion yen)

I. *Interest Paid on JDB Loans under the JECC System*

	JDB	Payments on Loans	Balance	JDB i [1] Rate (%)	Total i Paid
1961	.4	0	.4	6.50	.026
1962	.8	0	1.200	6.50	.078
1963	1.5	0	2.700	6.50	.176
1964	2.5	.200	5.000	6.50	.325
1965	5.5	.462	10.038	6.50	.652
1966	8.0	2.204	15.834	8.40	1.330
1967	6.0	1.024	20.810	7.50	1.561
1968	8.0	2.964	25.846	7.50	1.938
1969	18.0	8.206	35.640	7.50	2.673
1970	23.0	8.740	49.900	7.50	3.743
1971	41.0	12.260	78.640	7.50	5.898
1972	20.0	18.330	80.310	7.50	6.023
1973	11.5	10.930	80.880	7.50	6.066
1974	32.5	22.330	91.050	7.50	6.829
1975	46.0	16.410	120.640	7.50	9.048
1976	43.0	27.400	136.240	7.50	10.218
1977	35.5	30.000*	141.740	7.50	10.631
1978	53.5	59.160*	136.080	6.05	8.233
1979	45.0	37.680	143.400	6.05	8.676
1980	46.0	46.020	143.380	7.10	10.180
1981	44.0	29.780	157.600	7.50	11.82
TOTAL	491.7 [2]				106.124 [3]

II. *Estimated Interest Expense If JDB Loans had to be Gotten From Private Sources*

Year	Would Have Had to Borrow[4]	Payments	Balance	Prime i Rate (%)	i Due	Money in Compensating Balance (Cumulative)	i on Compensating Balance[5]	Total i Would Have Paid[6]
1961	.500	0	.500	8.7	.044	.100	.006	.038
1962	1.000	0	1.500	8.7	.131	.300	.017	.114
1963	1.875	0	3.375	8.7	.294	.675	.037	.257
1964	3.125	.200	6.300	8.7	.548	1.300	.072	.478
1965	6.875	.462	12.713	8.7	1.106	2.675	.147	.960
1966	10.000	2.204	20.509	8.4	1.723	4.675	.257	1.463
1967	7.500	1.024	26.985	8.2	2.213	6.175	.340	1.873
1968	10.000	2.964	34.021	8.2	2.79	8.175	.450	2.340
1969	22.500	8.206	48.315	8.2	3.962	12.675	.697	3.265
1970	28.750	8.740	68.325	8.5	5.807	18.425	1.013	4.794
1971	51.250	12.260	107.315	8.2	8.800	28.675	1.649	7.151
1972	25.000	18.330	113.985	8.0	9.119	33.675	1.936	7.183
1973	14.380	10.930	117.435	8.3	9.747	36.555	2.285	7.462
1974	40.630	22.330	135.735	9.4	12.761	44.685	3.240	9.521
1975	57.500	16.410	176.825	9.7	17.152	56.185	4.354	12.798
1976	53.750	27.400	203.175	9.2	18.692	66.935	4.518	14.174
1977	44.400	30.000*	217.575	8.2	17.841	75.835	4.361	13.480
1978	66.900	59.160*	225.315	7.1	15.997	89.235	4.016	11.981
1979	56.300	37.680	243.935	7.7	18.783	100.535	5.278	13.505
1980	57.500	46.020	255.415	9.5	24.264	112.035	7.842	16.422
1981	55.000	29.780	280.635	8.5	23.851	123.035	7.689	16.162
Total	614.740[7]							145.421[8]

III. Implicit Subsidy Resulting from Low-Interest JDB Loans
(unit: billion yen)

	Total Interest Would Have Paid (A)	Total Interest Paid (B)	Implicit Subsidy (A–B)
1961	.038	.026	.012
1962	.114	.078	.036
1963	.257	.176	.081
1964	.478	.325	.153
1965	.960	.652	.308
1966	1.463	1.330	.133
1967	1.873	1.561	.312
1968	2.340	1.938	.402
1969	3.265	2.673	.592
1970	4.794	3.743	1.051
1971	7.151	5.898	1.253
1972	7.183	6.023	1.160
1973	7.462	6.066	1.396
1974	9.521	6.829	2.692
1975	12.798	9.048	3.750
1976	14.174	10.218	3.956
1977	13.480	10.631	2.849
1978	11.981	8.233	3.748
1979	13.505	8.676	4.829
1980	16.422	10.180	6.242
1981	16.162	11.820	4.342
Total	145.421	106.124	39.297[9]

Sources: JECC *Kompyūtā Nōto;* JECC *10 Nenshi;* JECC annual financial reports. Prime rate and interest rate on money in compensating balance are from Bank of Japan, *Economic Statistics Annual.*
Notes
* data not available, estimated.
1. i = interest (rate).
2. $1.97 billion. 1961–1970 calculated at 360 yen to the dollar, 1971–1976 at 300, and 1977–1981 at 200 yen to the dollar.
3. $429.37 million using same exchange rates as in note 2.
4. Private banks required a 20% compensating balance on loans, whereas JDB did not. Thus, to get a $100 loan from a private bank, a firm had to borrow $125.00 and put 20%—$25.00—in a deposit at the bank. In effect, this requirement pushes up the interest rate.
5. Interest on the compensating balance is estimated by using a one year time deposit interest rate. From 1961–1970 it was 5.5%; from 1971–72: 5.75%; 1973: 6.25%; 1974: 7.25%; 1975: 7.75%; 1976: 6.75%; 1977: 5.75%; 1978: 4.5%; 1979: 5.25%; 1980: 7%; 1981: 6.25%.
6. "Total interest would have paid" equals: interest due minus interest on compensating balance.
7. $2.5 billion using exchange rates as in note 2.
8. $595.33 million using exchange rates as in note 2.
9. $165.96 million using exchange rates as in note 2.
Some discrepancies may occur due to rounding.

Appendix D Government Financial Assistance, 1970–1975 (unit: billion yen)

	1970	1971	1972	1973	1974	1975	Total ($1 = 330 yen) Billion Yen	Total ($1 = 330 yen) Million Dollars
I. SUBSIDIES								
1. 1966 Project	2.300	3.330					5.630	$ 17.061
2. DIPS—1 Project	7.500	7.500					15.000	$ 45.455
3. DIPS—11 Project				1.670	1.670	1.660	5.000	$ 15.152
4. Pattern Information Processing Recognition Project		0.200	1.070	1.630	2.180	3.370	8.450	$ 25.606
5. New Series Project (including subsidies for peripheral equipment and LSIs)			5.210	21.860	18.450	13.380	58.900	$178.485
6. Government Money Given to Set Up the I.P.A.	0.200	0.400	0.450				1.050	$ 3.182
7. Annual Subsidy to the I.P.A. (for software development consignment)	0.300	0.400	0.370	0.790	1.000	1.320	4.180	$ 12.667

Appendix D (cont.)

	1970	1971	1972	1973	1974	1975	Total ($1 = 330 yen) Billion Yen	Total ($1 = 330 yen) Million Dollars
I. SUBSIDIES								
8. Subsidies for R&D on Important Technologies (formerly called "Mining" Subsidies [computer-related])	0.570	0.630	0.570	0.650	0.480	0.220	3.120	$ 9.455
9. NTT's VLSI Project						6.670	6.670	$ 20.212
10. Subsidy due to JECC Advance	1.670	.310	.060	.730	2.110	1.340	6.220	$ 18.848
11. Interest Savings Because of JDB Low-Interest Loans to JECC	1.051	1.253	1.160	1.396	2.692	3.750	11.302	$ 34.25
12. Development of a Medical Information System				0.110[1]	0.200	0.280	0.590	$ 1.788
				0[2]	0.200	0.130	0.330	1.00
13. Development of a Video Information System			.030[1]	0.210	0.540	0.750	1.530	$ 4.636
14. Software Module Project			.072[2]	0.280	0.730	1.250	2.330	7.061
15. Development of Automobile Traffic Control System				0.600	1.200	1.200	3.000	$ 9.091
				0.200	0.840	2.010	3.050	$ 9.242

16.	Subsidies for Putting Traded-In Computers into Chamber of Commerce Offices					0.700	0.900	1.600	$ 4.848
17.	Development of Trade Information System						0.060	0.060	$ 0.182
18.	Special Research on Technology related to Information Processing (ETL Lab in AIST)		0.710	0.810	0.790	0.910	1.000	4.220	$ 12.788
19.	Development of Resource Recovery System				0.150	0.400	0.750	1.300	$ 3.939
20.	Information-Processing Technicians Test	0.040	0.033	0.033	0.034	0.038	0.044	0.222	$ 0.673
21.	Software Program Survey Register	.002	.003	.003	.004	.004	.004	.020	$ 0.061
22.	Surveys on the Current and Future Direction of Information Processing	.001	.002	.007	.010	.011	.015	.046	$ 0.139
23.	Survey on "Systemization"	.006	.008	.004	.004	.004	.006	.030	$ 0.091
24.	Survey on Computer Purchases and Trade-Ins				.004	.005	.005	.014	$ 0.042
25.	Survey on Legal Protection of Software		.001	.001	.001	.001	.001	.005	$ 0.015
26.	Survey on the Formation of Information Networks	.004	.004	.002	.002	.002	.002	.012	$ 0.036

Appendix D (cont.)

	1970	1971	1972	1973	1974	1975	Total ($1 = 330 yen)	
							Billion Yen	Million Dollars
I. SUBSIDIES								
27. Register of Information-Processing Service Firms			.001	.001	.001	.001	0.004	$ 0.012
28. Promotion of Standardization		.006	.011	.013	.007	Ø	.037	$ 0.112
29. Annual Week for Promoting Informationalization			.001	.001	.001	.001	.004	$ 0.012
30. Promotion of Information Processing in the Government	.530	.690	.810	1.120	1.620	2.270	7.040	$ 21.333
31. Survey of the Trends in Technology Development in the Electronics Industry	.001	.011	.009	.009	.010	Ø	0.040	0.121
32. Subsidies for Japan Patent Information Center		.033	.033	.033	.033	.04	0.172	0.521
TOTAL SUBSIDIES:							151.178	$458.116

II. TAX BENEFITS[3]

1. Computer Buyback Reserve	5.70	8.20	10.30	5.60	3.00	5.00	37.80	$114.545
2. Special Depreciation for Equipment used in Experimental R&D	13.00	15.80	8.80	19.80	21.00	21.00	99.40	301.212
( ) Assuming 10% for Computer Industry	(1.30)	(1.58)	(.88)	(1.98)	(2.10)	(2.10)	(9.94)	(30.121)
3. Special Depreciation for Equipment Important to Rationalization	9.70	15.40	31.20	12.50	17.00	12.00	97.80	296.364
( ) Assuming 10% for Computers	(.97)	(1.54)	(3.12)	(1.25)	(1.70)	(1.20)	(9.78)	(29.636)
TOTAL ESTIMATED TAX BENEFITS:							57.52	174.302
TOTAL ESTIMATED SUBSIDIES AND TAX BENEFITS:							208.698	$632.418

III. LOANS

1. To JECC from JDB	23.00	41.00	20.00	11.50	32.50	46.00	174.00	527.273
2. JDB Loans based on 1971 Law (for computers)	1.47	1.21	0.29	1.58	1.71	0.60	6.86	20.788
3. Loans from IBJ, LTCB, JREB, for Promotion of Information Processing	4.00	9.50	14.50	13.30	9.00	12.00	62.30	188.788
4. JDB Loans for Software Development	2.00	2.50	2.50	2.50	2.50	2.50	14.50	43.939

Appendix D (cont.)

	1970	1971	1972	1973	1974	1975	Total ($1 = 330 yen)	
							Billion Yen	Million Dollars

III. LOANS

	1970	1971	1972	1973	1974	1975	Billion Yen	Million Dollars
5. JDB Loans for Promotion of Domestic Technology ( ) Computers; assuming 50%	14.00 (7.00)	22.00 (11.00)	18.10 (9.05)	21.50 (10.75)	21.90 (10.95)	25.40 (12.70)	122.90 (61.45)	372.424 (186.212)
6. Up-front Cash (loan) through JECC	19.70	3.80	.80	8.80	22.40	13.80	69.30	210.00
7. JDB Loans for Consolidation of the Industry			0.68	0.86	1.98	1.13	4.65	14.091
8. JDB Loans for Structural Improvement of the Industry			0.85	1.00	2.20	1.92	5.97	18.091
9. JDB Loans for Equipment for Software Development	1.84	1.21	∅	1.70	.94	.85	6.54	19.818

10. JDB Loans for the Pro-motion of ON LINE Information Processing Systems	0.50	1.00	1.01	2.50	5.01	15.182
TOTAL LOANS:					410.580	$1,244.282 million
TOTAL SUBSIDIES, TAX BENEFITS, AND LOANS:					619.278	$1,876.600

Sources: JECC *Kompyūta Nōto;* Denshi Kōgyō Nenkan; Kompyūtā Hakusho; various issues of the monthly magazine *Kompyūtopia;* Zeisei Chōsa Kai, Zen Shiryō Shū, and Zeisei Chōsa Kai Kankei Shiryō Shū; Internal JDB and MITI documents without titles. There may be discrepancies due to rounding.

Notes

1. Top row is money directly from the government
2. Bottom row is money from bicycle-racing profits; the government controls bicycle racing to acquire funds for industry.
3. Tax Benefits are the reduction in government tax revenue due to these three tax measures.

Appendix E Private-Sector Investment in the Computer Industry, 1970–1975 (unit: billion yen)

	1970	1971	1972	1973	1974	1975	Billion Yen	Million Dollars
1. Computer Industry Investment in Plant and Equipment (Private Sector)	21.3	22.3	14.7	18.5	24.8	27.8	129.4	392.121
2. Computer Industry Investment in R&D (Private Sector)	29.7	40.2	33.0	45.1	37.7	52.8	238.5	722.727
Total Private Sector Investment:							367.9	$1,114.848

Total Direct Assistance: 208.698 billion yen ($632.418 million)

Direct Financial Assistance as Percent of Investment: 56.73%

Total Subsidies, Tax Benefits, and Loans, as Percent of Investment: 168.33%

Sources: *Shuyō Sangyō no Setsubi Tōshi Keikaku*; Sōrifu Tōkeikyoku, *Kagaku Gijutsu Kenkyū Chōsa Hōkoku*.
Note: There may be discrepancies due to rounding.

Appendix F Government Financial Assistance, 1976–1981 (unit: billion yen)

	1976	1977	1978	1979	1980	1981	Total $1 = 200 yen	
							Billion Yen	*Million Dollars*
1. New Series Project (including subsidies for peripheral equipment)	11.400						11.400	57.00
2. Pattern Information Processing Recognition Project	3.400	2.920	2.500	2.800	1.850	—	13.470	67.350
3. Annual Subsidy to the I.P.A. (including subsidies for software production technology development)	1.730	2.100	2.300	2.600	2.780	2.660	14.170	70.850
4. NTT's VLSI Project (first three years)	6.670	6.670					13.340	66.700
5. MITI's VLSI Project	3.500	8.640	10.100	6.900			29.140	145.700
6. Subsidies for R&D on Important Technologies (computer-related)	0.230	0.270	0.330	N.A.	N.A.	N.A.	0.830	4.150
7. Subsidy due to JECC Advance	.950	.300	-.110[1]	.57	2.870	1.930	6.510	32.550

Appendix F (cont.)

	1976	1977	1978	1979	1980	1981	Total $1 = 200 yen	
							Billion Yen	Million Dollars
8. Interest Savings because of JDB Low-Interest Loans to JECC	3.956	2.849	3.748	4.829	6.242	4.342	25.966	129.83
9. Development of a Medical Information System	0.440[2]	0.430	0.190	0.190	0.220	0.220	2.850	14.250
	0.460[2]	0.430	0.270					
10. Development of a Video Information System	0.540[2]	0.430	0.040	0.590			3.020	15.100
	0.690[2]	0.120	0.580	0.030				
11. Development of Automobile Traffic-Control System	2.150	1.470	0.580	0.150	∅	∅	4.350	21.750
12. Subsidy for Putting Traded-In Computers into Chamber of Commerce Offices	0.600	0.090	0.100	0.130	0.190	N.A.	1.110	5.550
13. Development of Trade Information System	0.100	0.042	0.033	0.025	0.034	—	0.234	1.170
14. Special Research on Technology related to Information Processing (ETL in AIST)	N.A.	0.610	0.710	0.650	0.690	0.710	3.370	16.85

15. Development of Resource Recovery Systems	0.944	2.100	2.630	0.880	—	—	6.554	32.770
16. Information Processing Technicians Test	0.470	0.520	0.570	0.620	0.680	0.840	3.700	18.500
17. Software Program Survey Register	0.003	0.002	0.002	0.002	0.002	0.002	0.013	0.065
18. Survey on the Current Situation in Information Processing	0.016	0.017	0.016	0.016	0.016	0.014	0.095	0.475
19. Survey on Computer Purchases and Trade-Ins	0.004	0.005	0.005	0.005	0.005	0.005	0.029	0.145
20. Survey on Legal Protection of Software	0.002	0.006	0.006	0.006	0.006	0.005	0.031	0.155
21. Survey on the Formation of Information Networks	0.002	0.002	0.002	—	—	—	0.006	0.030
22. Register of Information Processing Service Firms	0.001	0.001	0.001	0.001	0.001	0.001	0.006	0.030
23. Optoelectronics Project	—	—	—	0.051	0.930	2.420	3.401	17.005
24. Super Computer Project	—	—	—	—	—	0.030	0.030	0.150
25. Basic Technologies for Next Generation Industries	—	—	—	—	—	2.710	2.710	13.550
26. Basic Technologies for Next Generation Computers	—	—	—	1.700	5.790	6.200	13.690	68.450
27. Promotion of Information Processing in the Government	2.950	3.310	N.A.	N.A.	N.A.	N.A.	6.260	31.300
TOTAL SUBSIDIES:			N.A.	N.A.	N.A.	N.A.	166.285	$831.425

Appendix F (cont.)

	1976	1977	1978	1979	1980	1981	Total $1 = 200 yen	
							Billion Yen	Million Dollars

II. TAX BENEFITS

	1976	1977	1978	1979	1980	1981	Billion Yen	Million Dollars
1. Computer Buyback Reserve	5.0[3] 2.10[4]	3.00 1.10	∅	3.0	2.0	2.0	18.2	91.000
2. Special Depreciation for Equipment Important to Rationalization ( ) assuming 10% for computers	11.0[5] 4.2[6] (1.10)(.42)	9.00 (0.90) 3.40 (0.34)	15.00 (1.50)	14.00 (1.40)	16.00 (1.60)	16.00 (1.60)	88.60 (8.86)	443.000 (44.30)
3. Special Depreciation for Equipment used in Experimental R&D ( ) assuming 10% for computers	14.00 (1.40)	17.00 (1.70)	15.00 (1.50)	21.00 (2.10)	24.00 (2.40)	27.00 (2.70)	118.00 (11.80)	590.000 (59.00)
TOTAL ESTIMATED TAX BENEFITS:							38.86	$194.30
TOTAL ESTIMATED SUBSIDIES AND TAX BENEFITS:							205.145	$1,025.725

III. LOANS

	1976	1977	1978	1979	1980	1981	Billion Yen	Million Dollars
1. JDB Loans for JECC	43.00	35.50	53.50	45.00	46.00	44.00	267.00	1,335.000
2. Loans from IBJ, LTCB, JREB for Promotion of Information Processing	13.00	11.00	8.00	7.00	5.00	5.00	49.00	245.000

3. JDB Loans Based on 1971 and 1978 Laws (assume 40% for computers)	4.60 (1.84)	3.80 (1.52)	2.10 (0.84)	7.00 (2.80)	12.00 (4.80)	9.80 (3.92)	39.30 (15.72)	196.50 (78.60)
4. Up-Front Cash (loan) through JECC	10.30	3.60	-1.6^7	7.4	30.20	22.70	72.60	363.00
5. JDB Loans for Promotion of Domestic Technology (assuming 50% for computers)	28.00 (14.00)	24.70 (12.35)	65.90 (33.00)	51.20 (25.60)	26.50 (13.25)	44.00 (22.00)	240.30 (120.20)	1,201.50 (601.0)
6. JDB Loans for Structural Improvement and Software Development	4.00	16.50	2.50	5.00	2.00	2.00	32.00	160.00
TOTAL LOANS:							556.52	761.765
TOTAL SUBSIDIES, TAX BENEFITS AND LOANS:							2,782.60	3,808.325

Sources: JECC *Kompyūtā Nōto;* *Denshi Kōgyō Nenkan;* *Kompūtā Hakusho;* various issues of the monthly magazine *Kompyūtopia;* internal JDB and MITI documents without titles; *Zeisei Chōsa Kai,* *Zen Shiryō Shū;* and *Zeisei Chōsa Kai Kankei Shiryō Shū.*

Notes:

1. The JECC advance is the difference between the cash flow under JECC and the hypothetical cash flow under the firms' own rental systems. In 1978 and 1979, due to heavy computer trade-ins and sluggish new rentals, the cash flow under JECC was less than the hypothetical cash flow. The subsidy—the amount the firms would have had to pay in interest if they had borrowed the up-front cash (advance) at the prime rate—is thus negative in that year.

2. Top row is money directly from the government
   Bottom row is money from bicycle-racing profits; the government controls bicycle racing to receive funds for industry.

3. Decrease in National Tax Revenues due to the Computer Buyback Reserve.

4. Decrease in Local Tax Revenues due to the Computer Buyback Reserve.

5. Left column: Decrease in National Tax Revenues.

6. Right column: Decrease in Local Tax Revenues.

7. See explanation of JECC advance (up-front cash) in Note 1.
   Some discrepancies may occur due to rounding.

Appendix G Private-Sector Investment in the Computer Industry, 1976–1981 (unit: billion yen)

	1976	1977	1978	1979	1980	1981	Total	
							Billion Yen	Million Dollars
1. Computer Industry Investment in Plant and Equipment (Private Sector)	22.7	23.4	19.0	20.4	23.5	44.6	153.6	768.0
2. Computer Industry Investment in R&D (Private Sector)	65.3	81.9	88.5	118.0	140.8	168.6	663.1	3,315.5
							816.7	4,083.5

TOTAL INVESTMENT BY THE PRIVATE SECTOR:

TOTAL DIRECT FINANCIAL ASSISTANCE: 205.145 billion yen ($1,025.725 million)

DIRECT FINANCIAL ASSISTANCE AS PERCENT OF INVESTMENT: 25.12%

TOTAL SUBSIDIES, TAX BENEFITS, AND LOANS, AS PERCENT OF INVESTMENT: 93.2%

Sources: Shuyō Sangyō no Setsubi Tōshi Keikaku; Kagaku Gijutsu Kenkyū Chōsa Hōkoku.
Note: Some discrepancies may occur due to rounding.

Bibliography

Bibliography

Abegglen, James. "The Economic Growth of Japan," *Scientific American* 222.3:31–37 (March 1970).

——— and George Stalk, Jr. *Kaisha, The Japanese Corporation*. New York: Basic Books, 1985.

Adams, Walter. *The Structure of American Industry*. 5th ed. New York: Macmillan, 1977.

Aiso Hideo. "Overview of Japanese National Projects for Information Technology." Tōkyō: Keio University, 1976. [pamphlet]

Amaya Naohiro and Masamura Kimihiro. "Dokkinhō Kaisei Ryūzan to 'Nihonteki Keizai Fūdo' " (The failure to revise the anti-monopoly law and the "Japanese economic climate"), *Tōyōkeizai*, 19 July 1975, pp. 32–42.

Aono Tadao. *IBM no Hikari to Kage* (IBM's light and shadows). 7th ed. Tōkyō: Nihon Keizai Shimbunsha, 1979.

Atsuya Joji, Uekusa Masu, and Kinekata Kenji. "Karuteru no Tetteiteki Kenkyū" (A thorough study of cartels), *Chūō Kōron* 14.3:126–158 (autumn 1975).

Bain, Joe S. *Barriers to New Competition*. Cambridge: Harvard University Press, 1956.

Ballon, Robert. "Management Style." In *Business in Japan*, ed. Paul Norbury and Geoffrey Bownas. Boulder: Westview Press, 1980.

Bank of Japan. *Economic Statistics Annual*. Tokyo: Research and Statistics Department of the Bank of Japan.

Bonnell, Victoria E. "The Uses of Theory, Concepts and Comparison in Historical Sociology," *Comparative Studies in Society and History* (Cambridge University Press) 22.2:156–173 (April 1980).

Brock, Gerald W. *The U.S. Computer Industry, A Study of Market Power*. Cambridge: Ballinger, 1975.

Caves, Richard E. "Industrial Organization, Corporate Strategy and Structure," *Journal of Economic Literature* 18:64–92 (March 1980).

———— and Masu Vekusa. "Industrial Organization." In *Asia's New Giant,* ed. Hugh Patrick and Henry Rosovsky. Washington: The Brookings Institution, 1976.

————. *Industrial Organization in Japan.* Washington: The Brookings Institution, 1976.

Clark, Rodney. *The Japanese Company.* New Haven and London: Yale University Press, 1979.

Daiwa Shōken Chōsabu. "Jōhō Sangyō" (Information industries), *Daiwa Tōshi Shiryō* 410:34–83 (August 1969).

Denison, Edward F. and William K. Chung, "Economic Growth and its Sources." In *Asia's New Giant,* ed. Hugh Patrick and Henry Rosovsky. Washington: The Brookings Institution, 1976.

Denshi Kōgyō Nenkan (Electronics industry yearbook). Tōkyō: Dempa Shimbun.

Denshi Shijō Yōran (Survey of the computer market). Tōkyō: Kagaku Shimbun, annual.

Dokusen Bunseki Kenkyūkai, ed. *Nihon no Dokusen Kigyō* (Japan's monopolistic enterprises). Vol. I. Tōkyō: Shin Nihon Shuppansha, 1969.

————. "Nihon IBM" (IBM Japan). In *Nihon no Dokusen Kigyo* (Japan's monopolisitic enterprises), Vol. V. Tōkyō: Shin Nihon Shuppansha, 1971.

————. "Nihon Denshin Denwa Kōsha" (NTT). In *Nihon no Kōkigyō* (Japan's public companies). Tōkyō: Shin Nihon Shuppansha, 1973.

Dore, Ronald. *Flexible Rigidities, Industrial Policy and Structural Adjustment in the Japanese Economy 1970–80.* Stanford: Stanford University Press, 1986.

Ekonomisuto Editorial Board, ed. *Sengo Sangyō Shi e no Shōgen* (Interviews towards a history of postwar industry). Vols. I, II, and V. Tōkyō: Mainichi Shimbunsha, 1977.

Feigenbaum, Edward A. and Pamela McCorduck. *The Fifth Generation: Artificial Intelligence and Japan's Computer Challenge to the World.* New York: Signet Books, 1984.

Fisher, Franklin M., John J. McGowan, and Joen E. Greenwood. *Folded, Spindled, and Mutilated, Economic Analysis and U.S. vs. IBM.* Cambridge: MIT Press, 1983.

Fisher, Franklin M., James W. McKie, and Richard B. Mancke. *IBM and the U.S. Data Processing Industry, an Economic History.* New York: Praeger, 1983.

Fujitsu, Ltd. *Fujitsu Shashi* (A history of Fujitsu). Vols. I and II. Tōkyō: Joban Shoin, 1977.

Fujitsu no Gaikyō (Fujitsu's outlook). Tōkyō: Fujitsu, Ltd. 1987.

Galbraith, John Kenneth. *American Capitalism: The Concept of Countervailing Power.* Boston: Houghton Mifflin, 1952.

George, Alexander L. "Case Studies and Theory Development: The Method of Structured, Focused Comparison." In *Diplomacy: New Approaches in History,*

Theory, and Policy, ed. Paul Gordon Lauren. New York: Free Press, 1979.

Gresser, Julian. *High Technology and Japanese Industrial Policy: A Strategy for U.S. Policymakers.* Report for the Subcommittee on Trade of the Committee on Ways and Means, U.S. House of Representatives, 96th Congress, 2nd Session. Washington: U.S. Government Printing Office, 1 October 1980.

Hadley, Eleanor M. *Antitrust in Japan.* Princeton: Princeton University Press, 1970.

Helm, Leslie D. "The Japanese Computer Industry: A Case Study in Industrial Policy." Unpublished Masters Thesis, University of California, Berkeley, 1981.

Hilton, Barry. "Government Subsidized Computer, Software and Integrated Circuit Research and Development by Japanese Private Companies," *Scientific Bulletin,* Department of the Navy, Office of Naval Research Far East, October–December 1982.

Imai Kenichi. "Tekkō" (Steel). In his *Gendai Sangyō Soshiki* (Modern industrial organization). Tōkyō: Iwanami Shoten, 1976.

———. "Japan's Industrial Organization." In *Industry and Business in Japan,* ed. Kazuo Sato. White Plains: M.E. Sharpe, 1980.

———. "Gijutsu Kakushin kara mita Saikin no Sangyō Seisaku" (Recent industrial policy from the viewpoint of technological innovation). In *Nihon no Sangyō Seisaku* (Japan's industrial policy), eds. Komiya Ryūtarō, Okuno Masatatsu, and Suzumura Kōtarō. Tōkyō: Tōkyō Daigaku Shuppankai, 1984.

Industrial Bank of Japan. *Kōgyō Chōsa Geppō* (Industrial Bank of Japan Monthly survey). Tōkyō.

Isomura Takafumi. *Nihon gata Shijō Keizai* (Japanese-style market economy.) Tōkyō: Nihon Hyōronsha, 1982.

Itō Motoshige and Kiyono Kazuharu. "Bōeki to Chokusetsu Tōshi" (Trade and direct investment). In *Nihon no Sangyō Seisaku* (Japan's industrial policy), ed. Komiya Ryūtarō, Okuno Masatatsu, and Suzumura Kōtarō. Tōkyō: Tōkyō Daigaku Shuppankai, 1984.

Iwabuchi Akio. *Fujitsu no Chōsen—Kompyūtā Uozu Saizensen* (Fujitsu's challenge—the frontline of the computer wars). Tōkyō: Yamate Shobō, 1984.

Iwahori Y. *Hitachi no Keiei* (Hitachi's management). Tōkyō: Nihon Seihan Kabushiki Gaisha, 1978.

Japan Electronic Computer Company (JECC). *Japan Computer News.* Tōkyō, monthly newspaper.

———. *JECC 5 Nenshi* (Five-year history of JECC). Tōkyō, 1968.

———. *JECC 10 Nenshi,* (Ten-year history of JECC). Tōkyō, 1973.

———. JECC annual financial statements.

———. *EDP in Japan.* Tōkyō, annual.

———. *JECC Kompyūtā Nōto* (JECC computer notes). Tōkyō, annual.

———. *JECC Chōsa Kihō* (JECC quarterly survey). Tōkyō.

————. *Kokusan Denshikeisanki Nyūzu* (Domestic computer news). Tōkyō.

————. *Kompyūtā Jitsudo Jōkyō Chōsa* (Survey of computers currently in use). Tōkyō, annual.

Japan Information-Processing Development Center. *Computer White Paper.* Tōkyō, annual.

Johnson, Chalmers. "Who Governs? An Essay on Official Bureaucracy," *Journal of Japanese Studies* 2:1–28 (autumn 1975).

————. *Japan's Public Policy Companies.* Washington: American Enterprise for Public Policy Research, 1978.

————. "Japan Inc., Does it Exist?" Proceedings of a symposium, Kansai University of Foreign Studies, 1979.

————. *MITI And the Japanese Miracle.* Stanford: Stanford University Press, 1982.

————. ed. *The Industrial Policy Debate.* San Francisco: Institute for Contemporary Studies, 1984.

Jōhō Sangyō Shimbunsha. *Jōhō Sangyō Benran* (Information industries handbook). Tōkyō, annual.

————. *Nihon Jōhō Sangyō Nenkan* (Japan's information industries yearbook). Tōkyō, annual.

————. *Nihon Jōhō Sangyō Shimbun* (Japan information industries news).

Jōhō Shori Shinkō Jigyō Kyōkai. *IPA News,* A special edition commemorating the 15th anniversary of the establishment of the IPA. no. 13. Tōkyō, 1985.

Kaizuka Keimei. *Keizai Seisaku no Kadai* (Themes of economic policy). Tōkyō: Tōkyō Daigaku Shuppankai, 1973.

Kamien, Morton I. and Nancy L. Schwartz. "Market Structure and Innovation: A Survey," *Journal of Economic Literature* 13.1:1–37 (March 1975).

Kaplan, Eugene. *Japan: The Government-Business Relationship.* Washington: U.S. Department of Commerce, 1972.

Kashiwabara Hisashi. *IBM o Furueagaraseta Otoko, Ikeda Toshio to Fujitsu Yarōtachi* (The men who made IBM tremble, Ikeda Toshio and the Fujitsu fellows). Tōkyō: Kanki Shuppan, 1986.

Katzenstein, Peter, ed. *Between Power and Plenty.* Madison: The University of Wisconsin Press, 1978.

Kobayashi Taiyū. *Tomokaku Yatte Miro* (At any rate, try and do it!). Tōkyō: Tōyōkeizai Shimpōsha, 1983.

Kodama, Fumio. "A Framework of Retrospective Analysis of Industrial Policy." Institute for Policy Research Report no. 78-2, Saitama University, Graduate School of Policy Science. July 1978.

Komiya Ryūtarō, Okuno Masatatsu, and Suzumura Kōtarō, eds. *Nihon no Sangyō Seisaku* (Japan's industrial policy). Tōkyō: Tōkyō Daigaku Shuppankai, 1984.

Kompyūtopia (Computopia), Tōkyō: Kompyūtā Eijisha, monthly.

Kōsai Yutaka. " 'Nihon Kabushiki Gaisha Ron' no Tasogare" (The dusk of the "Japan Inc. theory"), *Tōyōkeizai* 57:56–63 10 July 1981.

————. "Fukkōki" (The period of [postwar] reconstruction). In *Nihon no Sangyō Seisaku* (Japan's industrial policy), ed. Komiya Ryūtarō, Okuno Masatatsu, and Suzumura Kōtarō. Tōkyō: Tōkyō Daigaku Shuppankai, 1984.

Kōsei Torihiki Iinkai Jimukyoku, eds. *Shuyō Sangyō ni okeru Chikuseki Seisan Shūchūdo to Hafindaru Shisū no Suii* (Changes in accumulated concentration and the Herfindahl index in major industries). Tōkyō: Kōsei Torihiki Kyōkai, annual.

Krugman, Paul, ed. *Strategic Trade Policy and the New International Economics.* Cambridge, MIT Press, 1986.

Kurihara Shōhei. *Kompyūta* (Computers). Tōkyō: Nihon Keizai Shimbunsha, 1985.

Lincoln, Edward J. *Japan's Industrial Policies.* Washington: Japan Economic Institute of America, 1984.

Lindblom, Charles E. *Politics and Markets.* New York: Basic Books, 1977.

Lynn, Leonard. *How Japan Innovates: A Comparison with the U.S. in the Case of Oxygen Steelmaking.* Boulder: Westview Press, 1982.

Magaziner, Ira C. and Thomas M. Hout. *Japanese Industrial Policy.* Policy papers in international affairs, no. 15. Berkeley: Institute of International Studies, 1980.

Magaziner, Ira C. and Robert B. Reich. *Minding America's Business.* New York: Vintage Books, 1982.

Markham, Jesse W. "Market Structure, Business Conduct, and Innovation," *American Economic Review* 55.22 (May 1965).

Matsuo Hiroshi. *Daitanna Chōsen, Fujitsu no Monogatari* (The Fujitsu story, a bold challenge). Tōkyō: Aoba Shuppan, 1978.

————. *IBM Ōkoku o Obiyakasu Fujitsu* (Fujitsu, threatening the IBM monarchy). Tōkyō: Asahi Sonorama, 1980.

McCraw, Thomas K. "Regulation in America: A Review Article," *Business History Review* 49.2:159–183 (summer 1975).

Minamisawa Noburō. *Nihon Kompyūtā Hatten Shi* (The history of the development of Japanese computers). Tōkyō: Nihon Keizai Shimbunsha, 1978.

Ministry of Finance. *Zeisei Chōsa Kai* (Tax-system survey committee). Zeisei Chōsa Kai Kihon Mondai Koiinkai. Tōkyō, 1970.

————. *Zeisei Chōsa Kai Kankei Shiryō Shū* (Collection of documents related to the tax-system survey committee). Tōkyō: Zeisei Chōsa Kai, annual.

————. *Zeisei Chōsa Kai, Zen Shiryō Shū* (Tax-system survey committee, collection of complete documents). Tōkyō: Gendai Burein, annual.

————. *Zaisei Kinyū Tōkei Geppō* (Monthly fiscal and monetary statistics.) Tōkyō.

————. Ōkura Shō Shukeikyoku Chōsaka, eds. *Zaisei Tōkei* (Financial statistics). Tōkyō, annual.

Ministry of International Trade and Industry (MITI) Chōsa Kai. *Genkō Yunyū Seido Ichiran* (A summary of the current import system). Tōkyō, annual.

Ministry of International Trade and Industry (MITI), Kōgyō Gijutsuin (AIST). *Ōgata Purojekuto ni yoru Chōkō Seinō Denshikeisanki* (The Super High-Performance Computer Project of the large-scale project). Tōkyō: Nihon Sangyō Gijutsu Shinkō Kyōkai, July 1972.

————. Kōgyō Gijutsuin, eds. *Kenkyū Kaihatsu Josei Seido* (The system of subsidizing R&D). Tōkyō: Tsūsan Seisaku Kōhōsha, 1975 and 1983 editions.

————. *Agency of Industrial Science and Technology (AIST)*. Tōkyō, 1983.

————. Kōgyō Gijutsuin, *Kōgyō Gijutsu* (Science and Technology). Monthly magazine.

————. Kōgyō Gijutsuin (AIST), *Ōgata Purojekuto, Patān Jōhōshori Shisutemu Kenkyū Kaihatsu Seika Happyōkai Ronbunshū* (The large-scale project, a collection of papers announcing the R&D results of the pattern-information-processing system). Tōkyō: Nihon Sangyō Gijutsu Shinkō Kyōkai, 1980.

————. Kōgyō Gijutsuin (AIST), Sōmubu Gijutsu Chōsaka, ed. *Wagakuni no Kenkyū Kaihatsu Katsudō Shuyō Shihyō no Dōkō* (Primary indicators of the direction of our nation's research and development activities). Tōkyō, 1982.

————. Kikai Jōhō Sangyōkyoku, ed. *Wagakuni Jōhōshori no Genjō* (The current state of information processing in our nation). Tōkyō: Ministry of Finance Printing Office, annual.

————. Sangyō Kōzō Chōsakai, eds. *Nihon no Sangyō Kōzō* (Japan's industrial organization). Vol. II. Tōkyō: Tsūshō Sangyō Kenkyūsha, 1965.

————. Sangyō Kōzō Shingikai Kankei Shiryō. "Waga Kuni Kikai Jōhō Sangyō no Genjō" (The current state of the machinery and information industries). Tōkyō: Kikai Jōhō Sangyō Kyoku, June 1977.

————. *Sangyō Kōzō no Chōki Bijion* (A long range vision of industrial structure). Tōkyō: Sangyō Kōzō Shingikai Hōkoku, annual.

————. *Shuyō Sangyō no Setsubi Tōshi Keikaku* (Plans for investment in plant and equipment in major industries). Tōkyō, annual.

————. *Tsūsan Jānaru* (MITI journal). Tōkyō, monthly.

————. Takatsuji Masumi and Tsuji Kiyoaki eds., together with other members of Tsūshō Sangyō Gyōsei Kenkyūkai. *Gendai Gyōseishū* (Series on modern administration). *Tsūshō Sangyō* (International trade and industry). nos. 1 and 2,Vols. XIV and XV. Tōkyō: Gyōsei, 1983.

————. Tsūshō Sangyōshō Jūkōgyōkyoku (MITI Heavy Industries Bureau) eds. *70 Nendai no Denshi Kikai Kōgyō, Kidenhō no Kaisetsu* (The electronics and machinery industries in the 1970s, an explanation of the law concerning temporary measures for the promotion of specified electronics and machinery industries). Tōkyō: Tsūshō Sangyō Chōsa kai, 1971.

Miyasaka Tokitsuke, Kaneko Akira, and Takahashi Iwakazu. *Dokusen Kinshi Kōrei Shiryōshū* (Collection of data on the anti-monopoly law). Tōkyō: Seibundo, 1977.

Miyazawa Kenichi and Takeuchi Hiroshi, eds. *Nihon Sangyō Kyōshitsu* (A lecture room on Japanese industry). Tōkyō: Yuhikaku Sōsho, 1976.

Mizusawa Tōru. *IBM no Senryaku—Nihon Shijō no Shihai o Nerau Tsūshin Kyojin* (IBM's strategy—the communications giant that aims to dominate the Japanese market). Tōkyō: Daiyamondosha, 1984.

Morozumi Yoshihiko. *Sangyō Seisaku no Riron* (A theory of industrial policy). Tōkyō: Nihon Keizai Shimbunsha, 1966.

Motooka Tōru and Kitsuregawa Masaru. *Dai Go Sedai Kompyūta* (5th-generation computers). Tōkyō: Iwanami Shoten, 1984.

Nakae Gōki. *Kompyūtā Sangyō no Shijō Senryaku* (Market strategy of the computer industry). Tōkyō: Chūō Keizaisha, 1977.

Nakamura Takafusa. "Sengo no Sangyō Seisaku, Jūkagaku Kōgyō o Chūshin ni" (Postwar industrial policy, with emphasis on the heavy chemical industries). In *Nihon no Sangyō Soshiki* (Japan's industrial organization), ed. Niida Hiroshi and Ono Asahi. Tōkyō: Iwanami Shoten, 1969.

———. "Nihon ni okeru Sangyō Seisaku no Tokushoku to Hyōka" (Special characteristics and evaluation of industrial policy in Japan), *Tōyōkeizai*, 18 June 1974, pp. 58–64.

———. *The Postwar Japanese Economy.* Tr. Jacqueline Kaminski. Tōkyō: University of Tōkyō Press, 1981.

Namiki Nobuyoshi. "Kigyō Kan Kyōsō to Seifu Kainyū" (Competition among firms and government intervention). In *Gendai Sangyō Ron 3: Sangyō Seisaku,* Vol. III, ed. Baba Masao and Shinohara Miyohei. Tōkyō: Nihon Keizai Shimbunsha, 1973.

Nano Hiko. *Nichibei Kompyūtā Sensō, IBM Sangyō Supai Jiken no Teiryū* (The U.S.-Japan computer war, the undercurrent of the IBM industrial spy case). Tōkyō: Nihon Keizai Shimbunsha, 1982.

Nelson, Richard R., Merton J. Peck, and Edward D. Kalachek. *Technology, Economic Growth and Public Policy.* Washington: The Brookings Institution, 1967.

Nihon Chōki Shinyō Ginkō Sangyō Kenkyūkai. *Shin Jidai ni Chōsen suru Nihon no Sangyō* (Japan's industries challenging the new era). Tōkyō: Mainichi Shimbunsha, 1968.

Nihon Chōki Shinyō Ginkō. *Shuyō Sangyō Sengo 25 Nenshi* (25-year history of major industries in the postwar period). Tōkyō: Kurihara Shigeo, 1972.

———. *Chōsa Geppō* (Monthly survey).

Nihon Densan Kikaku Kabushikigaisha. *Hojokin Benran* (Handbook of subsidies). Tōkyō, annual.

Nihon Denshi Kikai Kōgyōkai. *Denshi* (Electronics). Tōkyō, monthly.

———. *Denshi Kōgyō 30 Nenshi* (30-year history of the electronics industry). Tōkyō, 1979.

Nihon Denshi Kōgyō Shinkō Kyōkai. Denshikeisanki Chōsa Iinkai, ed. *Waga*

Kuni no Denshikeisanki Sangyō no Mondai Ten to Sono Taisaku (Policies to deal with the problems of our nation's computer industry). Tōkyō, 1970.

―――. *Denshi Kōgyō no Chōki Tenbō* (A long-term view of the electronics industry). Tōkyō, annual.

Nihon Denshin Denwa Kōsha 25 Nenshi Iinkai, eds. *Nihon Denshin Denwa Kōsha 25 Nenshi* (25-year history of NTT). 4 vols. Tōkyō: Denki Tsūshin Kyōkai, 1978.

Nihon Jōhō Shori Kaihatsu Kyōkai, eds. *Kompyūtā Hakusho* (Computer white paper). Tōkyō: Kompyūtā Eiji, annual.

Nihon Kaihatsu Ginkō. *Nihon Kaihatsu Ginkō 25 Nenshi* (25-year history of the Japan Development Bank). Tōkyō, 1976.

―――. *Nihon Kaihatsu Ginkō Tōkei Yōran* (Japan Development Bank summary of statistics). Tōkyō, annual.

Nihon Keizai Chōsa Kyōgikai. *Nihon no Sangyō Saihensei* (The reorganization of Japanese industry). Tōkyō: Shiseido, September 1967.

Nihon Keizai Shimbun, ed. *Kompyūtā Uōzu* (Computer wars). Tōkyō, 1987

Nikkō Shōken Kabushiki Gaisha Chōsabu. *Tōshi Geppō* (Investment monthly). Tōkyō.

Nishikiori Hisashi. *IBM tai Fujitsu, Sono Shitō* (IBM vs. Fujitsu, their life-or-death struggle). 2nd ed. Tōkyō: Yunion Shuppansha, 1980.

Nomura Securities Research Institute. *Zaikai Kansoku* (Observations of the business world). Tōkyō, monthly.

Ogura Masatatsu and Yoshino Naoyuki. "Zeisei to Zaisei Tōyūshi" (The tax system and the Fiscal Investment and Loan Plan). In *Nihon no Sangyō Seisaku,* (Japan's industrial policy), ed. Komiya Ryūtarō, Okuno Masatatsu, and Suzumura Kōtarō. Tōkyō: Tōkyō Daigaku Shuppankai, 1984.

Okawa Kazushi and Henry Rosovsky. *Japanese Economic Growth.* Stanford: Stanford University Press, 1973.

Ouchi, William. *The M-Form Society.* Reading: Addison-Wesley, 1984.

Ozaki, Robert S. *The Control of Imports and Foreign Capital in Japan.* New York: Praeger, 1972.

Patrick, Hugh. "Japanese Industrial Policy and Its Relevance for United States Industrial Policy." Prepared statement for the Joint Economic Committee, U.S. Congress. 13 July 1983.

――― and Henry Rosovsky, eds. *Asia's New Giant.* Washington: The Brookings Institution, 1976.

Pechman, Joseph and Keimei Kaizuka. "Taxation." In *Asia's New Giant,* ed. Hugh Patrick and Henry Rosovksy. Washington: The Brookings Institution, 1976.

Peck, Merton and Shuji Tamura. "Technology." In *Asia's New Giant,* ed. Hugh Patrick and Henry Rosovsky. Washington: The Brookings Institution, 1976.

Pempel, T.J. "Japanese Foreign Economic Policy: The Domestic Bases for International Behavior." In *Between Power and Plenty,* ed. Peter Katzenstein. Madison: University of Wisconsin Press, 1978.

————. *Policy and Politics in Japan: Creative Conservatism.* Philadelphia: Temple University Press, 1982.

Phillips, Almarin. *Market Structure, Organization, and Performance.* Cambridge: Harvard University Press, 1962.

Reich, Robert B. *The Next American Frontier.* New York: Times Books, 1983.

Richardson, G.B. *Information and Investment, A Study in the Working of the Competitive Economy.* London: Oxford University Press, 1960.

Sabashi Shigeru. *Ishoku Kanryō* (A unique bureaucrat). Tōkyō: Daiyamondosha, 1967.

Samuels, Richard J. *The Business of the Japanese State, Energy Markets in Comparative and Historical Perspective.* Ithaca and London: Cornell University Press, 1987.

Sangiin (The Upper House of the Japanese Parliament). Proceedings of a variety of committees.

Scherer, F.M. *Industrial Market Structure and Economic Performance.* 2nd ed. Chicago: Rand McNally College Publishing Company, 1980.

Schultz, Charles. "Industrial Policy: A Dissent," *The Brookings Review,* fall 1983.

Schumpeter, Joseph A. *Capitalism, Socialism, and Democracy.* 3rd ed. New York: Harper, 1950.

Scott, Bruce R. and George C. Lodge, eds. *U.S. Competitiveness in the World Economy.* Boston: Harvard Business School Press, 1985.

Shepherd, William G. *Market Power and Economic Welfare, An Introduction.* New York: Random House, 1970.

————. *The Treatment of Market Power.* New York: Columbia University Press, 1975.

————. *The Economics of Industrial Organization.* Englewood Cliffs: Prentice Hall, 1979.

Shimoda Hirotsugu. *IBM to no 10 nen Sensō* (The 10-year war with IBM). Kyōto: PHP Kenkyūjō, 1984.

————. *Kasumigaseki no Haiteku Kokka Senryaku* (Kasumigaseki's high-tech national strategy), Kyōto and Tōkyō: PHP Kenkyūjō, 1987.

Shimura Yukio. *IC Sangyō Daisensō.* (The IC industry's big war). Tōkyō: Daiyamondosha, 1979.

Shinohara Miyohei and Baba Masao, eds. *Gendai Sangyō Ron 3: Sangyō Seisaku* (Theory of modern industry, Vol. III: Industrial policy). Tōkyō: Nihon Keizai Shimbunsha, 1973.

Shūgiin (The Lower House of the Japanese Parliament), Proceedings of a variety of committees.

Skocpol, Theda and Margaret Somers. "The Uses of Comparative History in Macrosocial Inquiry," *Comparative Studies in Society and History.* April 1980, pp. 174–197.

Smith, Adam. *The Wealth of Nations.* New York: Random House, Modern Library, 1937.

Sōhyō Zenkoku Kinzoku Rōdō Kumiai Tōkyō Chihon, Nihon Sofutouea Shibu (The Japan Software Division of the Tokyo branch of the Sōhyō National Metalworking Union). *Ikarimote, Kompyūtopia no Tobira o Tatake* (In a rage, pounding on the door of computopia). Tōkyō: Yanagisawa Akiro, 1976.

Sōrifu Tōkeikyoku. *Kagaku Gijutsu Kenkyū Chōsa Hōkoku* (Report on the survey of R&D in science and technology). Tōkyō, annual.

Suzuki, Yoshio. *Money and Banking in Contemporary Japan.* Tr. John G. Greenwood. New Haven and London: Yale University Press, 1980.

Takahashi Kenkichi, Nishida Shōhei, and Ōhashi Takashi. *Kompyūtā Gyōkai* (The computer industry). Tōkyō: Kyōikusha, 1985.

Takashima Makoto. "Kompyūtā" (Computers). In *Nihon no Sangyō Soshiki* (Japan's industrial organization), ed. Kumagai Hisao, Vol. III. Tōkyō: Chīrō Kōronsha, 1976.

Takashima Setsuo. "Nihon no Sangyō Gyōsei to Kyōchō Hōshiki" (Japan's industrial administration and the method for cooperation), *Keizai Hyōron,* May 1963, pp. 26–33.

Takeda Yoshinori. *IBM no Subete* (Everything about IBM). Tōkyō: Nihon Jitsugyō Shuppansha, 1984.

Takenaka Kazuo. *Mirai Sangyō: Jōhō Sangyō* (Future industries: information industries). Vol. IX. Tōkyō: Tōyōkeizai Shimpōsha, 1971.

Takeuchi Hiroshi. "Kompyūtā Sangyō" (The computer industry). In *Nihon Sangyōron* (Industry in Japan), ed. Miyashita Takehei. Tōkyō: Yuhikaku Sōsho, 1971.

———. *Gendai no Sangyō: Denki Kikai Kōgyō* (Modern industry: The electric machinery industry). Tōkyō: Tōyōkeizai Shimpōsha, 1973.

Tarui Yasuo. *IC no Hanashi, Toranjisuta kara Chō LSI made* (The story of integrated circuits, from transistors to VLSI). 2nd ed. Tōkyō: Nihon Hōsō Shuppan Kyōkai, 1984.

Tawara Sōichirō. "IBM wa ya ni Hanatareta Tora da!" (IBM is a tiger let loose in a field), *Bungeishunjū,* September 1982.

Thurow, Lester. "The Case for Industrial Policies in America." In *Economic Policy and Development: New Perspectives,* ed. Toshio Shishido and Ryuzo Sato. Dover: Auburn Publishing Company, 1985.

Trezise, Philip H. and Yukio Suzuki. "Politics, Government, and Economic Growth in Japan." In *Asia's New Giant,* ed. Hugh Patrick and Henry Rosovsky. Washington: The Brookings Institution, 1976.

Tsuji Junji. *Jōhōshori Sangyōkai* (The information-processing industry). Industry

Series no. 519. Tōkyō: Kyōikusha Shuppan Sābisu Kabushikigaisha, 1987.

Tsuruta Toshimasa. *Sengo Nihon no Sangyō Seisaku* (Industrial policy in postwar Japan). Tōkyō: Nihon Keizai Shimbunsha, 1982.

Tyson Laura and John Zysman, eds. *American Industry in International Competition*. Ithaca: Cornell University Press, 1983.

Uekusa Masu. *Sangyō Soshikiron* (Industrial organization theory). Tōkyō: Chikuma Shobō, 1982.

Ueno Hiroya. *Nihon no Keizai Seido* (Japan's economic system). Tōkyō: Nihon Keizai Shimbunsha, 1978.

————. "Jiyū Shijō Kikō to Seifu no Kisei Kainyū" (The free-market mechanism and the government's restrictive intervention), in *Tōyōkeizai*, special edition, modern economy series no. 65, 9 February 1983, pp. 6–16.

————. and Mutō Hiromichi, "Jidōsha" (Automobiles). In *Nihon no Sangyō Soshiki* (Japan's industrial organization), ed. Kumagai Hisao, Vol. I. Tōkyō: Chūō Kōronsha, 1976.

Uozumi Tōru. *Kompyūtā Sensō* (The computer war). Tōkyō: Aoya Shoten, 1979.

Usui Kenji, Terasawa Yasuo, and Numakura Hōzo. *Nihon no Denshi Kōgyō— Shisutemuka no Ayumi* (Japan's electronics industry—the course of systemization). With editorial supervision from Nihon Denshi Kōgyō Shinkō Kyōkai. Tōkyō: Kompyūtā Eijisha, 1978.

Vernon, Raymond, ed. *Big Business and the State*. Cambridge: Harvard University Press, 1974.

Villard, Henry. "Competition, Oligopoly, and Research," *Journal of Political Economy* 66:483–497 (December 1958).

Vogel, David. "Why Businessmen Distrust Their State," *British Journal of Political Science* 8:45–78 (1978).

Vogel, Ezra. *Comeback*. New York: Simon and Schuster, 1985.

Wheeler, Jimmy W., Merit E. Janow, and Thomas Pepper. *Japanese Industrial Development Policies in the 1980s*. A Hudson Institute Research Report prepared for the U.S. Department of State. New York: Hudson Institute, October 1982.

Wiedenbaum, Murray. *Business, Government, and the Public*. 2nd ed. Englewood Cliffs: Prentice-Hall, 1981.

Yamamura, Kozo and Jan Vanderberg, "Japan's Rapid-Growth Policy on Trial: The Television Case." In *Law and Trade Issues of the Japanese Economy: American and Japanese Perspectives*, ed. Gary R. Saxonhouse and Kozo Yamamura. Seattle and London: University of Washington Press, 1986.

Yamawaki Hideki. "Tekkō Gyō" (The steel industry). In *Nihon no Sangyō Seisaku* (Japan's industrial policy), ed. Komiya Ryūtarō, Okuno Masatatsu, and Suzumura Kōtarō. Tōkyō: Tōkyō Daigaku Shuppankai, 1984.

Yokokura Takashi. "Sangyō Seisaku no Riron to Jittai" (Theory and reality of industrial policy), *Keizai Seminā,* June 1979, pp. 48–55.

Zysman, John. *Political Strategies for Industrial Order.* Berkeley: University of California Press, 1977.

Index

Index

Harvard East Asian Monographs

21. Kwang-Ching Liu, ed., *American Missionaries in China: Papers from Harvard Seminars*

22. George Moseley, *A Sino-Soviet Cultural Frontier: The Ili Kazakh Autonomous Chou*

23. Carl F. Nathan, *Plague Prevention and Politics in Manchuria, 1910–1931*

24. Adrian Arthur Bennett, *John Fryer: The Introduction of Western Science and Technology into Nineteenth-Century China*

25. Donald J. Friedman, *The Road from Isolation: The Campaign of the American Committee for Non-Participation in Japanese Aggression, 1938–1941*

26. Edward Le Fevour, *Western Enterprise in Late Ch'ing China: A Selective Survey of Jardine, Matheson and Company's Operations, 1842–1895*

27. Charles Neuhauser, *Third World Politics: China and the Afro-Asian People's Solidarity Organization, 1957–1967*

28. Kungtu C. Sun, assisted by Ralph W. Huenemann, *The Economic Development of Manchuria in the First Half of the Twentieth Century*

29. Shahid Javed Burki, *A Study of Chinese Communes, 1965*

30. John Carter Vincent, *The Extraterritorial System in China: Final Phase*

31. Madeleine Chi, *China Diplomacy, 1914–1918*

32. Clifton Jackson Phillips, *Protestant America and the Pagan World: The First Half Century of the American Board of Commissioners for Foreign Missions, 1810–1860*

33. James Pusey, *Wu Han: Attacking the Present through the Past*

34. Ying-wan Cheng, *Postal Communication in China and Its Modernization, 1860–1896*

35. Tuvia Blumenthal, *Saving in Postwar Japan*

36. Peter Frost, *The Bakumatsu Currency Crisis*

37. Stephen C. Lockwood, *Augustine Heard and Company, 1858–1862*

38. Robert R. Campbell, *James Duncan Campbell: A Memoir by His Son*

39. Jerome Alan Cohen, ed., *The Dynamics of China's Foreign Relations*

40. V. V. Vishnyakova-Akimova, *Two Years in Revolutionary China, 1925–1927*, tr. Steven I. Levine

41. Meron Medzini, *French Policy in Japan during the Closing Years of the Tokugawa Regime*

42. *The Cultural Revolution in the Provinces*

43. Sidney A. Forsythe, *An American Missionary Community in China, 1895–1905*

44. Benjamin I. Schwartz, ed., *Reflections on the May Fourth Movement: A Symposium*

45. Ching Young Choe, *The Rule of the Taewŏn'gun, 1864–1873: Restoration in Yi Korea*

46. W. P. J. Hall, *A Bibliographical Guide to Japanese Research on the Chinese Economy, 1958–1970*

47. Jack J. Gerson, *Horatio Nelson Lay and Sino-British Relations, 1854–1864*

48. Paul Richard Bohr, *Famine and the Missionary: Timothy Richard as Relief Administrator and Advocate of National Reform*